UPSTATE LITERATURE

A New York State Study

Thomas F. O'Donnell

UPSTATE LITERATURE
*Essays in Memory of
Thomas F. O'Donnell*

Edited by **FRANK BERGMANN**

SYRACUSE UNIVERSITY PRESS   1985

3/1986
Am. Lit

This book is published with the assistance
of a grant from the John Ben Snow Foundation.

Winner of the 1985 John Ben Snow Manuscript Prize.

Library of Congress Cataloging in Publication Data
Main entry under title:

Upstate literature.

   (A New York State study)
   Contents: Literary history of New York, 1650–1958 /
Thomas F. O'Donnell — Introduction to James Kirke
Paulding, The dutchman's fireside / Thomas F.
O'Donnell — Oneida County, literary highlights / Thomas
F. O'Donnell — [etc.]
   Includes bibliographies and index.
   1. American literature — New York (State) — History and
criticism — Addresses, essays, lectures. 2. New York
(State) in literature — Addresses, essays, lectures.
3. O'Donnell, Thomas Francis, 1915–1980. I. Bergmann,
Frank. II. Series.
PS253.N7U67   1985   810'.9'9747   84-26853
ISBN 0-8156-2333-X
ISBN 0-8156-2331-3 (pbk.)

Contents

Contributors

THOMAS F. O'DONNELL (1915–1980) taught English at Hamilton College, Syracuse University, Utica College (1949–1970), and State University of New York Brockport. His specialty was the regional fiction of upstate New York.

FRANK BERGMANN is Professor of English and German at Utica College of Syracuse University. He has published books on two New England writers, John William De Forest and Robert Grant. His most recent essays are on Harold Frederic and on Utica's Germans.

EDWIN H. CADY is Professor of English and Mellon Professor of Humanities at Duke University and chairman of the editorial board of *American Literature*. His most recent books are a revised edition of *Stephen Crane* and an edition, with Norma W. Cady, of *Critical Essays on W. D. Howells, 1866–1920*.

STANTON GARNER is Professor of American Literature at the University of Texas at Arlington. Born in Corning, New York, he has long been interested in two New York State writers: as General Editor of the Harold Frederic Edition, he has recently completed editions of *The Market-Place* and *The Damnation of Theron Ware or Illumination*; he has also been preparing a study of Herman Melville's Civil War years.

LOUIS C. JONES is retired after twenty-five years as Director of the New York State Historical Association, its Farmer's Museum, and the Cooperstown Graduate Programs sponsored by the Historical Association and

State University of New York Oneonta. He has published widely on New York folklore, and he was an early advocate of interdisciplinary approaches to the field of folk life.

JOHN M. REILLY, Professor of English at State University of New York Albany, regularly contributes the bibliographical survey on black literature to *American Literary Scholarship.* Other recent publications include essays on Ralph Ellison, Jean Toomer, and Richard Wright. He also writes on popular literary genres and is the editor of *Twentieth Century Crime and Mystery Writers,* winner of the Edgar Allan Poe Award in 1981.

PERRY D. WESTBROOK is Professor Emeritus of English, State University of New York Albany. His major interest is the regional literature of New York and New England. Among his recent books are *John Burroughs, William Bradford,* and *The New England Town in Fact and Fiction.*

KATE H. WINTER is a lecturer in the English department at State University of New York Albany. Her book *Marietta Holley: Life with "Josiah Allen's Wife"* was co-winner of the 1984 John Ben Snow Manuscript Prize. She is currently preparing a book on Adirondack women writers. She also writes fiction.

LIONEL D. WYLD has taught American Studies at Syracuse University, Notre Dame, and elsewhere. Among his major publications are *Low Bridge! Folklore and the Erie Canal* and *Walter D. Edmonds, Storyteller.*

Preface

THIS BOOK is not a *festschrift,* for lack of the proper occasion, yet it has many features of one, as it celebrates and carries on Tom O'Donnell's work instead of mourning his passing. Edwin Cady's remarks which follow take a fine and deep measure of the man and the scholar; nothing remains to be added except a few bare essentials of Tom's biography for the benefit of those whose misfortune it was never to have met him, some comments on this volume, the first literary history of upstate New York to appear in book form, and a note of thanks to everyone who helped this book to become a reality.

Born in Oneida in 1915, Thomas F. O'Donnell received his schooling in central New York. In 1942 he graduated from Hamilton, a college with which many distinguished upstate writers and scholars have been connected over the years. For his doctorate from Syracuse University in 1957 he wrote a dissertation on "The Regional Fiction of Upstate New York," a subject on which he would eventually be recognized as the foremost authority. He taught at Utica College of Syracuse University from 1949 to 1970 and at State University of New York Brockport from 1970 to shortly before his death in 1980. Since the late 1960s he had made plans to write the literary history of New York State, but the move to Brockport delayed the project and the untimely death denied it altogether.

Tom's first volume was to have chronicled the literature of the entire state until about 1840 and of Upstate from then until the present time; the second volume was to have covered the literature of New York City since 1840. The present book is an approximation to his first volume. But even this partial fulfillment of Tom's plans was problematic. There seemed to be no one as broadly knowledgeable about the literature of Upstate as he had been. It therefore seemed best to include some of Tom's own writings as Part I and to print as Part II original essays by scholars more than casually interested in upstate fiction and, in some instances, more than passingly acquainted with Tom.

O'Donnell's "Literary History of New York, 1650-1958" leads off Part I. It is reprinted from *Richards Atlas of New York State,* now out of print. In addition to surveying the fiction of Upstate, this long essay deals briefly with poetry and drama — genres either too diffuse or not well enough represented to call for special treatment in Part II — as well as with pertinent nonfiction and, very succinctly, the literature of New York City. Unfortunately, reproducing the three literary maps that accompany the text would have been too costly; the reader must enjoy them in those libraries circumspect enough to have acquired a copy of the *Atlas.* The second piece by O'Donnell is his "Introduction" to a reprint of Paulding's *The Dutchman's Fireside*; it is reprinted here as testimony to Paulding's key role in transmitting a lively and authentic picture of the state's Dutch heritage and as an example of Tom's most engaging writing. A shortened — in some ways even truncated — version of "Oneida County: Literary Highlights" appeared in Oneida County's bicentennial *History*; the full text — with its notes, broader background, and splendid local curlicues — is offered here as a challenge to those upstate counties without a similar work to their credit to go and do likewise. Six of the seven essays constituting Part II either deal with great figures among upstate novelists or else write thematic or subregional literary history; the seventh reminisces about folklore, a field which is more firmly linked to literature in the land of Irving and Cooper than in most other regions of America.

How is Upstate defined in this book? Where does Downstate begin? The leading historian on the subject, David Ellis, is a central New Yorker and consequently happily and hopelessly biased. One of his chapter headings in *New York, State and City,* "Upstate versus Downstate," does manage to acknowledge something down there, but his index lists only "Upstate," and how can something be said to exist that you can't index? On political evidence, Ellis includes everything in Upstate except New York City itself: "Upstate — an imprecise term applied to any area within the state, rural or urban, outside the boundaries of New York City, whether east to Montauk Point, north to Rouses Point, or west to Dunkirk — has provided a Republican majority since 1856. The citizens of New York City have voted strongly Democratic since 1800" (180). Carl Carmer is less land hungry but even more nationalistic; he locates "this land north of Manhattan and west of New England" and brandishes his book as "a literary shotgun" to persuade the reader that Upstate is not just a state but "a country" (vii). The present editor has long had a secret hankering for

marking Upstate by the snow line, which careful observation of the win-
try landscape through train windows has convinced him runs through
Poughkeepsie. Since, however, he does not wish to forfeit Washington Irving to the slickers, he'll stick 'em up for Carmer and has Upstate begin
north of the city.

More vital than Irvingesque mock battles over Upstate's boundaries
is a reflection on the character of regional literature and on the validity
of offering to the public the sort of study here attempted. In Carlos Baker's
finely tuned phrase from *Literary History of the United States,* regional
writers, at a time of rapid and drastic change in the decades following the
Civil War, captured "the feel and flavor of things as they were, and would
never be again" (861). Immediately one thinks of Irving's "Rip Van Winkle"
and "The Legend of Sleepy Hollow," only to realize that those stories an-
tedate the local-color movement by half a century and that their lasting
appeal lies not only in their atmospheric charm but also in their deep
awareness of the complexities of change. If regional literature turns in
upon itself and degenerates into miniaturizing for its own sake, it is apt —
as Larzer Ziff has argued — to become purely antiquarian, to slip "into an
ignoring of deeper social differences" (18). The literature of upstate New
York, so the present book would persuade the reader, is largely free of gra-
tuitous sentimentality and introspection. To be sure, this literature can be
nostalgic over the passing of that which was — or was perceived to be —
good in the good old days, but it also knows the dry bread of the field
hands and mill workers, the loneliness of women in the hills and hovels.
It is certainly not parochial, and its concern with larger social issues is
immediately evident in the work of Harold Frederic, who figures positively
and prominently in Ziff's study. Above all, this literature is resilient and
dynamic; its province, as the peddler says of the Erie Canal in Walter D.
Edmonds' *Rome Haul,* is "the whole shebang of life" (8). From Washington Irving to William Kennedy, the literature of upstate New York bears
out in its own vibrant ways what even the Florentines in Dante's transcend-
ing *Divine Comedy* prove, that the "literary imagination is incurably local"
(Vendler 349).

The purpose, then, of the present volume is clear. All of the contributors share the philosophical assumptions about the sociocultural basis of the literature of this country which underlie the magisterial *Literary
History of the United States,* already referred to. They also believe in the
broad caution and mandate of *LHUS* that "scholars can no longer be content to write for scholars; they must make their knowledge meaningful and
applicable to humanity" (vii). This statement dates from 1947 but has lost
none of its urgency. Current critical discourse, particularly as it relates to
the writing of literary history, is excessively theoretical and, in the way of

practical suggestions, singularly unhelpful. The present book is avowedly not an attempt to add to that discourse. The contributors were asked to write narrative-descriptive literary history with enough critical and analytical detail to add depth to the breadth of O'Donnell's opening survey. They were asked to keep footnotes and technical terms to a minimum and to avoid literary jargon. In short, this book was written for the educated and interested general reader, although we hope and think that the scholar will find it useful too. It is not a contribution to critical theory, nor does it lay claim to being exhaustive in its coverage. It does attempt to present the rich heritage and continuing vitality of upstate New York literature, and nothing could please us better than to see our readers reach for some of the books we have put before them.

Without the help and support of some special people, this book would still be only a vague idea in the editor's head. Gert O'Donnell was most cooperative in making Tom's materials available and in helping in countless other ways. Arpena S. Mesrobian, director and editor of Syracuse University Press, encouraged and guided the project from the beginning. The contributors allowed me to persuade them to make room in their busy schedules for this work. Perry D. Westbrook furnished not only the longest individual essay but also the name of another contributor as well as much moral support; I am deeply grateful for his unfailing courtesy. I am equally grateful for Edwin H. Cady's willingness to share his personal recollection of Tom O'Donnell with the readers of this book. I am happy to acknowledge help closer to home: Jill Ziemann Bergmann, M.L.S., verified the selective checklist of Tom O'Donnell's publications which concludes Part I and resourcefully and dependably took care of all other queries. My distinguished colleague Eugene Paul Nassar was deeply interested in the book from the start and helped it along by conceptual and practical advice. Lansing G. Baker, President of Utica College, and Robert W. Millett, Chairman of its Division of Humanities, offered welcome tangible support. Eleanor Hazard and her associates made room in their work schedules for much typing and retyping. The staff of Syracuse University Press proved once more that it is second to none. Finally, it is a pleasure to record the following permissions to reprint previously published material by Tom O'Donnell: by The Frank E. Richards Publishing Co., Inc., of Phoenix, New York, for "Literary History of New York, 1650–1958"; by the New College and University Press of New Haven, Connecticut, for "Introduction to James Kirke Paulding, *The Dutchman's Fireside*"; by the Oneida County Board of Legislators and John D. Plumley, Oneida County Executive, for "Oneida County: Literary Highlights." Mrs.

O'Donnell gave permission to print the previously unpublished portions of the Oneida County essay.

Utica, New York   FRANK BERGMANN
November 1984

Works Cited

Baker, Carlos. "Delineation of Life and Character." In *Literary History of the United States: History.* Edited by Robert E. Spiller *et al.* 4th ed., rev. New York: Macmillan, 1974, pp. 843–61.

Carmer, Carl. *The Tavern Lamps Are Burning.* New York: McKay, 1964.

Edmonds, Walter D. *Rome Haul.* Boston: Little, Brown, 1929.

Ellis, David Maldwyn. *New York, State and City.* Ithaca: Cornell University Press, 1979.

Vendler, Helen. "Presidential Address 1980." *PMLA* 96.3 (May 1981): 344–50.

Ziff, Larzer. *The American 1890s.* New York: Viking, 1966.

Tom O'Donnell

Tom O'Donnell did me the honor of being one of the very first of "my" graduate students. Together with the assorted "G.I." and other people in his group, he was so good he spoiled me for life. I have never, in spite of all that reason and experience could teach, forgotten the standard they set. Pre-consciously, I have always expected later groups to rise to equal them. None has ever done so. I have, and in more prestigious graduate programs, taught individuals who could have "made O'Donnell's team." That is all.

It shocked me a bit when his answers to examination papers came forth needing only a little polish here, a little expansion there, to be publishable. Soon, of course, I began to expect it. He had an enviable career as teacher and administrator where the going was, every day, hard. He made enviable friends of many sorts. He never began, in print, to fulfill anything like the potential that was in him when I first knew him; and I never knew a man whose manhood, his deep character, I respect more than I respect Tom's.

There are stories one may tell but, as I am old enough to think, stories one may not tell. The one about Tom which reruns itself most often in my memory is the true legend of his M.A. oral. In the years after World War II, Syracuse University continued its tradition of being downright serious about the M.A. It was the tradition still that for an M.A. one wrote a substantial thesis, though it did not need to be "original." And one faced a searching oral examination into the graduate work pursued to that point. Often enough, though the thesis would do, the oral stumbled and erred its way from one embarrassment to another and died away, leaving the examiners with weighty problems of integrity on their hands. Not O'Donnell's.

Tom had, in the first place, written on an author with strong Syracuse connections and chosen an aspect of his work that left no doubt of the originality of his thesis on "Stephen Crane's Poetry." Had he been free to drive ahead and make a book of it, he would in large part have anticipated Daniel Hoffman's standard work by many years. The oral sparkled along, never dull, never dragging, the candidate in top form, the professors unwilling to look at their watches. It was the onset of the typically long and somehow deep Syracuse spring twilight that made us realize we were far past the statutory limits and must stop. When, ever so briefly, the candidate was "discussed," the visitor from another department, a distinguished sociologist, spoke for us all. "That," he said, "was one of the most satisfactory intellectual conversations I have ever been privileged to take part in."

In what must be thirty-five years of it since, I have not had the luck to sit in on any Ph.D. oral which matched Tom O'Donnell's M.A. oral. I wish I might, but I do not expect it.

In the years when it would have been easy to do, Tom never would let me try to place him in easier, better-paying, more visible posts. "I will not live outside the Mohawk Valley," he told me — smiling, and yet in a tone of voice which showed that he meant it. Though at last he left Utica College for a better job west of his valley but still on his beloved "Canawl," his affection for Utica was as real as it was incomprehensible to me.

His writing and his projects were those of a man of letters, not of a chic-chasing careerist. The work he finished and published — like the work finished which will one day be published — won him national respect as a scholar along with nationwide delight in his wit. Every once in a while someone comes along to say, "You don't know me. But I worked with Tom O'Donnell, and he helped me get myself together." All the way through him, Tom had what we retain in the language of ballplayers, having eschewed the nobler words: Tom had class. So far as I am personally concerned, he stands in my own inmost hall of honor, with few beside him.

Therefore I am pleased that this book is being made to join together a number of the people who, not knowing one another, wish to unite in expressing their admiration. "The world will little note . . ." But that is a matter of course and not the point. Syracuse University, Utica College, and that otherwise mysterious Club of O'Donnell's People unite to salute him.

EDWIN H. CADY

Part 1

1 Literary History of New York, 1650-1958

THOMAS F. O'DONNELL

New York's Role in American Literature, 1650-1865

MOST OF THE COLONISTS who settled in New York State in the years before the Revolution had little time or use for the luxury of literature. The Dutch, who ruled the colony from 1609 until 1664, did leave many documents of various kinds describing their workaday lives along the Hudson. A few French Jesuits—Fathers Isaac Jogues and Simon Le Moyne among them—wrote vivid accounts of their experiences among the Iroquois in the heart of the state. Readable and interesting as they are, however, most of these early Dutch and French documents are of more value to the historian than to the student of literature.

Although most of the writing left by the Dutch is in the form of official records, a few educated Dutch colonists managed to produce a small amount of what deserves to be called literature. The first of these was Adriaen van der Donck, a leader in the futile attempt to attract more settlers from Holland. Although it failed in its original purpose, van der Donck's book-length *Description of New Netherland* was a sparkling and affectionate treatment of what he called "this naturally beautiful and noble province." Three other prominent residents of New Amsterdam—Jacob Steendam, Nicasius de Sille, and Henricus Selyns—left enough worthy poetry to indicate that some Dutchmen, at least, were concerned with other things than guilder-grubbing. The combined work of these four men who wrote in a language that is strange to all but a handful of modern New Yorkers constitutes the faltering beginning of a literary tradition in this state.[1]

For many years the English who seized and renamed the colony in

3

1664 showed little more interest in literature than their Dutch predecessors had shown. Except for a few short descriptive pieces, such as Daniel Denton's *A Brief Description of New York,* published in London in 1670, no significant literature was produced in New York until well into the eighteenth century. In 1720, however, when Cadwallader Colden came to New York as its surveyor general, the colony acquired its first intellectual. Throughout his fifty-six years of service to the colony — chiefly as its unpopular lieutenant governor — Colden wrote with such energy and scope that his voluminous output has not even yet been thoroughly evaluated. Although he was never a "literary" writer, his work helped immeasurably to establish the kind of intellectual climate that must exist before a literature can flourish.

Such a climate was beginning to form — thanks to Colden and a few others, like the historian William Smith — in the decade before the Revolution. In 1769 a French immigrant, Hector St. John de Crèvecoeur, was happily settling on a farm in Orange County. In his spare time during the next few years Crèvecoeur wrote a number of engaging essays which were later to become a part of his widely read *Letters from an American Farmer* (first published in 1782) and *Sketches of Eighteenth Century America* (first published in 1925). A New Yorker for only about six years (he was driven from his farm as a loyalist in 1775), Crèvecoeur nevertheless deserves an honored place in the literary history of the state.

So, too, does Mrs. Anne Grant, whose *Memoirs of an American Lady* is the most detailed and intimate first-hand account of colonial New York life and manners available to us. Although it was not published until 1810 — long after its author's six-year stay in the home of Margarita Schuyler, near Albany — the book belongs properly to the pre-Revolutionary period which it describes. Mrs. Grant's chatty treatment of the New York landscape, of social customs in the upper Hudson Valley, and of eighteenth-century personalities great and small has made her *Memoirs* a favorite of generations and a valuable source book for writers from Cooper and Paulding (both of whom acknowledged indebtedness to it) down into our own time.

The threat and eventual outbreak of revolution provided Americans of the 1760s and 1770s — including New Yorkers, both loyalists and patriots — with reasons for writing as they had never written before. In New York ardent loyalists like Samuel Seabury ("the Westchester Farmer") and Myles Cooper (president of King's College), attempted, in vigorously rhetorical pamphlets, to hush the hum of rebellion that was growing more audible in the colony. In equally vigorous answers, New York patriots, including seventeen-year-old Alexander Hamilton, spoke up in firm rebuttal. Then, as war broke out and dragged on, and as New York became an increasingly bloody battleground, loyalist spokesmen like Joseph Stansbury and Jonathan Odell taunted their enemies in clever satirical poetry, prose, and even plays. The patriots retorted chiefly with ballads, most of them anonymous, based on actions or episodes like the murder of Jane McCrea and the surrender of Burgoyne—subjects that the British and Tories would have preferred to forget. Though fleeting in appeal, this literature provided valuable precedent for writers yet to come.[2]

The Revolution, furthermore, like all transoceanic wars, resulted in significant cultural exchanges on both sides. British soldiers brought with them talents and tastes, especially for the theater, which transplanted easily to New York soil. When the long war ended, New York had a substantial body of indigenous prose and poetry, and a liking for satire and drama. Most important of all, perhaps, the new state had a proud history, a roster of stalwart heroes and heroines, and a mine of exciting lore and tradition—the stuff, in other words, of which literature is made.

During the last fifteen years of the eighteenth century, busy New Yorkers began to move into new areas of all kinds, intellectual and cultural as well as geographical. In 1787 in New York City, delighted audiences applauded Royall Tyler's *The Contrast* as the first American comedy and an early expression of the new nation's literary independence. In the same year, a larger audience discussed the brilliant letters addressed "To the People of the State of New York" that were currently appearing in New York journals. These letters, the work of Alexander Hamilton, John Jay, and James Madison, were to be published in 1788 as *The Federalist* and recognized as classics not only of political theory but of literary art. Other letters, too, were widely read and discussed, sometimes even before they were published. From the heart of the state in 1792, for example, Francis Adrian Van der Kemp wrote like a prophet new-inspired of upstate New York's marvelous destiny in a series of widely circulated letters to his friend, Adam Mappa.[3] And finally, the new vogue of the novel with native theme, characters, and setting—a vogue already established in America by books like *The Power of Sympathy, Charlotte Temple,* and *The Coquette* —came to New York in 1798 with the publication of *The Fortunate Discovery; or The History of Henry Villars,* by "A Young Lady of the State of New York."

Meanwhile, the generation of New Yorkers born during and shortly after the Revolution was growing up. One of them, Washington Irving (1783–1859), was to develop into New York's—and America's—first major literary figure. A number of others, ambitious young followers of Irving, gathered together in the thriving metropolis to form New York's first coterie of writers, the "Knickerbocker School." Dedicated, versatile, and energetic, these men were to make New York City—for three decades, at least — the literary capital of the nation. Their collective efforts, marked by a concern for the craft as well as the art of writing, were to produce not only a body of literature valuable in its own right, but a healthy tradition for later writers to follow.

Irving scored his first success in the *Salmagundi* papers of 1807 and 1808. It was, however, in *Diedrich Knickerbocker's History of New York* (to use its familiar title), published in 1809, that his talent really declared itself, as Van Wyck Brooks has said, "the first high literary talent the country had known." In this serio-comic masterpiece and a pair of marvelous short stories in *The Sketch Book* (1819-20), Irving accomplished a feat which has been matched only by the greatest of storytellers: he made a great stretch of land — the lower Hudson Valley — forever his own, and peopled it with characters whom age cannot wither nor custom stale.

It has never mattered that "Rip Van Winkle," "The Legend of Sleepy Hollow," and some of the sketches later published in *Wolfert's Roost* (1855) are actually Irving's versions of legends he had found in German literature. Transported to the New World, naturalized, and set down among the Catskills and along the river, old Rip and his dwarfish bowling companions, Brom Bones, the "blooming Katrina," and the Yankee interloper Ichabod Crane have become almost as much a part of the great valley as the Hudson itself.

In spite of Irving's great popularity, however, it was the eldest of the Knickerbockers, James Kirke Paulding (1778-1860), rather than Irving himself, who left the only authentic full-length fictional portrait of the Dutch society that flourished along the Hudson in the days before the Revolution. In the best of his work — a series of fine tales collected in *The Book of St. Nicholas* (1836) and a novel, *The Dutchman's Fireside* (1831) — Paulding saved "the distinct characteristicks" of an older generation from oblivion. In his fiction the fading Dutch strain was solidly woven into the fabric of New York's cultural and literary heritage.

Among the other Knickerbockers, Fitz-Greene Halleck (1790-1867) and Joseph Rodman Drake (1795-1820) led the way in poetry. Drake's "The Culprit Fay," a Hudson River fairy tale, still charms many readers, while Halleck is best remembered today for his stirring "Marco Bozzaris" and a moving tribute to the memory of his friend, "On the Death of Joseph Rodman Drake." Other figures in the group include the playwright John Howard Payne (1791-1852), author of "Home, Sweet Home"; Samuel Woodworth (1784-1842), best known for a poem that came to be sung as "The Old Oaken Bucket"; and George Pope Morris (1802-64), whom Poe called "very decidedly, our best writer of songs," but who is remembered now only for one of them, "Woodman, Spare That Tree."

Hard upon the heels of these men came another group of younger writers who, more frequently than their elders, looked beyond the metropolis for their subject matter. Of these, Nathaniel Parker Willis (1806-67) achieved a solid contemporary reputation as poet, critic, and editor. Charles Fenno Hoffmann's novel, *Greyslaer: a Romance of the Mohawk* (1840), contains the first of what were to be many fictional descriptions of the battle of Oriskany. Lewis Gaylord Clark (1808-73), born and raised in Onondaga County, built his *Knickerbocker Magazine* into the most influential periodical of the day, while his twin brother Willis (1808-41) earned fame in its "Ollapodiana" columns.

The literary atmosphere that now enveloped New York City meanwhile had begun to spread to other parts of the state. In Poughkeepsie in 1811 Isaac Mitchell wrote a novel entitled *The Asylum: or Alonzo and Melissa,* only to see it plagiarized in the same year by Daniel Jackson of Plattsburgh as *Alonzo and Melissa,* the title under which the book achieved enormous popularity. In the same village of Plattsburgh two short-lived sisters — Lucretia (1808-24) and Margaret Davidson (1823-38) — wrote poetry which, when it was collected and edited by Washington Irving, drew kind words from many critics, including Robert Southey, Maria Sedgwick, and Edgar Allan Poe. These, however, were feeble voices. In contrast, another infinitely stronger voice was about to speak up for the great upstate area.

The extent to which James Fenimore Cooper (1789-1851) contributed to the native literary tradition of New York State is difficult to measure. In all, he wrote thirteen novels, ranging from *The Spy* (1821) to *Ways of the Hour* (1850), in which a considerable amount of action takes place upstate. In these novels — especially in *The Pioneers, The Last of the Mohicans, The Pathfinder, The Deerslayer, Satanstoe,* and *Wyandotté* — he scored two remarkable accomplishments. First, he created what might be called a Region Visible. When Cooper was finished, New Yorkers — and all the world, for that matter — could see the state, in all its versatile expanse, as it had never been seen before. As Howard Mumford Jones has pointed out, these novels "fixed the image of America for thousands of Europeans" who dreamed of the New World in terms of the New York landscape that Cooper described so vividly.

Cooper's second great accomplishment resulted from his explorations, in time as well as space. In novels ranging (in order of action) from *Satanstoe* to *The Pioneers* he dramatized the process by which frontier settlements of New York had developed into civilized communities. As he did so, Cooper enriched the already exciting history of his state by endowing it with a body of myth that gave new meaning to the ancient land itself. Natty Bumppo and Chingachgook, Hurry Harry and Judge Marmaduke Temple — citizens all of the Region Invisible that Cooper created — have long since blended into the frame of reference by which New York considers its own past.

Just as Cooper's career as a novelist was getting well under way, New York state acquired its third major literary figure. William Cullen Bryant (1794-1878) was already an established poet in 1825 when he moved from his native Massachusetts to New York City. For the rest of his long life Bryant was to belong to New York, both city and state. Like his colleagues, Irving and Cooper, Bryant loved the majestic face of the Hudson Valley, and his frequent walks through the Catskill country inspired some of his best-loved poetry. This, in turn, inspired his artist friends — Thomas Cole, Asher B. Durand, and other members of what came to be called the "Hudson River School" of painting — to produce the distinctive and romantic landscapes which, like Cooper's novels, helped to "fix the image of America" in the minds of generations of Europeans.

During this rich period in New York's literary history when the reigns of the three giants — Irving, Cooper, and Bryant — so happily overlapped, a number of lesser figures were also contributing substantially to the body of the state's indigenous literature. Playwrights dramatized various events in the state's history in such successes as Mordecai M. Noah's *Marion; or the Hero of Lake George* (1822); Charles S. Talbot's anti-Masonic *Captain Morgan; or the Conspiracy Unveiled* (1827); Richard Penn Smith's *The Triumph at Plattsburgh* (1830); and W. W. Lord's *André: A Tragedy* (1856).

As early as 1829 Rip Van Winkle had begun his long theatrical career in John Kerr's *Rip van Winkle; or the Demon of the Catskill Mountains,* the first of numerous acting versions of the beloved story. Less memorable was the work of the poets. The state had its quota of pretty little gift books, full of imitations of Byron, Bryant, and Moore (to name only three standard models) and published over pseudonyms like "Amica Religionis" and "Tacita." Of these minor bards hard-working Alfred B. Street deserves to be remembered for verse-narratives like "The Burning of Schenectady" (1842) and "Frontenac" (1849).

The host of minor novelists who followed Cooper were especially attracted to the Revolution, which had left its scars on almost every part of the state. Most were content with recreating such episodes as the siege of Fort Stanwix, the battle of Saratoga, and Benedict Arnold's treason. Others, however, like Josiah Priest and Edward E. Z. Judson (known to his innumerable readers as "Ned Buntline") turned to unhistorical, but vivid and salable melodrama. A great American institution, the dime novel, was born in 1860 with the publication by Erastus Beadle of Mrs. Ann Stephens' *Malaeska, the Indian Wife of the White Hunter,* a thriller set in traditionally sleepy Catskill country.

During the "Feminine Fifties," as Fred L. Pattee labeled the decade,

New York also produced its share of sentimental ladies — members of what Hawthorne grumpily called "a d———d mob of scribbling women." Emily Chubbock Judson ("Fanny Forester") and Sarah J. Clarke ("Grace Greenwood") both lived and wrote in upstate New York. So did Susan Fenimore Cooper, the novelist's daughter, who deserves more acclaim than she has received for her idyllic *Rural Hours* (1850). Susan Warner's *The Wide, Wide World* (1851), written on Constitution Island, became one of the most popular novels of the century. Almost as widely read, but very different in tone, was Mrs. F. M. Whitcher's *The Widow Bedott Papers,* a searing piece of social criticism written mainly in Whitesboro and published posthumously in 1855.

As the 1850s went on, however, there was a pronounced lull in the literary activity that had characterized the state since Irving's first appearance. By 1852 Cooper was dead, Bryant was traveling abroad, and Irving was planning his last major work, *The Life of Washington.* A small army of local and state historians, led by E. B. O'Callaghan and J. R. Brodhead, were busy at work that was destined to make the 1850s a golden decade in New York historiography. Except for them, however, New York's had suddenly become a "sluggard intellect," and no new novelists or poets appeared. Over most of the state the creative impulse, so strong only thirty years before, by 1855 had apparently burned out.

Not so in Brooklyn, however. There the atmosphere was electric, crackling with ideas — at least for one man, an unknown printer-poet named Walt Whitman. Some of these ideas were his own; some had drifted to him on strong breezes from Concord, across the sound. But whatever their origin, Whitman's expression of these new ideas in new and bold fashion was to constitute New York's most important contribution yet to American poetry. To late editions of *Leaves of Grass,* the state has at best a slight claim. But the poems that made up the first three editions of *Leaves* (1855–60) came straight from Long Island beaches and lanes, and from crowded Brooklyn streets. Whitman's vision began, at least, in his own state. Few contemporaries, however, even noticed the publication of *Leaves of Grass* in 1855. Fewer still realized that its publication was actually to be the last exciting literary event to occur in New York State until after the Civil War.

New York Literature from Reconstruction to the Great Depression

During the twenty years that followed the Civil War, the only literature to come out of New York State was the product of minor talents. The older generation of writers was gone—all except for Bryant, whose twilight years were largely devoted to translating Homer. Whitman, after the first few editions of *Leaves of Grass,* no longer belonged to the state, but to the larger world. No exciting new leaders appeared to replace the dead giants, Irving and Cooper. For a brief time in 1870 New York's literary future looked brighter when Mark Twain and his bride settled in Buffalo. But after only a few months, he too was gone—off to Hartford, Connecticut, to spend his most productive years.

In New York City, to be sure, there was bustling activity in the areas related to literature: newspapers, magazines, and publishing houses bloomed and flourished as the city's population increased at a fantastic rate. But even there the only new creative voices to be heard were thin and quavering. "Literature is not in any great favor here," lamented the *Nation* in 1866, "and literary men do not abound." A full decade later, New York's John Bigelow was still complaining: "It looks as if we should have to get New England to do our writing for some time yet." And in 1881 a writer for the *Critic* noted that while New York could produce Vanderbilts, she could not produce Emersons.

What literary leadership there was in New York during these years was provided by men like Richard Henry Stoddard (1825-1903), Edmund Clarence Stedman (1833-1908), and Richard Watson Gilder (1844-1909). Besides being influential as critics and editors—this is especially true of Stedman—these men were also widely respected in their own time as poets. Posterity, however, has found their verse genteel, eclectic, and generally unexciting. Remembered even less vividly is the work of one of their contemporaries, Edgar Fawcett (1847-1904), who satirized New York society of the early Gilded Age in a novel, *Purple and Fine Linen* (1873), and in plays like *The False Friend* and *Our First Families* (both 1880).

Though short on literary talent of a high order during these years, the state did shelter its full quota of popular writers whose subliterary works attracted huge and enthusiastic audiences. Best remembered among these was Horatio Alger, Jr. (1834-99), a New England-born, Harvard-trained Unitarian minister whose first great success was with *Ragged Dick* (1867). When Alger died, some thirty-two years and about 130 novels later, he had reached what was almost certainly the largest audience of any American author up to his time. Although he is remembered now chiefly for his unvarying perversions of Benjamin Franklin's success formula, Alger's image of New York City as a huge, dangerous, and temptation-ridden metropolis undoubtedly thrilled countless thousands of readers, both young and old, whose only acquaintance with the city came through his novels.

Besides Alger, at least three other New York writers working in different parts of the state also achieved great popularity with formula fiction that they turned out with machinelike regularity during the 1870s and beyond. In Highland Falls, Edward Payson Roe (1838–88) — like Alger, a minister — discovered his formula in *Barriers Burned Away* (1872). This first effort and its successor, *Opening a Chestnut Burr* (1874) were so successful that Roe resigned his pulpit, moved to Cornwall, and devoted the rest of his life to writing other novels on the same plan, all of them notable for their sentimental piety.

Across the state in Adams, near Watertown, a determined spinster had also found a formula that was to endear her to an international audience almost as large as Alger's, and a whit more respectable. This was Marietta Holley (1836–1926), whose *My Opinions and Betsey Bobbet's* (1873) was the first of more than two dozen popular favorites in which Miss Holley propagandized for her favorite causes, including temperance and woman's suffrage. For forty long and lucrative years Miss Holley kept her homespun heroine, Samantha, in zealous motion. While the author herself seldom left her home in Jefferson County, Samantha went everywhere, and her admirers followed her in works like *Samantha at the Centennial* (1877), *Samantha at Saratoga* (1887), *Samantha at the World's Fair* (1893), and a score of others.

Not quite so popular, perhaps, but fully as prolific as the other two, was the third member of this trio of writing machines, Charles Austen Fosdick (1842–1915), known to his readers as "Harry Castlemon." Fosdick wrote his first successful boy's book, *Frank the Young Naturalist* (1864) while living in Cairo, Illinois. In 1875, however, he returned to his native New York and settled in Westfield, in Chatauqua County, where he wrote almost fifty adventure novels — including the Boy Trappers Series, the Sportsman Club Series, and the Pony Express and Rocky Mountain Series — which won him a juvenile and adolescent audience that was second in size only to Horatio Alger's.

Although the state's chief literary export during the 1870s and 1880s was mass production formula fiction, a few New Yorkers were honestly — and in one case, effectively — dedicated to writing of a different kind. John Burroughs (1837–1921), after several years in Washington, D.C., returned to his native Catskills in 1873 and settled near Esopus. Here at "Riverby," and later at his picturesque retreat, "Slabsides," he lived a modified version of the life preached by Emerson and practised by Thoreau. Here also, in the house that Whitman loved to visit, Burroughs wrote the volumes of nature essays that won for him a large and appreciative audience. In *Wake-Robin* (1871) — his first volume, actually written before he came to Riverby — through *Winter Sunshine* (1875), *Locusts and Wild Honey* (1879), and a dozen other volumes, Burroughs' ability to mix moral idealism and scientific observation made him the most popular nature writer of the century.

Not so successful, on the other hand, were the comparatively few New York writers who were attracted to the "local-color" movement of the 1870s. Throughout the nation, spokesmen for various geographical areas were producing fiction and poetry that bore the area's own distinctive stamp: Bret Harte in California, Edward Eggleston in Indiana, Harriet Beecher Stowe in New England, to name only a few. In New York, it is true, a few isolated works with local flavor of a kind also appeared. In 1870, for example, Charles R. Edwards wrote of smuggling on the frontier in a novel entitled *A Story of Niagara*; in 1877 appeared Sireno French's *Down the Banks: A Romance of the Genesee* and James Kent's *The Johnson Manor*; and in 1878 Robert T. S. Lowell—elder brother of the poet, and a one-time professor at Union College—wrote of life in Schenectady in *A Tale or Two from an Old Dutch Town*. But these were insular works, and only questionably a part of the swell of local color that was flooding the nation's books and periodicals.

One authentic talent did appear briefly, however, to represent New York state in the local-color movement; this was Philander Deming (1829–1915) of Albany, whose first story was accepted by William Dean Howells for the *Atlantic Monthly* in 1872. In this, and in the handful of somber stories that followed, Deming described the harsh surfaces of life as he had seen it in remote Adirondack and Champlain Valley communities. Unfortunately, after publishing two volumes of these—*Adirondack Stories* (1880) and *Tompkins and Other Folks* (1885)—Deming had little more to offer except a few less impressive sketches that were to appear as *The Story of a Pathfinder* in 1905. With these his writing career, so promising in its early stage, was over. Meager as his output was, however, Deming's honest portrayal of the grim aspects of life in upstate hamlets and villages prepared the way for a more effective realist who was about to appear.

In 1887 the long literary drought that had bedeviled the whole state since before the Civil War finally came to an end with the simultaneous appearance of two novels: Henry Cuyler Bunner's *The Story of a New York House* and Harold Frederic's *Seth's Brother's Wife*. Both men already had established reputations, Bunner (1855–96) as editor of *Puck* and Frederic (1856–98) as a foreign correspondent for the New York *Times*. It was as novelists, however, that they were to make their most significant marks on New York literary history. Bunner's *The Story of a New York House,* while not particularly significant in itself, was a pioneer excursion in the fictional portrayal of New York City's complicated personality. In this work, and in his later stories and sketches about the city, Bunner was, in the words of Brander Matthews, "one of the first American writers of fiction to find a fertile field in the sprawling metropolis, so multiplex in its aspects and so tumultuous in its manifestations; and here he was truly a pioneer, driving a furrow of his own in soil scarcely scratched before he tilled it." After the appearance of *The Story of a New York House,* New York City, with its own overpowering personality, was to become the favorite setting — and often a favorite character — for dozens of writers.

Frederic's *Seth's Brother's Wife,* appropriately published at the same time as Bunner's book, demonstrated that the upstate area also had a personality of its own that warranted the attention of the writer of fiction. *Seth's Brother's Wife,* a realistic treatment of the kind of political and editorial warfare Frederic had witnessed in his native Mohawk Valley, brought to upstate New York a literary vitality that had been missing since the death of Cooper. Encouraged by the moderate success of his first novel, Frederic continued his study of upstate society in a historical romance, *In the Valley* (1890). Uncomfortable as a romanticist, however, he returned to realistic techniques in *The Lawton Girl* (also 1890), *The Copperhead* (1893), and his masterpiece, *The Damnation of Theron Ware* (1896), which became an international best-seller in the year of its publication.

In these novels, and in a group of short stories, *In the Sixties* (1897), Frederic protrayed his own upstate area in just about all its aspects: historical, political, sociological, economic, religious, and even aesthetic. Except for his expressed admiration for Howells, Frederic professed allegiance to no school and seemed to pay little attention to literary theorists. His three novels of contemporary life, however, laid the same foundation for subsequent New York realists that Cooper had laid for romanticists. No mere "local colorist," Frederic probed to the roots of upstate life; his interest in social genetics prompted him to explore the diverse forces that made his region what it was. His artistic analysis of those forces constitutes a comprehensive portrait of upstate New York society during the Gilded Age — a portrait all the more effective because it is revealed in the unflattering, but not unkindly light of realism. After Cooper, upstate New York could be seen; after Frederic, it could be understood.

With the appearance of these two men — Bunner speaking for the metropolis and Frederic for upstate — the fragile thread that had bound the city and the upstate area together in a common literary history seemed to snap. Actually, of course, the great city had long ago ceased to be the peculiar property of New York State. Culturally and economically, it had begun to grow away from the rest of the state as far back as 1850; now, as the nineteenth century drew toward a close, the city was independent in every sense except politically. From now on, there was to be no more literature of New York State; there was to be, instead, a literature of New York City and a literature of upstate New York.

From about 1885 on, New York City became not only the publishing center of the nation, but once more a city of novelists, poets, and playwrights. H. C. Bunner, having shown the way originally, soon gave up his brief leadership to more impressive figures. In 1889 Howells himself, the high priest of American realism, forsook Boston for New York and celebrated his move in *A Hazard of New Fortunes* (1890), the first of his New York City novels. Young Stephen Crane, fascinated by aspects of life that repelled Howells, examined the city with the naturalist's eye in his grim novels of the tenements, *Maggie* (1893), and *Bowery Tales* (1900). Henry Harland ("Sidney Luska"), who had begun his study of immigrant Jews in *As It Was Written* (1885), continued with *Mrs. Peixada* (1886), *The Yoke of Torah* (1888), and other novels.

Through the 1890s and into the new century more and more writers, both native and adoptive, continued to reveal new facets of life in the city. Richard Harding Davis' *Van Bibber and Others* (1892), Paul Leicester Ford's *The Honorable Peter Stirling* (1894), Edward Townsend's *Chimmie Fadden* (1895), Theodore Dreiser's *Sister Carrie* (1900), Edwin Lefevre's *Wall Street Stories* (1901), and Edith Wharton's *House of Mirth* (1905) are representative of the range of perspective from which the city was observed by the novelists who became increasingly fascinated with its enormity and complexity. The reading public was well prepared for the appearance of "O. Henry" (William Sidney Porter, 1862–1910), whose second book, *The Four Million* (1906), created the popular image of the city during the first decade of the twentieth century.

Meanwhile, there had been literary activity in upstate New York as well as in the city. During the 1880s and 1890s, as Frederic was drawing his fictional portrait of the whole upstate area, other writers were at work, too. Some of them were turning to the state's rich history for their material. Jane Marsh Parker, for example, described the Millerite movement and the Genesee country of the 1840s in her *The Midnight Cry* (1886). Molly Seawell went to the War of 1812 and the battle of Lake Champlain for *Midshipman Paulding* (1891). Other novels with local attachments appeared in various parts of the state, such as D. S. Foster's *Elinor Fenton: An Adirondack Story* (1893), Charles King's *Cadet Days: A Story of West Point* (1894), and Robert C. Rogers' *Old Dorset: Chronicles of a New York Countryside* (1897). Stephen Crane's last stories, too, published in 1900 as *Whilomville Stories,* were based on his own boyhood in Port Jervis.

Widely read as some of these were, by far the most popular work of fiction to come out of upstate New York since Cooper's day was *David Harum* (1898), by Edward Noyes Westcott (1846–98), a Syracuse banker who died before his book was published. Amateurishly inept as a novel, *David Harum* nevertheless became almost immediately a national best-seller, capturing the enthusiastic fancy of contemporary reviewers and public alike. The character of Harum himself, the small town banker who delights in horsetrading, soon stepped out of the confining pages of Westcott's clumsy novel and moved into the misty realm of American mythology, where he is still recognizable — after Natty Bumppo, Rip Van Winkle, and Ichabod Crane, probably the best-known upstate New Yorker in all fiction.

Only two years after *David Harum,* a second contribution to the so-called "B'gosh" school of fiction appeared. *Eben Holden* (1900), a folksy tale of life in the northern part of New York, was the first of a series of popular novels that Irving Bacheller (1859–1950) was to set against his native St. Lawrence County. In *D'ri and I* (1901), *Darrell of the Blessed Isles* (1903), *Silas Strong* (1906), and their successors, which continued to appear until 1941, Bacheller continued as a literary spokesman for a part of the state that had been ignored by other writers.

The wave of historical romance, meanwhile, that had swept over the nation in the early years of the century had found its upstate New York practitioner in Robert W. Chambers (1865–1933). At his home in Broadalbin, in Fulton County — a home for which he had abandoned a busy and successful life in New York City — Chambers reveled in the history of his adopted area. Here William Johnson had once ruled over Indians and whites alike, and here the Revolution in New York had been fought. In a series starting with *Cardigan* (1901) and continuing through *The Maid-at-Arms* (1902), *The Reckoning* (1907), *The Hidden Children* (1914), and *The Little Red Foot* (1921), Chambers retold the story of the Revolution in New York State in vividly romantic terms. He breathed new life into old villains like Walter Butler and Joseph Brant, and created new heroes whose marvelous derring-do delighted a generation of New Yorkers who, like the rest of the nation, had grown weary of realism.

Bacheller, with his pseudorealistic novels of the North Country, and Chambers, with his flagrantly romantic tales of the Mohawk Valley, were the last two writers of real significance to flourish in upstate New York before the coming of the New Regionalists in 1929. A few others appeared sporadically, it is true, but their efforts were minor and of fleeting interest. In Oneida County, for example, Clinton Scollard produced one competent historical romance, *The Son of a Tory* (1901), and a fine local-color tale set in the hop fields near his home, *A Knight of the Highway* (1908). After these, however, Scollard returned to his first love, the production of pleasant, but decidedly minor verse. Grace Miller White's *Tess of the Storm Country* (1909), and other tales of life in the land of the squatter colony near Ithaca attracted some brief, shocked attention. Other single works, like Myra Kelly's *Little Citizens* (1909) and Robert E. Knowles' *The*

Dawn at Shanty Bay (1907), appeared, but were soon read and forgotten. Only Bacheller and Chambers kept on writing and being read. And as the first quarter of the century moved on, upstate New York seemed headed back toward the state of literary torpidity from which Frederic had aroused it in 1887.

Things were entirely different in New York City, of course. By now, writing about the city had become a recognized career, and novelists were going into every alley, listening to every accent, following every ambulance, shuddering at every crime — all in an attempt to get the character of this behemoth among cities on paper. New developments in psychology, the social sciences, and biology, as well as in literature itself, gave these writers new perspectives. From Montague Glass' *Potash and Perlmutter* (1910) to John Dos Passos' *Manhattan Transfer* (1925), the novelists marveled, chuckled, and scolded at what they saw going on in the sun and in the shadows. But if any of them had visions of what the city was to be like only a short time later, in 1930 and beyond, they had no words for their visions, and kept them out of books.

New York in Literature: The Renaissance after 1929

Walter D. Edmonds' first novel, *Rome Haul,* published in February 1929, marked the beginning of a remarkably fruitful period in New York's literary history. His book started a flood of novels that continues in the late 1950s, and the old "awareness of place" that had added dimension to the works of Cooper and Irving a century before returned once more to literary fashion. The writers who appeared after 1929 roamed the state freely in both time and space, finding new attractions not only in its rich history, but in its variety of landscape and local tradition. They dramatized New York's society in every stage of its development from an unambitious, fur-trading Dutch colony to a prosperous modern state. They found materials for fiction in every corner of the state, from Long Island to the Niagara Frontier, and at all levels of social existence — on the farm, in the villages and small cities, in the upstate metropolises, and in New York City itself. And having found their material, they wove it carefully into their fiction in a variety of ways, using any number of recognizable techniques ranging from the historical romance to the realistic novel of social purpose. Despite all their diversity of techniques, however, the host of new writers had one purpose in common: to create literature from materials that were part of American life as it was lived in New York State.

This burst of creative energy did not occur in a vacuum. On the contrary, the emerging literature, distinctive in tone and unprecedented in quantity, was the inevitable result of the mingling of two intellectual currents that had been stirring in New York for some time. The first of these was the continuing discovery of many exciting aspects of New York history, tradition, and manners; the second was the search for appropriate ways to write about these things. By 1929 these two currents were ready to be united in literature. The new writers had at their disposal not only unused material, but fresh ways to use that material. The time was ripe for the arrival of the "new regionalists."

When these two currents—the "new regionalism" and the massive rediscovery of New York by the social historians—came together at the end of the 1920s, the result was a broad cultural movement that not even the Great Depression of the 1930s could stop. On the contrary, the injustices and inequities that they saw in the economic wasteland of the early depression years moved some to write who might have been silent in more prosperous times. The federal relief funds that started to come in 1936 also accelerated the movement. Amateurs worked side by side with trained professionals on intelligently administered TERA [Temporary Emergency Relief Administration] and WPA [Works Progress Administration] projects, and accumulated forgotten or overlooked historical records, painted appropriate historical murals on the walls of post offices and city halls, and wrote informative guides to all sections of the state. More than one writer and artist who later achieved distinction in his medium served an early apprenticeship on some kind of WPA program either in New York or elsewhere. Culturally, if not economically, the depression—not only in New York but in other areas—was a kind of *felix culpa,* a "fortunate fall," from which future generations were to benefit.

Edmonds, having established the tone of the new literature in *Rome Haul* (1929), set a vigorous pace during the next few years. *The Big Barn* appeared in 1930, *Erie Water* in 1933, *Mostly Canallers*—a collection of short stories—in 1934, and *Drums Along the Mohawk* in 1936. When *Drums* was enthusiastically hailed by readers and reviewers alike, Edmonds received an honorary degree from Union College, whose new president, appropriately enough, was the same Dixon Ryan Fox who had helped to prepare the way for the novelist. Edmonds, said Fox in his ceremonial charge, was being honored as "the second builder of our Grand Canal"—as the writer whose novels had restored the world of the Erie to bustling fictional life. Actually, Edmonds had done that and was to do more. Later he was to refer to his own work as "chronicles of the life and times of the ordinary citizen through two hundred-odd years, and the growth and change of their section of Central New York. . . . It is the story of the people and the land . . . and it reaches from the time the first white men went into the Iroquois country to my own day and crossroads." His plan, then, was for a series of historical novels — as carefully distinguished from historical romances like Chambers' — which would constitute a vertical examination of upstate New York society, just as Harold Frederic's work had constituted a horizontal, or comprehensive examination of that same society in the 1870s.

With the publication of *Chad Hanna* (1940), *In the Hands of the Senecas* and *The Wedding Journey* (both published in 1947) and *The Boyds of Black River* (1953), Edmonds continued his chronicle. Read in the order of their action, his novels now traced the growth of "the plain people" of New York, as he called them, from their day of bloody glory at Oriskany in 1777 (*Drums Along the Mohawk*) through the great days of the canal era to the coming of the automobile (*The Boyds of Black River*). The capstone of this well-planned structure — the final novel in which Edmonds looks at his own generation of upstate New York — is still to come.

While Edmonds was "rebuilding our Grand Canal," other writers were finding inspiration in different aspects of the state's evolving culture. Some novelists focussed their attention on particular sections — on counties, cities, and villages with which they were especially familiar and for which they usually had a quiet affection that shines through their novels.[4] A few, however, angered by the economic bleakness around them, described the grim effects of the depression on life in their cities and on their farms.[5] Others found their material in episodes from the state's colorful religious history: in the story of the Shakers at New Lebanon, of the early Mormons near Palmyra, of the Quakers at Crum Elbow, and of the Perfectionists at John Humphrey Noyes' Oneida Community.[6]

Not all the writing of the thirties was done by the novelists. One of the most significant books of the decade was Carl Carmer's *Listen for a Lonesome Drum* (1936), a rich collection of folklore and folk history that was important not only in its own right, but as a stimulus for more of its kind. Carmer, besides bringing a distinctive tone to his indigenous material, added grist to the regionalists' already busy mill by uncovering fascinating episodes and characters that had been ignored by the more formal historians. His book represented a triumph for the folklorists who had been working busily in New York for years, but with scant recognition or encouragement. After 1936 the folklorists were to play an increasingly important role in the New York renaissance. *Listen for a Lonesome Drum* and Carmer's later works — *The Hudson* (1939), *Dark Trees to the Wind* (1949), and *The Susquehanna* (1955), together with his single novel, *Genesee Fever* (1942) — were to establish him as another major figure in the new literature of the state.

Another significant nonfictional work was Edward Hungerford's *Pathway of Empire* (1935), which Professor Harold W. Thompson has called "the best literary trip around the state." Josephine Young Case's *Midnight on the Thirty-First of March* (1938) is a long narrative fantasy, written entirely in blank verse, describing the manner in which a small New York village of modern times reacts when the rest of civilization suddenly disappears, leaving the village and its people completely alone in a new and silent world. Interesting too, for different reasons, is *Country Lawyer* (1939), by Bellamy Partridge, the first of several entertaining volumes in which the village of Phelps comes into its own.

Certainly one of the most memorable literary events of the thirties was the publication in 1937 of the ten-volume *History of the State of New York,* under the general editorship of Alexander C. Flick. This massive work, ten years in preparation, was the result of the combined efforts of seventy-eight scholars and writers in all parts of the state. Carefully organized and uniformly well written, the Flick history was welcomed not only by historians, but by the novelists, who recognized its value as a source for background material.

The decade of the 1940s opened with the publication of two other important nonfiction works. Dixon Ryan Fox's *Yankees and Yorkers* (1940) is a stimulating and provocative study of the long-standing feud between New England and New York — a feud which alternately smoulders and flares in the work of New York writers from Irving and Cooper on. In the same year appeared Harold W. Thompson's *Body, Boots and Britches,* another masterful collection of folklore and ballads that are a savory part of New York's heritage.

The novelists were even more productive in the forties than in the thirties. Some went on with work they had begun in the previous decade: Alice B. Parsons and Frank O. Hough, for example, continued to use the lower Hudson Valley, and Margaret Widdemer the Mohawk Valley, as background for new novels. Even as World War II erupted, new writers looked for and found material in previously unexploited parts of the state. Edward Havill discovered the grape country near Keuka Lake; Herbert Best, the Champlain Valley, where "some years the winter comes down like an enemy that pitches its white tents and lies down to a long siege." Roger Burke Dooley and Sister Consolata Carroll both told their stories against a background of Irish Catholic family life — one in Buffalo, the other in Rome — during the early years of this century. Harriet McDoual Daniels told her stories of the Loomis Gang and of the mysterious Lewis Anathe Muller against the background of Madison and Oneida Counties. Anne Miller Downes used the Mohawk Valley; Taylor Caldwell, western New York. Oriana Atkinson's *Big Eyes* (1949) was the first of a fine series of novels set in the Catskill country, "thirty miles back from the Hudson."[7]

Religious colonies, the activities of both Abolitionists and Copperheads, and especially the Erie Canal continued to attract the novelists.[8] In 1944 Samuel Hopkins Adams, long a writer of established stature, joined the new regionalists with *Canal Town,* a story of Palmyra in 1820. Happy in his new career, the beloved "old pro" soon followed with *Banner by the Wayside* (1947), a tale about a floating theatrical troupe in the 1840s. These, together with his later works, were to win for Adams a place with his younger colleagues, Edmonds and Carmer, among the most distinguished spokesmen for the new literature.

Other novelists of the forties contributed single works in which they scrutinized life in different parts of the state. Edmund Gilligan's *Strangers in the Vly* (1941), for example, is a fanciful story of three dwarfs, exiles from Europe, transplanted to Rip Van Winkle country; "it belongs," said a New York *Times* reviewer, "somewhere between old Rip Van Winkle himself and *The Crock of Gold.*" Jerre Mangione's *Mount Allegro* (1943), based on the author's boyhood in the Italian section of Rochester, also won high praise not only as a fine novel, but as a good sociological study. In addition to these, the novels of the forties included studies of life in Malone, in Saranac Lake, in the Susquehanna valley in the 1750s, in Orange County during the Revolution, in Saratoga Springs in the 1880s, on a Wayne County tobacco farm in the 1890s, and in Otsego County before World War I.[9]

A new kind of indigenous drama also came into its own during the 1940s, chiefly at the careful prompting of Professor A. M. Drummond of Cornell University. Sponsored by the University Theater and a Rockefeller Foundation grant "to encourage the writing of plays of regional interest and of New York State flavor," some of the work of Drummond's students — and some of Drummond's own — was published in *The Lake Guns of Seneca and Cayuga and Eight Other Plays of Upstate New York* (1942), edited by Drummond and Robert E. Gard. Their *Cardiff Giant,* a striking dramatization of one of the most fabulous episodes in the state's history, was also published later, in 1949, although it had been produced originally in 1939.

During the first half of the 1950s the makers of the new literature showed little signs of tiring. The decade opened with a distinguished work of nonfiction, Whitney Cross' *The Burned-Over District* (1950), a scholarly but highly readable study of the tumultuous religious history of central New York. Samuel Hopkins Adams contributed two new works, *From Sunrise to Sunset* (1950), a story of the Troy textile industry, and *Grandfather Stories* (1955), tales of the canal. John Brick, who promises to be the most prolific New York novelist since Cooper, made an impressive debut with *Troubled Spring* (1950), and soon followed with *The Raid* (1951), *Homer*

Crist (1952), *The Rifleman* (1953), and others. Edward Havill continued to look to the grape country, and William B. Meloney to Dutchess County for background for new novels. Clyde B. Davis, one-time Buffalo reporter, used western New York for the background of his ironical *Thudbury* (1952), which he subtitled "An American Comedy." The hop fields of southern Madison County served as background for two works, *The Covered Bridge* (1950) and *The Road* (1952), by a promising newcomer, Herman Peterson. John Vrooman looked to Fulton and Schenectady counties for his material; Edward R. Eastman to Cherry Valley. The twelve "Arcadian tales" of Charles Jackson's *The Sunnier Side* are set appropriately enough in the town of Arcadia, in Wayne County. Another newcomer, Howard Breslin, contributed *Bright Battalions* (1953), a tale of the French and Indian wars near Lake Champlain, and *Shad Run* (1955), a vivid story of Poughkeepsie in 1788.[10]

After 1955, however, the number of novels with upstate New York background began to decline slightly. Constance Noyes Robertson's *Go and Catch a Falling Star* (1957), the story of an octagon house in central New York, is one of comparatively few recent novels by established writers. New names have appeared, of course. Janet O'Daniel contributed what Carmer has called "a new and psychologically interesting Leather-Stocking" in the character of Marcus Hook, in *O Genesee* (1958), a novel of western New York in 1813. Donald Braider's *The Palace Guard* (1958) continues the Leatherstocking motif by opening with the funeral of a man who had jumped from the cliff above Natty Bumppo's cave near Cooperstown. Claude Koch's *Light in Silence* (1958) is a story of the College of Saint Bardolph, which seems to resemble Niagara University. And Haniel Long's *Spring Returns* (1958) is the story of a young seer and healer of the Finger Lakes country. Other novelists who seem to be following in the upstate tradition include Mary L. MacKinnon, W. E. Barrett, Martin Caidin, Emma Louise Mally, Frederic F. Van de Water, and Harvey Swados.[11]

During these three decades the writers of upstate New York were no busier and certainly no more productive than their counterparts in New York City. The activity upstate was perhaps the more remarkable, but only because it contrasted so sharply with the comparative silence of the previous generation. In New York City that same generation, far from being silent, had produced a steady flow of fiction, drama, and poetry — much of it about the city itself — during the first thirty years of the century. From 1930 on, through the forties and fifties, therefore, a new group of writers continued to explore their city-world and to write about it in greater quantity than ever.

The New York City fiction of this period, however, was different from the upstate fiction in at least one significant respect: it was less rooted in the past. New York City writers, not so conscious of historical tradition as their upstate brethren, produced fewer historical novels; in the midst of such a teeming present, there was little reason to look to the past. And so the bulk of their material came from the pulsing life around them: from Wall Street and Broadway, from Park and Madison avenues, from Brooklyn and the Bronx, and from the numerous ethnic islands that still flourish in cultural isolation in various parts of the most cosmopolitan of cities.

The range of their diverse interests is apparent in the list of fifty representative novels that accompanies the map of this period. The earliest title on the list is Maxwell Bodenheim's *Ninth Avenue* (1930), a grim picture of Harlem dives; the latest is John Brooks' *The Man Who Broke Things* (1958), a story of latter-day financial manipulations. In between are dozens of novels about life in almost every part of all five New York boroughs; about big business on Wall Street and Madison Avenue; about delinquency and crime; and about every racial, religious, and national group large enough to produce a spokesman.

The list of poets, too, who found inspiration somewhere in the city during this period would be a long one. It would include, certainly, such names as Conrad Aiken, Stephen Vincent Benét, Countee Cullen, Babette Deutsch, Richard Eberhart, Kenneth Fearing, Horace Gregory, Langston Hughes, Marianne Moore, Karl Shapiro, Wallace Stevens, Mark van Doren, Peter Viereck, John Hall Wheelock, William Carlos Williams, Samuel Yellen, and many others, native and adopted.

And so the great wave of indigenous literature that started with Edmonds' *Rome Haul* in 1929 continues into 1959, New York's "Year of History." If the upstate writers have been slightly less productive since 1955, their colleagues in New York City continue to be as articulate as ever. The tradition established by Cooper and Irving goes on, firmly anchored in the three centuries that have passed since an eloquent Dutchman, Adriaen van der Donck, became the first to capture in words the marvelous promise of "this naturally beautiful and noble province."

Notes

1. Early Dutch documents may be found in a number of places, including Vols. I and II of *Documents Relating to the Colonial History of the State of New York* (1856–58); *Documentary History of the State of New York* (1849–51); *Narratives of New Netherland, 1609–1664* (1909); and *Van Rensselaer Bouwier Manuscripts* (1908). For accounts of the Jesuits see the monumental *Jesuit Relations*

and Allied Documents, edited by R. G. Thwaites (1896–1901), or a selection in *The Indians of North America,* edited by Edna Kenton (1927). For Adriaen van der Donck's *Description of New Netherland,* see Jeremiah Johnson's admirable translation in *Collections of the New York Historical Society,* 2nd series, Vol. I (1841). For the poetry of Steendam, de Sille, and Selyns, see *Anthology of New Netherland and New York,* translated and edited by Henry C. Murphy (1865).

    2. For New York's part in this aspect of the Revolution see Moses Coit Tyler, *The Literary History of the American Revolution,* 2 vol. (1897).

    3. These letters can be found in John F. Seymour, *Trenton, N.Y.: Its First Settlement* (Utica, 1877), and in Samuel Durant, *History of Oneida County* (1878), pp. 542–57.

    4. Most of Alice Beal Parsons' work, for example, is set in Rockland County. Her novels include *John Merrill's Pleasant Life* (1930) and *A Lady Who Lost* (1932); *The Mountain* (1944) and *The World Around the Mountain* (1947) are collections of short stories. William Brown Meloney's *Rush to the Sun* (1937), *Mooney* (1950), and *Many Are the Travelers* (1954) are set in Dutchess County. Frank O. Hough's *Renown* (1938), *If Not Victory* (1939), and *The Neutral Ground* (1941) are set in Westchester County during the Revolution. Margaret Widdemer's *Hand on Her Shoulder* (1938), *Red Cloak Flying* (1950), *Lady of the Mohawks* (1951), and other novels are set in the Mohawk Valley, most of them in the days of Sir William Johnson. Don Cameron Shafer's *Smokefires in Schoharie* (1938) tells the story of the settlement of the Palatine Germans in the Schoharie Valley. Paul Horgan's *Fault of Angels* (1933), a Harper Prize-winning novel, stems from the author's knowledge of Rochester. Valma Clark's *Their Own Country* (1934) is set in Finger Lakes country; Zona Gale's *Light Woman* (1937) in Cattaraugus County; Clair Perry and John Pell's *Hell's Acres* (1938) tells the story of lawless doings, including a fabulous heavyweight championship prize fight, on twelve hundred acres of unclaimed land near Boston Corners in the 1850s. See also Charles Bonner's *Fanatics* (1932) and Paul Hoffman's *Seven Yesterdays* (1933), an autobiographical novel with a Utica setting. Roger Burlingame's *Three Bags Full* (1936), Nickerson Bangs' *The Ormsteads,* Hilda Morris' *The Main Stream,* and Chard Powers Smith's *Artillery of Time* (all published in 1939) are chronicles of multigeneration family life in various parts of the state.

    5. See Clara W. Overton's *The Road to the Left* (1935) and Joseph Vogel's *Man's Courage* (1938), the latter set in the Polish section of Utica during the depression.

    6. The Shakers figure in R. W. McCulloch's *Me and Thee* (1937) and later in Ann G. Leslie's *Dancing Saints* (1943); the beginnings of Mormonism in G. D. Snell's *Root, Hog and Die* (1937) and Vardis Fisher's *Children of God* (1939); the Hudson River Quakers in *Crum Elbow Folks* (1938), Constance Noyes Robertson's *Seek-No-Further* (1938) presents a composite picture of nineteenth-century communal life with physical details from the Oneida Community, founded by the author's grandfather, John Humphrey Noyes. Oneida Community also provides background for Rhoda Truax's *Green Is the Golden Tree* (1943), and Worth Tuttle Hedden's *Wives of High Pasture* (1944), as well as for a play, *Suzanna and the*

Elders, by Lawrence Langner and Arminia Marshall, produced in New York in 1940.

7. See Edward Havill's *Tell It to the Laughing Stars* (1942), *Low Road* (1944), and *The Pinnacle* (1951); Herbert Best's *Young 'Un* (1944) and *Whistle, Daughter, Whistle* (1947); Roger Burke Dooley's *Less Than Angels* (1946), *Days Beyond Recall* (1949), and *House of Shanahan* (1952); Sister Consolata Carroll's *Pray, Love, Remember* (1947) and *I Hear in My Heart* (1949); Harriet McDoual Daniels' *Nine Mile Swamp* (1941) and *Muller Hill* (1943); Anne Miller Downes' *Until the Shearing* (1940) and *Eagle's Song* (1949); Taylor Caldwell's *Wide House* (1945), *This Side of Innocence* (1946) and others; and Oriana Atkinson's *Twin Cousins* (1951) and *Golden Season* (1953).

8. Constance Noyes Robertson's *Fire Bell in the Night* (1944) is based on the famous "Jerry rescue" in Syracuse; her *The Unterrified* (1946) describes the draft riots and the activities of the "Knights of the Golden Circle," a Copperhead society. James M. Fitch's *The Ring Buster* (1940) is a story of tough life on the Erie Canal and in New York City during the Cleveland administration.

9. For Malone background see Francine Findley's *From What Dark Roots* (1940); for Saranac Lake, see Dorothy P. Hines' *No Wind of Healing* (1946); for the Susquehanna Valley, Waverly, and Elmira, see Ray D. Herrington's *The Western Gateway* (1944); for Orange County see Burke Boyce's *The Perilous Night* (1942); for Saratoga Springs, see Edna Ferber's *Saratoga Trunk* (1941); for Wayne County, see Jane Cuddeback's *Unquiet Seed* (1947); for Otsego County, see Mateel Farnham's *The Tollivers* (1944). See also Anya Seton's *Dragonwyck* (1944) for Hudson Valley setting.

10. See John Vrooman's *Clarissa Putnam of Tribe's Hill* (1950) and *The Massacre* (1954); Edward R. Eastman's *The Destroyers* (1947) and *The Settlers* (1950).

11. See Mary L. MacKinnon's *One Small Candle* (1956); W. E. Barrett's *The Sudden Strangers* (1956); Martin Caidin's *Long Night* (1956); Emma Louise Mally's *Abigail* (1956); Frederic F. Van de Water's *This Day's Madness* (1957); and Harvey Swados' *On the Line* (1957).

Introduction to
James Kirke Paulding,
The Dutchman's Fireside

2

THOMAS F. O'DONNELL

SINCE ITS FIRST APPEARANCE in 1831 *The Dutchman's Fireside*—like a number of minor masterpieces in American literature—has had a well-balanced share of critical yeas and nays. In the original and in the half-dozen subsequent editions that followed during the 1830s and 1840s, all the western world loved this pleasant tale of life among the Hudson River Dutch in pre-Revolutionary War days. Published almost simultaneously in America and England, it was generally well received in both countries; and within seven years it had been translated into French, German, Swedish, Danish, and Dutch. For two full decades readers on both sides of the Atlantic admired James Kirke Paulding's novel, with its differently shaded picture of the same New York landscape that Cooper's earlier works— *The Spy, The Pioneers,* and *The Last of the Mohicans*—had made so familiar.

New editions of *The Dutchman's Fireside* continued to appear until 1852. Midcentury America, however, had developed new tastes, talents, and troubles; and as the decade moved on, the popularity of Paulding's novel declined inevitably before a rush of new concerns and attitudes. During the brief period that saw the appearance of such widely different works as *The Scarlet Letter, Uncle Tom's Cabin,* and *Ten Nights in a Barroom,* Paulding's leisurely pastoral moved toward the Dark Shelf of American libraries. Even before drums began to roll, *The Dutchman's Fireside* was all but forgotten.

In 1867—seven years after Paulding's death—his son, William Paulding, attempted to revive interest in his father's work in a curiously inept memoir, *The Literary Life of James K. Paulding.* Despite the ominous coolness of the critics toward this book, William Paulding published in

1868 four volumes of his father's tales and novels, including *The Dutchman's Fireside*. The younger Paulding's project, for all its good intentions, was foredoomed for at least two reasons. First, the time was not right; a public already hearkening to young William Dean Howells' demands for a new kind of literature was not interested in literary revivals. Second, the new version of *The Dutchman's Fireside,* with the mark of William Paulding's heavy editorial hand on virtually every page, hardly constituted an improvement over an original that had pleased a generation of American and European readers.

In his Preface to the 1868 edition, William Paulding observed that *The Dutchman's Fireside* had been "written heedlessly, as the rest of Mr. Paulding's works were." He failed to tell the reader about the changes he had made, and implied that he had merely corrected the punctuation and spelling. The changes he did in fact make in the original are, however, much more serious. He not only tampered gratuitously with the diction, but also painstakingly expurgated some of his father's earthy—but never indelicate—imagery. "Massa Ariel," says Aunt Nauntje in the original edition, "don't know no more about bees dan a bull's foot." In William Paulding's edition, Ariel "don' know no more about bees dan a chipmonk." At the death of the slave-companion Tjerck, Paulding in the original edition wrote: "Peace to his *manes,* black as they were!" This becomes, in William Paulding's edition, "Peace to his soul!" Weakened in scores of places by prissy editing like this, the 1868 edition of *The Dutchman's Fireside* is a poor reflection of the blunt vigor that his contemporaries admired in Paulding's novels—even when they were "written heedlessly."

Needless to say, William Paulding's vitiated edition of *The Dutchman's Fireside* did little to restore the book to its old place among America's favorites. To the next two generations, James Kirke Paulding was merely another member of the group of writers whose names lived dimly on, not because of their work, but because of their association with Washington Irving. Except for James Grant Wilson's friendly memoir in *Bryant and His Friends* (1886)—in which Wilson tells of meeting with a copy of the first edition of *The Dutchman's Fireside* in Northern Africa in 1882 —Paulding's name and work drew scant mention from the critics and literary historians of the Gilded Age and beyond.

In the decade after World War I, however, as a new and searching interest in its own innocent past began to stir America, Paulding's reputation set out on the long road back from oblivion. The way was prepared by such sympathetic scholars as Oscar Wegelin, with his bibliography of Paulding, published in 1918; Carl Van Doren, in *The American Novel* (1921); and Fred Lewis Pattee, in *The Development of the American Short Story* (1923). At last, in 1926, the first book-length study appeared: Amos

Herold's *James Kirke Paulding, Versatile American.* Herold's book—a brief but objective and judicious critical biography—straightened out much of the confusion of William Paulding's *Literary Life,* and made a clear case for the revival of interest in Paulding's work, especially *The Dutchman's Fireside.*

By the time Herold's book appeared, Vernon L. Parrington had discovered and was writing with characteristic relish about the Jeffersonian and Jacksonian strain that runs through Paulding's work. Although Parrington preferred *Koningsmarke* (Paulding's first novel, published in 1823) to *The Dutchman's Fireside,* he found in Paulding the voice of "the authentic New York, not of Broadway merchants or Wall Street bankers, but of the plain rank and file of the people." To Parrington, Paulding—unlike his friend and early collaborator, Washington Irving—was a confirmed agrarian, a "political philosopher with clear-cut doctrines."

After 1930, some form of tribute to Paulding and his work began to appear with increasing frequency in the writings of scholars and critics of American literature. In *The Indian in American Literature* (1933), Albert Keiser devoted a chapter of appreciative analysis to *Koningsmarke,* in which he found, among other things, "a rather comprehensive picture of the natives." Van Wyck Brooks preferred *The Dutchman's Fireside,* with its authentic picture of the fading New York Dutch tradition. This "charming tale," as Brooks described it in *The World of Washington Irving* (1944), "opened a window on an otherwise irrecoverable scene of the past." Alexander Cowie, in *The Rise of the American Novel* (1948), agreed with Brooks; he found *The Dutchman's Fireside* "a livelier and more varied book" than Cooper's *Satanstoe* (1845), although less masterful in its treatment of "sheer adventure." Ernest E. Leisy also praised the book in *The American Historical Novel* (1950), noting that *"The Dutchman's Fireside* combines the attractive features of a frontier novel by Cooper with something of the mellow style of Irving."

More recently Benjamin T. Spencer, in *The Quest for Nationality* (1957), saw in Paulding's consistent use of themes from "normal American experience" an anticipation of at least one aspect of Howellsian realism. On the other hand, James N. Tidwell and Daniel G. Hoffman have both been more interested in Paulding's lost play, *The Lion of the West,* first produced in 1831, the same year in which *The Dutchman's Fireside* was published. *The Lion of the West,* as Tidwell points out in his introduction to the revised version of the play (published in 1954), has long been recognized as important in the history of American drama because it was "the first American comedy to use an uncouth frontiersman as its central character." Hoffman used the adapted version of the play to illustrate the thesis so convincingly developed in *Form and Fable in American Fiction*

(1961). For some reason, however, Hoffman treats *The Dutchman's Fireside* lightly, neglecting to point out that the novel is — at one level, at least — an early version of the "bumpkin *vs.* slicker" theme that *Form and Fable* traces in American literature from Irving through Twain.

The strongest impetus of all to a revival of interest in Paulding came with the publication in 1962 of *The Letters of James Kirke Paulding,* edited by Ralph M. Aderman. In this collection of more than four hundred letters, well edited and annotated, Paulding makes his own claim for further attention.

The consensus of modern critics, then, is that Paulding's work clearly needs revaluation. The growing circle of his friendly readers — including a number not cited above — may not agree unanimously that *The Dutchman's Fireside* is his best work; they will agree, however, that it deserves to be brought out of the darkness where it has languished for over a century. And they agree, too, with Luther S. Mansfield's observation in *The Literary History of the United States* (1948) that

> In his range of interest and materials, in his capacity for "innovations," in the breadth of his view of the resources out of which America could bring her own literature, and in his formulation and practice of a literary creed, Paulding represents the catholicity and inclusiveness, the fusion of divergent strains, for which the whole body of literature produced in the middle states from 1810 to 1860 is most distinguished, and by which it is best characterized.

At the time of the publication of *The Dutchman's Fireside,* on June 10, 1831, James Kirke Paulding was in the middle of a long and productive career. Fifty-two years old, he already enjoyed a substantial reputation as one of America's most versatile writers. Abroad as well as at home he was known as a satirist and wit; as a poet, a literary and social critic, a writer of stories and sketches; and as a prize-winning playwright, as well as a novelist. His American audience, however, knew him best of all as the inveterate and implacable hammer of the early British travelers, whose careless reporting Paulding had excoriated in five separate books published between 1812 and 1825.

One of these books — *The United States and England* (1815) — had caught the attention of President James Madison, and it won for Paulding an appointment to the Board of Navy Commissioners. In 1830, as he finished writing *The Dutchman's Fireside,* Paulding was rounding out fifteen years of government service and was heading toward a cabinet post as Secretary of the Navy under Martin Van Buren. But that appointment was still seven years away, and Paulding was happy with what he had accomplished in his first fifty-two years. Already he had been the intimate friend of Presidents Madison and Monroe; he knew and was known by everyone in his beloved city of New York; he had married well; and his creative powers were as strong as ever. Of all the American writers at work in 1831, only Irving and Cooper were more widely read and admired.

Paulding's life had begun inauspiciously enough. Born on August 22, 1778, in the war-torn lower Hudson Valley, Paulding was in a real sense a child of the American Revolution. His earliest memories were of a kind that his younger contemporaries, born after Yorktown, could never share or fully understand: memories of a family sundered, first by the misfortunes of war and later by the ironies of peace. In the early days of the Revolution, his father — Commissary of the New York militia — had moved his family from its comfortable home in Tarrytown to Great Nine Partners, a spot more safely distant from threatening British forces. Here James Kirke Paulding was born in a kind of exile. When he was seven years old, the peace proved as troublesome as the war had been. During the Revolution, his father had used his own credit to obtain supplies for the beleaguered New York troops; by 1785, the neglectful new nation had failed to assume those obligations. In that year the elder Paulding not only lost his home and property to clamoring creditors but actually spent months in prison for debts he had incurred in the name of the infant government. The memory of an unpleasant childhood remained with Paulding for the rest of his life. "From the experience of my early life," he wrote later, "I never wish to be young again."

Paulding's young manhood — and for that matter, the rest of his life — was to be brighter than his childhood. At the turn of the century he was in New York City happily cavorting with the bright young "Lads of Kilkenny," a group sparked by Washington Irving, to whom Paulding was now related by marriage (his sister, Julia, had married William, the oldest of the Irving brothers). In 1802 his writing career began — as did Washington Irving's — with a group of modest contributions to the *Morning Chronicle,* a paper operated by Peter, still another of the Irving brothers. This close association with the Irvings culminated in 1807 when Paulding joined with Washington and William Irving to produce the precocious *Salmagundi* papers that delighted New York.

Much as Paulding enjoyed and profited from working with the younger Irving, the two men differed in fundamental ways. They were destined to be friends for life, but never again collaborators. Blunter by nature and firmer in his convictions than Irving, Paulding was from the beginning a burly democrat, "fashioned out of the wool from the fireside loom and domestic dye-pot," as Parrington described him. More aggressive than artistic, Paulding was always ready to abrogate the Treaty of Paris and to blast at Britain with a vigor and directness that dismayed Irving. When the pleasant, witty, but innocuous *Salmagundi* papers were finished, so was the possibility of any further collaboration between the two men. From now on, Paulding was on his own.

Between 1812 and 1818, his reputation grew with five book-length works, including three that established him as one of America's doughtiest champions in the "paper war" with British travelers and journals, particularly the august *Quarterly Review*. In the *Diverting History of John Bull and Brother Jonathan* (1812), Paulding proved himself a successor to Philip Freneau in his ripostes at foreign critics of democracy and in his demands for an indigenous literature as completely free of foreign influence as English-speaking America could make it. Calmer and less headstrong than the irascible old "Poet of the Revolution," who was then living in comparative obscurity, Paulding won a wider audience than Freneau had ever been able to reach. Even Paulding's two long poems, *The Lay of the Scottish Fiddle* (1813) and *The Backwoodsman* (1818) — both of them consistent with his developing theories of a national literature — were widely read and discussed, although not always favorably, in periodicals both at home and abroad. The *British Review* in August 1819, for example, remarked with a carelessness that Paulding would have labeled as typical: "The most recent, as well as the best specimen of American poesy is unquestionably the 'Backwoodsman' of Mr. Paulsen [sic], to whom the transatlantic poets have awarded the highest place among their native poets."

Only a year later, when Paulding launched his own series of *Salmagundi* papers, he found himself in unfortunate competition with his old friend and one-time collaborator, Washington Irving. The years 1819 and 1820 are most memorable, perhaps, for the appearance of Irving's *Sketch Book*; Paulding's *Salmagundi, Second Series* suffered — and still suffers — by comparison. Nevertheless, his essay "National Literature," which appeared in 1820 as part of that series, remains one of the most forceful and perceptive pieces of criticism that America had yet produced. In this essay Paulding dismissed the laments, already numerous, that the history, tradition, and lore of the young nation provided scant material for the writers of romantic fiction. "Wherever there are men," said Paulding firmly, "there will be materials for romantic adventure." The fortunes and misfortunes of men provide such materials — not superstition, ghosts, fairies, goblins "and all that antiquated machinery which till lately was confined to the nursery." In the character of earlier Americans, he pointed out, "in the motives which produced the resolution to emigrate to the wilderness; in the courage and perseverance with which they consummated this gallant enterprise; and in . . . their adventures, and their contests with the savages" will be found plenty of material for "those higher works of the imagination, which may be called Rational Fictions."

Addressing these words to Americans in whose hearts the contemptuous question of Sidney Smith, "Who reads an American book?" still rankled, Paulding insisted that the state of American literature was the fault of the writers themselves. They had been misled by bad models and by "docile" critics; instead of turning to their own rich resources, they had been content to sponge upon "the exhausted treasury of our impoverished neighbours." The hope for an American literature now lay in the willingness of young writers to free themselves from "servile imitation" of foreign models and to turn to "domestic subjects." As an example for American writers, Paulding cited the work of Charles Brockden Brown, almost forgotten since his death in 1810. Brown's work would be rediscovered, Paulding accurately predicted, and his "future fate will furnish a bright contrast to the darkness in which he is now enveloped."

The strong convictions of "National Literature" are central to the whole body of Paulding's work, early and late. And yet, in the novels, short stories, and plays that followed, he often found it difficult to follow his own admonitions. At the same time that he was warning American authors against the influence of contemporary English romanticists — including the still anonymous author of *Waverly* — Paulding himself was looking backward to eighteenth-century England for his own models. Of Fielding, Goldsmith, and Smollett he could write in *A Sketch of Old England* (1822):

> Each of these writers, without going out of the bounds of probability, or offending against "the modesty of nature," by extravagant and incongruous events, or boisterous, uncontrolled passion, had produced works, that appeal far more powerfully to the heart and the imagination, than the dashing succession of characters and events, that only hang together by a chain of improbabilities, or by the thread of history, exhibited in the work of the Great Unknown.

Tom Jones, he believed, is "one of the most consummate works of fiction that ever the world saw."

Only a year later, Paulding again openly expressed his admiration for Fielding in *Koningsmarke, the Long Finne* (1823), his first novel. A picaresque tale of life in the Swedish colony in Delaware and among the Indians of Pennsylvania, *Koningsmarke* is admittedly an imitation of *Tom Jones* not only in structure but in technique. Following Fielding's example, Paulding divided the novel into books; each book opens with a chapter in which he frequently comments on the art of writing and complains about the incredibilities of contemporary romantic fiction. On the other hand *Koningsmarke,* an unidealized picture of life in a wilderness settlement, also fits Paulding's definition of what he had previously designated in "National Literature" as "Rational Fiction." It represents Paulding's first sustained attempt to adapt eighteenth-century realism to American purposes, to invest "ordinary characters and everyday incidents . . . with charms a thousand times more engaging and interesting, than the monstrous creations, or copies of a Maturin or even a Great Unknown."

Although *Koningsmarke* was moderately successful from the first, Paulding did not turn immediately to another novel. Except for *John Bull in America* (1825), in which he brought his private war with Britain and her travelers to a good-natured close, the next several years were largely devoted to writing short fiction. Ever since 1807, Paulding had been experimenting with fictional sketches and short tales. By 1830, while Hawthorne and Poe were still studying their art, Paulding had published three volumes of short fiction of various kinds, as well as a number of fugitive pieces that were not reprinted in book form. So consistently did these stories appear during the years between 1820 and 1832, when Irving was busy with other efforts, that this period, as Amos Herold has pointed out, "may be fairly named the Paulding decade of the short story."

Despite his success with short fiction, however, Paulding was well aware of the demand for full-length novels. And so, even as one of his volumes of short stories, *Chronicles of the City of Gotham* (1830), was in press, he was busy on his second novel—another work of the kind that he later advised Poe to write: "a tale in a couple of volumes, for that is the magical number."

Paulding tells us in the brief "Advertisement" that prefaces *The Dutchman's Fireside* that he had started to write the novel many years before, after reading Mrs. Anne Grant's *Memoirs of an American Lady,* "one of the finest sketches of early American manners ever drawn." Since the first American edition of Mrs. Grant's book appeared in 1809 (a year after the first English edition), it is possible that Paulding worked irregularly on *The Dutchman's Fireside* for almost twenty years before completing it in January 1830. In view of his well-known work habits, however, it is more probable that after a hasty start, Paulding put the tale away, forgot it for some years, and then finally finished it in one extended stint in 1829 and 1830. Whatever the case, Mrs. Grant's marvelously detailed picture of life in and around colonial Albany proved to be a mine for him—as it was later for other New York novelists like Cooper, who also acknowledged his debt to Mrs. Grant, and Harold Frederic, who did not.

There is some irony in the fact that Paulding, the most aggressively American writer of his time, should have been so thoroughly captivated by — and indebted to — *Memoirs of an American Lady.* A high Tory from birth, Mrs. Grant was still alive in 1831 — even though Paulding probably did not know this as he penned his tribute to her book — and was still ruling her small bluestocking roost in literary London. Only seven years before, in 1824, she had been such a formidable figure that Sir Walter Scott himself could write in a letter to Maria Edgeworth: "good Mrs. Grant is so very cerulean, and surrounded by so many fetch-and-carry mistresses and misses . . . that though I would do her any kindness in my power, yet I should be afraid to be very intimate with a woman whose tongue and pen are rather overpowering." Fortunately, Paulding knew Mrs. Grant only through her book; and even though his democratic hackles must have risen as he read those parts of *Memoirs of an American Lady* where Mrs. Grant's aristocratic convictions are most evident, he could still recognize the book's charm and its value to his purposes. It was a source book crammed with materials waiting to be fashioned into distinctively American fiction.

Memoirs of an American Lady is a chatty, intimate account of the author's childhood years, from 1758 to 1768, in and around colonial Albany. Her father, a captain in a Scottish regiment, was stationed near Claverack on the Hudson near Albany, when his wife and three-year-old daughter joined him there. Here, in a community predominantly Dutch, the child started to grow up with the widowed granddame of the Hudson Valley, Catalina Schuyler, who had been attracted by the young Scottish girl's precocity. For the next six years Anne grew up as one of the Schuyler household, storing away in her remarkable memory the sights and sounds of life on the New York frontier. In 1768 her father, no longer in the British army, decided to return to Scotland; at the age of thirteen, Anne left America, never to see it again.

Almost forty years later, Anne MacVicar Grant — now a middle-aged widow herself — turned to her childhood experience and wrote *Memoirs of an American Lady* as if she were gazing out a window at the eighteenth-century colonial scenes and citizens she described. The predominantly Dutch society of the Hudson Valley she remembered as being "so peculiar, so utterly dissimilar to any other that I have heard, or read of, that it exhibits human nature in a new aspect, and is so far, an object of rational curiosity, as well as a kind of phenomenon in the history of colonization." Dates she sometimes forgot or confused; but details of social custom, of natural surroundings, of personalities great and small, and of what Paulding called "domestic subjects" — all these came from her pen as brightly as if she had observed them yesterday.

Of the large audience of admiring readers that *Memoirs of an Ameri-*

can Lady won for Mrs. Grant, perhaps none was so thoroughly enchanted by the book as James Kirke Paulding. It was a reliable account of the daily existence of Paulding's own forebears, the Hudson Valley Dutch; of the education and "early habits" of Albany children; of social rituals like the Dutch boy's first fur-trading expedition; of Dutch courtship and marriage customs; of popular sports and amusements; of the character – obnoxious to Mrs. Grant – of the wandering New Englanders; and of the social upheaval attending the arrival in the area of a regiment of British troops with handsome and sophisticated officers. Here too were first-hand reminiscences of such shapers of colonial New York history as Sir William Johnson, superintendent of Indian affairs, "an uncommonly tall, well-made man, with a fine countenance" who not only dressed like the Indians but dealt with them so honorably that he "taught them to repose entire confidence in him."

With the wealth of detail he found in *Memoirs of an American Lady,* including some evidence of the character of the shadowy Sir William, Paulding had all the background material he needed for *The Dutchman's Fireside.* Now he had only to supply a hero and heroine, lead them through a series of conventional adventures in both forest and town, and bring them happily together at the end. In doing this, Paulding turned once more to his favorite eighteenth-century model, *Tom Jones,* rather than to the contemporary examples of Scott and Cooper. Sybrandt Westbrook and Catalina Vancour – "romantic cognomens!" sighed one contemporary reviewer – are brought together, separated by circumstance and misunderstanding, and then reunited in ways that Fielding himself would have approved of as being both possible and probable.

Throughout *The Dutchman's Fireside* Paulding tried manfully to write the "probable and consistent" fiction that he had praised in "National Literature" and to avoid the excesses of contemporary romanticism. He did not completely succeed, of course. The character of Sir William Johnson – whom Paulding knew only through legend – emerges as a kind of aristocratic Leatherstocking, an idealized figure whose high coloring belies Paulding's dislike for the romantic. On the other hand, most of his minor characters – including Indians Hans Pipe and Paskingoe, and "Indian-hater" Timothy Weasel – are carefully drawn to realistic rather than romantic dimensions. *The Dutchman's Fireside,* then, may be read as modified realism that points backward to the fiction of eighteenth-century England and forward to that of post-Civil War America.

Whatever its relationship to the fiction of other times, however, *The Dutchman's Fireside* was an immediate success in Paulding's own time. On June 4, 1831 – a week before the book was available to the public – the *New York Mirror* printed a friendly prepublication review, praising Paulding generally for his refusal to cater "to the prevailing tastes and fashions of the day" and for his devotion to the cause of a national literature. Two weeks later, as if to atone for the vagueness of the first notice, the *Mirror* printed a second, more explicit review of the book. "We admire it," said the reviewer (probably George Pope Morris), "for its manly and healthy tone of *Americanism,* in which our native writers are lamentably deficient; for its absolute freedom from affectation, and for the powerful interest which is excited . . . without violating the probability of time and place, or wandering away from the routine of life." The *Mirror,* the review remarked significantly, was grateful to observe "the unanimity of approbation with which this production has been noticed by the public press."

Despite this general approval, however, Paulding was scolded — in the *Mirror,* as well as in other periodicals — for his sometimes shoddy writing. "Words occasionally find their way as if by accident where they have no business," complained one reviewer in a charge that was echoed by others. The *New England Magazine* observed that with more care and attention to his style Paulding "might do infinitely better for his own literary reputation, and for that of the country, by producing something worth putting aside for a second perusal."

The reaction of British critics to the English edition of the novel was less consistent than that of their American counterparts. The *Literary Gazette* found the story old and the style "often inelegant and florid." The *Edinburgh Literary Journal,* on the other hand, thought the tale was "elegantly told, and full of incident." The *Monthly Review* archly observed that Paulding had chosen "a subject for his theme, which could hardly be expected to be much in unison with English ideas." With this restrained opinion, however, the *Westminster Review* — traditionally more friendly to America than other British journals — did not agree. The anonymous *Westminster* reviewer (possibly John Bowring) was enchanted with *The Dutchman's Fireside,* and he said so plainly in the longest, most laudatory essay to appear on either side of the Atlantic. As a stylist, said the *Westminster,* Paulding "is neither too elaborate like Irving, nor too diffuse like Cooper . . . ; he is just, neat, fanciful, and descriptive." Offering liberal excerpts from the novel to document his judgment that Paulding was both a poet and a thinker, the *Westminster* reviewer concluded by praising the book for its "moral remarks," characterization, and narrative — "but, above all, for its correct and spirited views of Red-Indian manners and morals."

With the critical reception of his book both at home and abroad, Paulding was generally gratified. Ironically, however, he was never to read the words of praise that he would have cherished above all others: praise from his countryman and literary rival, James Fenimore Cooper. "Did you publish Paulding's book?" asked Cooper in a letter to his own publishers from Paris in November 1831. "I have just read it, and I think it quite good — some parts excellent, but very unequal. . . . It is the only American novel that I have read since I left home [in 1826], and I must say the species improves." Cooper did not approve of Paulding's picture of Sir William Johnson, and he predicted that the book would not go well in England, "for it hits John too hard (not for the truth) but for that gentleman's taste." Nevertheless, for Cooper — not always so magnanimous when his own domain was invaded — *The Dutchman's Fireside* had "capital things in it."

With this judgment the reading public agreed. Long before the critical vote had been fully tabulated, *The Dutchman's Fireside* was a popular success. Even in England Paulding's anglophobia, most evident in his characterization of Sir Thicknesse Throgmorton, failed to disturb his general audience.

From 1831 until his virtual retirement in 1849, Paulding continued to be one of the busiest of American writers. Except for a period of service from 1838 to 1841 as Secretary of the Navy in the cabinet of President Van Buren — a fellow Hudson Valley Dutchman — he continued to produce plays, poems, stories, and novels. For a time in the 1830s, the continuing success of his prize-winning play, *The Lion of the West,* prompted a vision of himself as the savior of the faltering American theater. "Paulding puts into my hands a manuscript comedy called . . . 'The Bucktails or Americans in England,'" wrote William Dunlap in his journal for October 17, 1832. "He suggests our uniting to produce Comedies and upholding the American Stage." In the same year appeared Paulding's third novel, *Westward Ho!,* set in Virginia and Kentucky. At the same time, he was preparing a two-volume *Life of Washington* (1835), destined to go through nine American editions and at least one British. Short pieces, both fiction and nonfiction, continued to pour in profusion from his pen until 1846, when he returned to the novel in *The Old Continental,* a fictional dramatization of Revolutionary days in Westchester County. Finally in 1849, when Paulding was in his seventy-second year, appeared his last sustained fictional effort, *The Puritan and His Daughter.*

For all his prodigious activity, however, Paulding was never again to know the success that came to him in 1831 with *The Dutchman's Fireside.* Although he was to live on until 1860, during his final decade Paulding was almost completely forgotten. Like Freneau before him and Howells after, Paulding was destined to outlive his own contemporaries and his literary reputation. His warnings against the dangers of romanticism had gone unheeded, although he could observe with some satisfaction that the American version had at least taken its own vigorous direction. The battle for national literary independence had, in effect, been won — although there were few fellow warriors still alive to recall Paulding's part in it. America was no longer concerned with independence, but with slavery — and Paulding, like Hawthorne, could not share the antislavery fervor of his northern countrymen. Time and his stubborn adherence to principle — even to an unpopular one — had caught up with him. Even as he died, on April 6, 1860, Paulding the writer was already a shadow in America's literary limbo.

Understandably forgotten as much of his voluminous work is, a small part of it — especially *The Dutchman's Fireside* — still retains a freshness that modern readers will appreciate as fully as Paulding's contemporaries did. Here is both realism and romance, quiet humor and occasionally sharp wit; here is a picture of the New York Dutch as Irving never saw them — the only authentic full-length fictional portrait, in fact, of a society that flourished along the Hudson for generations before it produced its first significant spokesman in James Kirke Paulding.

3   Oneida County
Literary Highlights

THOMAS F. O'DONNELL

THANKS TO A COMBINATION of fortunate circumstances, geographic as well as social and sociological, Oneida County has always been able to contribute its share in the development of the national culture, including literature. Situated on the main road to the West throughout the nineteenth century, the county was a stopping-off place not only for goods and people from both east and west, but for ideas, concepts, tastes, and attitudes that are part of the civilizing process and necessary to the growth of an intellectual and literary climate. During the century after the Revolution, the river, the canal, good turnpikes, and the railroad all helped to quicken in Oneida County people a desire to do more than survive and prosper on their rich lands.

The first generation of Yankees who poured into "Whitestown Country" starting in 1784 were not writers but doers. Although they had little time for the luxury of literature themselves, they quickly made certain that both reading and writing would be part of the future way of life in this westernmost settlement of the Puritan hive. They built not only schools, academies, and seminaries, but a college—the third in the state and the first west of Schenectady. Newspapers began to appear in 1793[1]—five years before the county itself was officially formed. And after 1808, when William Williams became a master printer, Utica developed rapidly into a publishing center [2] as well as a training spot for young men who studied printing under Williams and then carried their craft throughout the state. Thus, even before the opening of the Erie Canal, Oneida County was preparing an audience for whatever intellectual or literary patterns might follow in the wake of the continuing westward movement.

Insistent as they were on literacy in their frontier community, the first

39

transplanted New Englanders brought with them no true literary tradition. The chattel they lugged into the wilderness included books, to be sure: the Bible and some commentary by New England divines; a few copies of Mr. Webster's new *Spelling Book*; perhaps some histories and inspirational biographies; copies of Robert Bailey Thomas' *Farmer's Almanack.* But whatever small private libraries began to accrue along the Mohawk or the Oriskany or the Sauquoit certainly contained no fiction or drama. If they contained any poetry, it was in the form of Michael Wigglesworth's versified minatory sermon, *The Day of Doom*; Milton's *Paradise Lost,* which latter-day Puritans could still read with approval; or the staunchly orthodox Calvinistic and federal poetry of the young "Connecticut Wits," men like Timothy Dwight, Joel Barlow, and John Trumbull.

If there were no examples of fiction or belletristic writing in early Oneida County homes, however, it was not entirely the fault of the settlers. American fiction had not yet been born. On an April evening in 1789, as a group of Oneida settlers held their first town meeting in Hugh White's barn in Whitesboro, none knew (or would have seriously cared to know) that a Boston man, William Hill Brown, was about to publish a shocking narrative entitled *The Power of Sympathy,* now commonly recognized as the first American novel. In New York City a boy named Washington Irving was six years old; in Burlington, New Jersey, another boy, to be named James, was about to be born to the Cooper family, and would move, a year later, to Cooperstown.

Until Irving and Cooper grew up to help change the direction of American literature, Oneida County—and other "colonies from New-England," to use Timothy Dwight's term—continued to believe, like their Puritan ancestors, that writing was a means to an end, a tool to be used for informing, exhorting, moralizing—but never for dramatizing or merely entertaining. If copies of books like *Charlotte Temple* (1791), Brackenridge's *Modern Chivalry* (1792), or new American editions of English gothic romances (Mrs. Ann Radcliffe's *Mysteries of Udolpho,* 1794; Matthew G. Lewis' *The Monk,* 1799) appeared in central New York, they were read secretly, perhaps concealed behind the covers of more respectable works.

Whatever they thought of the new kind of writing, Oneida County people continued to build a literate audience for the future. Ironically, however, the first writers to appear in their midst were not transplanted Yankees nor even the children of Yankees. The sons and daughters of Connecticut, Massachusetts, and Vermont continued to build schools, to print newspapers, to publish books and to preach sermons—but they did not, for many years, produce any imaginative (or even secular) literature. That remained to be done by members of the non-Yankee minority—settlers and children of settlers who came to Oneida County from places other than

New England. The first two "writers" of significance to appear in Oneida County were not even American-born; one was a Dutch refugee for whom English was a recently acquired second language; the other was an English immigrant who professed scorn for fiction, but managed nevertheless to write a considerable amount of it.

The first Oneida County resident to whom writing was not only a skill but something of an art appeared—appropriately enough, since he was Dutch—in Oldenbarneveld (now Trenton) in 1797. When he arrived in Oneida County, Francis Adrian Van der Kemp was forty-five years old, an ordained Baptist minister and ex-soldier exiled from his native Holland for having rebelled against the ruling House of Orange. Encouraged by John Adams and Lafayette, Van der Kemp emigrated to America in 1788, lived first on a farm near Kingston, then on the north shore of Oneida Lake near what is now Bernhard's Bay. His friendship with Gerrit Boon and Adam Mappa, agents for the Holland Land Company, drew him eventually to Oldenbarneveld, where he was to live for more than three decades.

To his cottage near Mappa's impressive house, Van der Kemp brought the finest collection of books in the area—"Belles lettres, ancient and modern languages, first and magnificent editions neatly bound." In 1794, in a letter to John Adams, Van der Kemp valued his library at "between 400 and 500£."[3] But perhaps even more important than his books, Van der Kemp brought his own scholarship, curiosity, and skills to the small village and the surrounding area, where he was soon recognized not only as a scholar but as an intellectual leader. For the rest of his life he devoted much of his time to writing and publishing on "politics, religion, history, government, scientific agriculture, geology, the Erie Canal, the conduct of the War of 1812, and any threat to political or religious freedom."[4]

In 1818, at the request of his close friend Governor DeWitt Clinton, the sixty-six-year-old Van der Kemp took on the monumental task of translating into English the forty volumes of bound documents that served as a reminder that from 1609 until 1664 New York had been a Dutch colony. Doing much of his work at home in Oldenbarneveld, Van der Kemp was able to complete over twelve thousand pages of the Dutch records in the next five years. Unfortunately, these translations were destroyed in the devastating Albany fire in 1911; only short passages remain as quoted by nineteenth-century state historians who were able to examine them before the fire.

Readily available to the modern reader, however, is a series of remarkable letters Van der Kemp wrote to Adam Mappa in 1792. Although they were originally written in Dutch and before he settled in Oneida County, Van der Kemp later translated them into English as he busied himself with other projects in Oldenbarneveld. The collection, in English translation

entitled "Letters on a Tour Through a Part of the Western District of New
York in 1792," was read and admired by both DeWitt Clinton and John
Adams but was not published until 1877.[5]

Van der Kemp's letters to Mappa differ from most other epistolary
or journal accounts of trips into the New York wilderness that were being
written by numerous other travelers at the time. Most such accounts are
of factual rather than of literary interest. Van der Kemp's letters are informative, to be sure; but they also bear the touch of the poet-prophet. In
them he reveals himself as a kind of Dutch Crèvecoeur, whose *Letters from
an American Farmer* had been published in 1782. Van der Kemp's letters,
despite occasional faulty English idiom, constitute his vision of the future
of New York and a statement of what might be called "The Yorker Dream,"
an eloquent expression of hope and faith in the abundant future that was
in the hearts of thousands of settlers as the great interior of central and
western New York opened to them in the 1790s. Before he died in Oldenbarneveld in 1829, Van der Kemp saw a good part of his vision become
a reality. And had he written nothing except his letters to Mappa, the
doughty scholar-soldier would still deserve to be remembered as the first
real man of letters in Oneida County, or, indeed, in all of central New York.

"If my prognostics are of any avail," wrote the aging Van der Kemp
on July 24, 1824, "the name of A. B. Johnson will do honor to our country."[6] The man to whom he wrote was Alexander Bryan Johnson of Utica,
like Van der Kemp himself, a comparatively recent immigrant to America.
Johnson — born in Gosport, England, in 1786 — had arrived in Utica, a village of about 500 people, in 1801, when he was fifteen. His father, Bryan
Johnson, had already made his mark in the wilderness village as a merchant. At the time Van der Kemp wrote his approving note, Alexander Bryan
Johnson was a successful banker and a lawyer as well — although he was
never to practice law. He was also the author of an impressive book on
banking and of two pamphlets — one an attack on slavery — that prompted
Van der Kemp's admiration. Furthermore, Johnson was married to Abigail
Adams, granddaughter of Van der Kemp's long-time friend and patron,
John Adams.

Despite his success in banking, Johnson always maintained that he
"adopted that profession in order to have time and opportunity to write"
and that the great study of his life was "language with reference to its meaning in something other than words."[7] His primary interest was, to put it
another way, in what today is known as semantics — a branch of linguistics
concerned with the actual meaning of words. In this interest Johnson was
a true pioneer — "the first man to recognize what are now called semantic
problems,"[8] says Stillman Drake, and "one of America's most profound
and original thinkers, the Philosophical Banker of Utica."[9]

Between 1828 and 1864 Johnson wrote and published in a quantity that is amazing in view of his time-consuming business and commercial interests. Most of his work developed ideas about language originally presented in his second book, *The Philosophy of Human Knowledge, or a Treatise on Language* (1828).[10] For many years Johnson expressed nothing but scorn for fiction and romance: he ridiculed Scott's novels, with their "snares preparing trapdoors constructed to immire to destruction some beautiful and faultless woman"; he had "never read any of Cooper's trash" and never would; he belittled Irving's "pretty stories" as "nursery amusements." Fiction, he maintained again and again, is the enemy of knowledge because it distorts reality.

Suddenly in 1841, however, Johnson changed his mind. In this year he published anonymously and at his own expense a small book entitled *The Philosophical Emperor: A Political Experiment,* an allegory in which he attempted to explain the defeat of Martin Van Buren by William Henry Harrison in the presidential election of 1840. This defeat stemmed, Johnson maintained, from the earlier conflict between Nicholas Biddle and President Andrew Jackson, the "Philosophical Emperor" of Johnson's tale. Thinly veiled as its message is, the work comes closer to being fiction than anything Johnson had previously written, and warrants historian David Millar's praise as "a brilliant political satire which alone should earn Johnson a place in American letters."[11]

But, like his earlier work, *The Philosophical Emperor* failed to bring him either fame or the large audience he admittedly wanted. And so between 1849 and 1857 he produced a number of fictional pieces designed to dramatize and perhaps sugarcoat his original ideas about the nature of language. Most of these appeared in the widely read *Knickerbocker Magazine* starting in November 1849, when Johnson was sixty-three years old. Many of the pieces are set against Oneida County backgrounds reflected in such titles as "How to Live Where You Like, A Legend of Utica" (November 1849); "The Hermit of Utica" (March 1850); "A Day at Utica: or, the First House-warming" (September 1850); and "The Threefold Nature of Man: A Legend of the Oneida Indians" (September 1851). Despite their regular appearance in a national magazine, the stories failed to stir comment or build an audience for what Johnson undoubtedly considered his more important work. As a student of language, Johnson was a century ahead of his time; but as a writer of fiction, he was a generation behind. After 1857 he abandoned fiction and returned to straight exposition of his ideas in books, pamphlets, and articles.[12]

When he died in Utica in 1867, Johnson probably considered himself a failure as a thinker and writer. But his career was not yet over. A century after his death, a number of modern admirers of Johnson, some with international reputations—semanticists, philosophers, economists, and historians—gathered in Utica (September 8 and 9, 1967) at a conference to mark the centennial of his death. Out of this conference—cosponsored by Hamilton College and Munson-Williams-Proctor Institute—came not only a volume of proceedings, *Language and Value,* but arrangements to reprint a number of his near-forgotten works.[13] Consequently, much of Johnson's writing is more readily available today than at any time since his death.

In 1846, as Alexander Bryan Johnson was beginning to fret about a lack of audience, a younger contemporary in nearby Whitesboro was embarking on a writing career that was to be quite different from his. Johnson complained that his audience was too small and apathetic; Frances Miriam Berry's complaint was quite the reverse: in a short time her audience became both too large and too critical. Johnson's career as a published writer spanned some forty-eight years; the young Whitesboro woman's lasted a scant seven or eight. With one book, published three years after her death, Frances Miriam Berry—now remembered as Mrs. F. M. Whitcher, author of *The Widow Bedott Papers* (1855)—acquired a much larger audience than Johnson had during his lifetime, or, indeed, beyond.

Francis Adrian Van der Kemp, Alexander Bryan Johnson, and Mrs. Whitcher had at least two things in common: they lived and wrote in Oneida County, and they were of anomalous roots. None inherited any part of New England; none—with the possible exception of Johnson, who married an Adams—was touched by the Puritan flame. But they differed, as well. Both Van der Kemp and Johnson used their writing skills to instruct and inform; Mrs. Whitcher insisted on entertaining as well as instructing.

The village of Whitesboro in which Frances Miriam Berry was born in 1811 was a promising outpost on the road to the West, inhabited almost entirely by migrants from Connecticut and Vermont. The Berry family— like the Coopers in Otsego County—had come, however, from New Jersey. Family tradition had it that the first Berry in America was a Cavalier rather than a Puritan. And so, although she grew up in the midst of a Puritan "hive," Miriam Berry inherited traditions and attitudes not shared by her transplanted Yankee neighbors. She was educated—apparently very well—in the local school, where she demonstrated little of the perversity that marked her later writings. In the 1840s, however, as she joined the "Moeonian Society"—a reading club—her writing talents and her sharp critical attitudes began to surface. Some of her sketches and poems appeared in both Utica and Rome newspapers. In 1846 one of her friends sent some of her work to *Neal's Saturday Gazette,* where it was published with such editorial praise that she was prompted to attempt more ambitious work. The result was the first group of "The Widow Bedott Papers," in which Miriam Berry (whose name was not attached to the sketches) sharply satirized the manners and morals of her Yankee neighbors in Whitesboro.

In January 1847, Miriam Berry married the Rev. Benjamin W. Whitcher, an Episcopal minister who had recently organized St. John's Church in Whitesboro. The newlyweds shortly moved to a new pastoral assignment in Elmira, where Mrs. F. M. Whitcher continued writing—but now for the famous *Godey's Lady's Book*. Although her work was still appearing anonymously, Mrs. Whitcher was soon identified as the author of articles that offended some of her husband's ultrarespectable parishioners. The resulting storm led, in 1849, to the Whitchers' departure from Elmira and return to Whitesboro, where Mrs. Whitcher wrote only a few more sketches and then, no doubt frightened by what her pen had accomplished, gave up her writing career. She died in January, 1852, without ever having seen any of her writing in book form.

Three years after her death, her husband arranged for the publication as a book of most of his dead wife's "sketches." In the project he was ably assisted by his second wife, Mrs. Martha L. W. Whitcher, herself a writer of some talent. When Mrs. F. M. Whitcher's book, *The Widow Bedott Papers,* appeared in 1855, it was a nationwide success; even in Utica and Rome (as well as Elmira), where readers had once seen themselves sharply caricatured in Mrs. Whitcher's work, the book was acclaimed. It was rendered into a moderately successful Broadway play, and went on to gather new readers for the dozen different editions that appeared before the century was over. But while the nation laughed and winced and guffawed at the coarseness of "the widow Bedott," and at Mrs. Whitcher's sharp thrusts at nineteenth-century American society and its foibles— especially at "moving-on" New Englanders—Frances Miriam Berry Whitcher slept quietly in her grave in Whitesboro, on a hill that looks down on the spot where she was born. She never knew what happened.[14]

One who *did* know what happened, however, was Mrs. Whitcher's sister. Kate Berry (1817–65) was never to produce a best seller or a "widow Bedott"; but she was to become a competent writer, with an audience of her own in the same magazines—including *Godey's Lady's Book*—that published her sister's work. In the 1840s and 1850s Kate Berry wrote for national magazines pieces (including a memoir of her posthumously famous sister) that indicate that she did not—any more than her sister—belong to what a grumpy Nathaniel Hawthorne called the "damned mob of scribbling women" who dominated magazine publications in America in the 1850s. But Kate Berry's talents were never fully developed; she lacked the sharp eye and ear, and the even sharper pen of her sister. Nevertheless, her name deserves a place in the developing story of literature in Oneida County.

Even though the Berry sisters did not belong to the group that Hawthorne complained about, Oneida County produced its share of women writers who did. One of the first was Mrs. Elizabeth Jesup Eames of New Hartford. Mrs. Eames, a native of the Hudson Valley, moved with her new husband into central New York in 1837. Her position and inclinations gave her opportunity to read widely, especially in the classics, and to develop a talent for bookish poetry. Whereas Mrs. F. M. Whitcher kept her eyes on her Whitesboro neighbors, Mrs. Eames looked to Tasso and Petrarch for her inspiration. There was a town square in her village, but she did not walk in it; her neighbors spoke Yankee, but she did not listen to them; if their manners were bad, she did not notice. She stayed with her books and respectable models. The poetry she produced in what must have been a good home library reflects all this. If the verse was genteel, it was competent, and Mrs. Eames had little trouble in placing it with *Graham's, The Southern Literary Messenger,* and other reputable national magazines. The highest contemporary tribute to her work came perhaps when Rufus W. Griswold gave prominent and permanent exposure to a number of her poems in an anthology that is still extremely valuable despite its title, *The Female Poets of America* (1860)[15] — although it should be noted that Griswold omitted her work from his earlier anthology, *The Poets and Poetry of America.*

Another young woman of talent who responded to the taste of her times was Emily Chubbock (1817–54), who was for a short time during the 1840s a teacher in a Utica "female seminary." Actually, Oneida County has but slight claim on her. She was a native of next-door Madison County and, during her Utica stay, was en route to a career in faraway places. Nevertheless, her experience in Utica provided some material for the sentimental and lugubrious pieces she wrote under the pseudonym of "Fanny Forester." Published originally in the 1840s in the *New York Mirror,* her sketches and poems were collected in 1847 in *Alderbrook,* a volume that went through nine editions in the next three years. In 1846 she married the Rev. Adoniram Judson, a leading Baptist missionary of the time, and accompanied him to Burma; there she helped him to compile the first Burmese-English dictionary. Back in America after her husband's death in 1850, she wrote his biography before her own death in 1854.[16]

The production of literature in Oneida County before the Civil War was certainly not restricted to the authors discussed above. They were the ones, however, who achieved some degree of national recognition as writers. Throughout the county there were numerous other literary-minded citizens whose efforts were regularly published in Oneida County newspapers. Almost always these efforts — poems, short pieces of fiction, and essays — appeared anonymously or under a pseudonym impossible to cut through today. A good example of the way early Oneida County residents attempted to fictionize their own history can be found in Pomroy Jones' *Annals and Recollections of Oneida County,* pp. 664–70.[17] Countless other examples appear in the pages of antebellum newspapers like the Utica *Gazette* and the *Roman Citizen.*

Nor were the authors of poetry and fiction the only writers at work during this period. Some of the most stirring writing was done, in fact, by Oneidans who shared their Puritan forefathers' belief that writing must be useful, must serve some strong moral purpose. Perhaps the most notable was the Rev. Beriah Green (1795–1874) of Whitesboro, second president of the Oneida Institute (forerunner of the famous Whitestown Seminary). Green's fiery sermons, many of which were later published in book form, were often marked by dramatic rhetoric — especially when he was expounding on educational theory or attacking slavery. A glance at his *Sermons and Discourses* (1860), for instance, reveals that Green — especially when angry — was a latter-day, local Jeremiah, capable of verbal effects that poets and dramatists might well envy. Toward the end of his stormy career, Green was a scarred warrior, veteran of numerous moral and religious campaigns; he even died in a kind of battle — of a heart attack in Whitesboro Town Hall, where he was warning an audience of the evils of drink.[18]

Turbulent as its political and social climate was at mid-nineteenth century, Oneida County produced no literature worthy of comparison with what was being written in New England. Central New York writers were silent at the very time that Emerson, Thoreau, and Hawthorne were shaping American letters during the early 1850s — a half-decade that F. O. Matthiessen labeled "the American Renaissance." Two New Yorkers — Herman Melville and Walt Whitman — were, to be sure, central to this "Renaissance"; but Oneida County had no part in it. The seeds of Emersonian transcendentalism drifted across Long Island Sound and sprouted into *Leaves of Grass*; but they did not drift westward on the Mohawk. If Oneida County writers were aware of Emerson and Thoreau, their awareness did not show in writing. Neither A. B. Johnson nor Mrs. F. M. Whitcher seems to have been touched by New England transcendentalism.

On the other hand, Melville — on whom Oneida County has no claim whatever — did contribute to what might be called Oneida mythology by eulogizing his grandfather, Peter Gansevoort, the sturdy commander of Fort Stanwix during the Burgoyne campaign of 1777. Colonel Gansevoort was dead years before Melville was born, but his name and fame were around young Melville as he grew up in New York City and Albany. In *Pierre* — an ill-starred novel published in 1852, only a year after *Moby-Dick* — Melville canonized Gansevoort as "grand old Pierre," whose superb

portrait by Gilbert Stuart had dominated homes in which the future novelist lived as a child. Gansevoort, never a resident of Oneida County, is nevertheless a local or regional hero, and Melville's question, "Where is grand
old Pierre?" is easily answered: grand old Pierre — or at least his famous
portrait — is still in Oneida County, hung carefully and impressively in
Utica's Munson-Williams-Proctor Institute, only thirteen miles from the
spot where he first earned fame.

Meanwhile, during the 1840s and 1850s, other writers — not Oneida
County born or bred — became aware of the dramatic potential of the fierce
battle fought near Oriskany on 6 August 1777 between Nicholas Herkimer's untrained militia and Colonel Barry St. Leger's force of British regu-
lars, Mohawk Valley Tories, and Indians — a force that was charged with
joining General Burgoyne's main British army near Albany, there to cut
off New England from the rest of the rebelling colonies. What happened
at Oriskany on that hot August day is still something of a mystery; Herkimer's men and St. Leger's fought to what seems to have been a standoff.
But as a result of the refusal of Herkimer's untrained men to give way,
St. Leger and his badly needed reinforcements never reached Burgoyne,
who was forced to surrender at Saratoga in October 1777.

For half a century the significance of the battle of Oriskany was generally overlooked; then, thanks to diligent local historians of the eastern
end of the valley — men like W. W. Campbell *(Annals of Tryon County)*,
W. L. Stone *(The Life of Joseph Brant),* and others — some kind of truth
came to be known. Charles Fenno Hoffman, a promising Albany writer,
was the first to dramatize Oriskany in a novel, *Greyslaer* (1840). Some
years later, Thomas Dunn English, a New Jersey poet best remembered
today for his poem "Ben Bolt," wrote a long narrative poem, "The Fight
at Oriskany," that appeared in *Harper's New Monthly* in August 1861.
Hoffman and English thus were two of the first to dramatize Oriskany
on a national scale; the fierce battle would later attract the imaginative
attention of numerous American writers, including a number of Oneida
County residents.

Long before the Civil War the geography, as well as the military history, of the county received admiring treatment by numerous writers, including Europeans who passed through the area. One of the great tourist
attractions in America before the Civil War (and after, as well) was Trenton Falls, on West Canada Creek. Among the thousands of awed visitors
to the falls who later recorded their reactions in writing was Mrs. Frances
Trollope, an Englishwoman who described the rugged beauty of the area
in her provocative *Domestic Manners of the Americans,* first published
in 1832. Even before Mrs. Trollope's book appeared, another famous English traveler, Captain Basil Hall, had told the English-speaking world about

Trenton Falls. A score of poets were inspired by the "leaping water" that leaps today only when permitted by the power industry.[19]

During the war, and for years afterward, little imaginative writing of consequence came out of Oneida County — or, for that matter, out of the nation itself, slow to recover (at least artistically) from the recent trauma. Whitman went on, although few as yet recognized his genius; other writers whose careers were established before Harper's Ferry were now either dead, hushed, or so shaken that they began to move (like W. C. Bryant and J. R. Lowell) in different directions. A new generation with new attitudes toward literature began to appear when young William Dean Howells took over the prestigious *Atlantic Monthly* in 1871 and called for a new kind of writing in America. In many parts of the nation there was healthy response in the form of what is now called "local-color" fiction — but New York was slow to react. In Brockport, Monroe County, Mary Jane Holmes went back to writing fabulously successful domestic novels of the kind she had turned out since *Lena Rivers* (1856). In 1873, in Adams (south of Watertown, in Jefferson County), Marietta Holley produced the first of her "Samantha" novels that would make her rich and briefly famous. At about the same time, a clear-eyed solitary named Philander Deming, working in Albany, started to write a series of stark short stories about life in the North Country that would appear in the *Atlantic* in the 1870s. From Oneida County, however, came no new voices. But one was soon to be heard.

In 1880 a twenty-four-year-old youngster named Harold Frederic became editor of the Utica *Observer* after having served an apprenticeship of only five years. During the next eighteen years, until his death in London in 1898, Frederic was to prove himself not only a great journalist but a novelist of high order. Born on South Street, Utica, in 1856, Frederic graduated from the old Advanced School and shortly thereafter began his newspaper career. After two years as editor of the *Observer,* he served another two years as editor of the Albany *Journal* before becoming European correspondent for the *New York Times* in 1884. Between 1887 and 1896, despite demanding journalistic responsibilities in late Victorian England, Frederic produced a series of novels and shorter works that portrayed his native Oneida County and the Mohawk Valley with incomparable dramatic effectiveness.

Responding to William Dean Howells' plea for realistic — as opposed to romantic — treatment of contemporary American life, Frederic first wrote *Seth's Brother's Wife* (1887), which reflected his newspaper experience in both Utica and Albany as well as his thorough knowledge of New York State politics in the turbulent early 1880s. In 1890, he followed with two more novels. One, *The Lawton Girl,* is set in an Oneida County village (in Frederic's fiction Oneida County is always called "Dearborn" County) beset by economic problems caused by ruthless outside manipulators who seek to gain control of a mine that is the mainstay of the local economy. In this novel Frederic also dramatized some of the reform or social movements of the 1880s and laid the foundation for the attention he was to pay in later novels to the role of the emerging "new woman" in both American and English society of the last decade of the century.

Published in the same year (1890) was *In the Valley,* which Stephen Crane later praised as "easily the best historical novel that our country has borne." Actually, Frederic had started to write this tale as early as 1877, the year of the great centennial celebration of the battle of Oriskany, which he had covered as a young reporter. But technical problems and other demands on his time had postponed completion of the novel for a dozen years. Applauded in both America and England when it finally appeared, *In the Valley* was the first full-length fictional treatment of the American Revolution as it was fought in the Mohawk Valley through 1777. The novel is romantic in concept but realistic in technique — perhaps the first revisionist novel in American historical fiction. In it, Frederic's sympathies are obviously with the Palatine-German farmers who worried about a future dominated by the Johnson and Butler Tories, and who joined Nicholas Herkimer's ranks to stop St. Leger at Oriskany. *In the Valley* contains the most vivid and accurate account of the battle of Oriskany in fiction. But the farmers in Frederic's book are not all heroes, and the British and Tories are not all villains. Even Walter Butler, the whipping boy scoundrel for a century up and down the valley, receives judicious treatment in *In the Valley* — the first he had been accorded since his death on the West Canada Creek in November 1781. *In the Valley,* even with an interwoven love story that some critics find banal, remains the best fictional treatment of the complicated issues that racked the valley in the years following the death of Sir William Johnson in 1774. It also provides depth — a historical context — against which Frederic's novels about contemporary Oneida County can be more appreciatively read.

In the early 1890s Frederic turned from both the present and the distant past to write a group of stories stemming from his small-boy memories of Oneida County during the Civil War — "the dreadful time," as he called the period, when a boy's "own relatives were being killed, and his school-fellows orphaned, and women of his neighborhood forced into mourning and despair." These stories — including two novelettes, "The Copperhead" and "The Deserter," as well as five shorter pieces — are actually unique in American literature. Nowhere else has a writer of fiction recorded so vividly and thoroughly, even from a distance in time, the way a single northern community received the shock of news from the faraway

South during those dismal years. The stories are, to use again the words of Stephen Crane, of "the great country back of the line of fight—the waiting women, the lightless windows, the tables set for three instead of five." More recently, the distinguished critic Edmund Wilson praised the stories as containing "in general no melodrama, no romance, and very little sentiment. The anguish and bitterness caused by the disruption of domestic life and the discordance of once quiet communities [in Oneida County] is treated with sober and ironic restraint."

Even as he was finishing the series of Civil War stories, Frederic was busy at a novel that would win him his greatest fame. Published in 1896 in America as *The Damnation of Theron Ware* and in England as *Illumination,* this work quickly became a best seller on both sides of the Atlantic. The novel is set in "Octavius" (i.e., Utica) and dramatizes the problems of an unsophisticated young minister who is not prepared to cope with intellectual, moral, and sexual problems that confront him in a new environment. Into his story Frederic introduced a number of memorable characters, including an urbane and erudite Catholic priest (the first fully drawn priest in American fiction); a brilliant, beautiful, rich, and liberated young woman whose ideas about life and art fascinate Theron Ware; and a strange husband-wife team of professional fund raisers to whom Ware turns when his own moral fibre disintegrates. The novel also contains a number of brilliant scenes against backgrounds that modern Oneida County readers will easily recognize. The opening chapter describes action in what is now Utica's Central Methodist Church. Following are scenes in what Uticans will recognize as St. John's Church and rectory on Bleecker Street. And the long, climactic scene describes both a Methodist meeting at Trenton Assembly Park and an Irish Catholic picnic at nearby Downer's Grove, near Trenton Falls.

At the core of *The Damnation of Theron Ware* is Frederic's dramatic treatment of the way in which new ideas about religion, art, and science found their way into a small, basically conservative community like Utica and bewildered a bright young clergyman trained in an older, passing tradition. Years after its publication, Frederic's novel was enthusiastically praised by F. Scott Fitzgerald and Sinclair Lewis, who admittedly felt Frederic's influence as he wrote his own *Elmer Gantry.* But Frederic himself had now completed his fictional scrutiny of Oneida County and the valley. In a unified body of work he had considered the history, politics, economics, and religious patterns of his native area. After 1896—until his early death two years later—he turned to England for material for his last works.[20] When it was all over, he returned in death to his beloved Oneida County to be buried in Forest Hills cemetery, a mile or so from his birthplace.

At the very time Harold Frederic sat brooding in London, looking westward across the Atlantic and planning his first novels about the Mohawk Valley, a number of other Oneida County writers were either beginning or continuing literary careers of their own, quite different from Frederic's. One of these was Rose Elizabeth Cleveland (1846–1918) of Holland Patent, youngest sister of President Grover Cleveland. Born in Fayetteville, New York, Rose grew up in Holland Patent, where her father served briefly as pastor of the Presbyterian Church until his death in 1853. After their father's death, young Grover Cleveland moved on to Buffalo, there to study law and begin his career in politics. When he was elected governor of New York in 1882, Rose joined him in Albany to serve as hostess in his bachelor's mansion. There both Clevelands met Harold Frederic, newly appointed editor of the Albany *Journal*, and a lasting friendship resulted. When Grover Cleveland moved into the White House in 1884, still a bachelor, Rose stayed with him to serve as temporary First Lady until the President's marriage in 1885, when she returned to her mother's home in Holland Patent.

But Rose Cleveland was no mere assistant or servant to a distinguished brother. Well-educated and articulate, she produced — even while busy with her duties in the White House — a volume of criticism, *George Eliot's Poetry and Other Studies* (1885) that was well received. Shortly after her return to Holland Patent she published a novel, *The Long Run* (1886). Later she wrote children's books and, in 1910, an English translation of the *Soliloquies of St. Augustine*. Always an intrepid and compassionate woman, she was, at the time of her death in 1918 at the age of seventy-two, engaged in social work in war-ravaged Lucca, Italy; there she lies buried — three thousand miles from the Oneida County village where she is still remembered in her own right as a personality and author, as well as a First Lady whose intelligence and general demeanor was of invaluable assistance to her brother, the President.[21]

Another Oneida County writer busy in the 1870s and 1880s was an aging man whose career had begun long before either Harold Frederic or Rose Cleveland was born. Leicester Ambrose Sawyer (1807–98) was born in Lewis County, graduated from Hamilton College as valedictorian of the class of 1828, from Princeton Theological Seminary in 1831, and moved about in various assignments until 1854, when he became pastor of the Congregational Church in Westmoreland. In 1860, having declared himself an "independent Christian minister," he moved to Whitesboro, where he was to spend the rest of his life writing, lecturing, and — for a time — serving as night editor and religious columnist for the Utica *Morning Herald*. In this last capacity, which he filled from 1868 to 1883, he must certainly have known young Harold Frederic, although there is no documentary evidence of their acquaintance. Sawyer was already sixty-eight when Frederic began a brief stint with the Utica *Herald* as a boy of nineteen. Riding the horse-cars to Utica daily from his home on the park in Whitesboro, Sawyer carried with him ideas about the Bible and the history of Christianity that would later appear in Frederic's masterpiece, *The Damnation of Theron Ware*.

Sawyer was hardly an "imaginative" or "creative" writer; he wrote no fiction or poetry. He was, rather, a fearless scholar-intellectual whose mind led him — during a life that encompassed all but nine years of the entire nineteenth century — into strange seas of religious thought, and whose constantly busy pen produced a quantity of articles and books that startled his more orthodox neighbors — at least those who were aware that in his Whitesboro home he had produced new translations of both the Old and New Testaments that differed substantially from conventional translations. In essence, he maintained that existing translations of the Bible were inaccurate and that, with the exception of five of Paul's epistles, the entire New Testament was a fiction — that the other nine letters ascribed to Paul were written long after his death. In a dozen books, the brave old ex-minister strove to get at what he hoped was the truth of holy scripture. Few people read him or listened to his lectures in Whitesboro on "Sacred History and the Sacred Books" in 1874. But the venerable battler remained undaunted. In the dedication, to his cousin, of his volume entitled *The Final Theology,* Volume I, Sawyer wrote: "My life has been given chiefly to the study and exposition of the Christian religion, its sacred books, its early and medieval history, its later developments and conflicts. . . . My work, if successful, will be revolutionary, but not destructive. It assails nothing that is true, nothing that is good. Its aim is to build up for all coming ages." In an editorial the day after Sawyer's death in 1898, at the age of ninety-one, the Utica *Morning Herald* — somewhat bewildered as to how to evaluate Sawyer's career — correctly pointed out that long before anything was heard about the "higher criticism" [i.e., historical investigation of the Bible] Sawyer had led the way.[22]

In 1887, as the indomitable Sawyer struggled with Biblical problems in his Whitesboro home, a younger Utican, David Skaats Foster (1852–1920), turned to writing — perhaps as a relief from the tedium of his coal and iron business. Before his death, Foster produced twelve books, most of them novels. Although few attracted wide readership, *Elinor Fenton, an Adirondack Story* (1893), tells an interesting story of the lumber industry in and around "Fentondale," a hamlet on the edge of the Adirondacks that could be the village of Lyons Falls. *Elinor Fenton* was successful enough to prompt Foster to rewrite it, changing the names of the characters, and to republish it in 1915 as *Our Uncle William; also, Nate Sawyer*. Foster's other books — including the first, *The Romance of the Unexpected* (1887) —

are so varied in theme, technique, and subject matter that they cannot be categorized.[23]

Unlike Foster's, the work of Clinton Scollard (1860–1932), both poetry and prose, reflects a strong unifying principle. Scollard was born in the village of Clinton, graduated from Hamilton College in 1881 and later taught there (1888–96, 1911–12), after graduate work at Columbia and Cambridge universities. Although he traveled considerably, most of his life was spent in his native village. From his first volume of poetry, *Pictures in Song* (1884) until his last, *The Singing Heart,* published posthumously in 1934, Scollard remained true to his late-romantic principles, admitting that the major influences on his own poetry were Keats and Shelley and that his favorite later poets included Dante Gabriel Rossetti and Sidney Lanier. As a result of these interests, and perhaps his own academic training and experience, Scollard's poetry over the years remained eclectic: technically skillful but never original or experimental. In the more than thirty thin volumes that came from his pen, Scollard pleased his readers with French forms, neat lyrics of the long ago and far away, and semimystical verse that reflects an outdated pantheism. The bulk of his poetry now represents a futile attempt to breathe new life into a literary tradition that was terminally ill even as his first volume appeared in the middle of what American literary historians call our poetic "doldrums." In a review of Scollard's *Old and New World Lyrics* (1888), William Dean Howells remarked pointedly that "It is useless to blink the fact that both [Frank Dempster Sherman] and Mr. Scollard have been influenced by the agreeable masters of the modern English school of rondeau and triolet makers." This was obviously a dismissal of Scollard's verse by a critic who was calling for new patterns in American literature.

But Scollard was not always looking to exotic lands and practising outworn techniques. Occasionally he looked out the window of his home on College Street in Clinton and saw parts of contemporary, as well as historical, America. It is possible, for instance, to find scattered throughout his ultraromantic verse a poem such as "Harding Hill," a picture of part of the noble escarpment that rises sharply to the west of Clinton; or a tribute to the Oneida chief contained in *Skenandoa* (1896); or a rousing ballad, entitled "St. Leger, August, 1777" that recalls the battle of Oriskany. Even more memorable are two light but readable novels set in Oneida County. The first of these, *The Son of a Tory* (1901), retells the story of the siege of Fort Stanwix and the battle in "bloody gulch." The second, *A Knight of the Highway* (1908), set in contemporary times, recalls vividly that the growing of hops was once a major industry in Oneida County. This pleasant story tells the modern reader more about the customs and traditions of hop-growing and hop-picking than any other source now readily available. After enjoying it, the reader wishes that Clinton Scollard had looked more often to places like Deansboro and Waterville for his material, rather than to the kind of Graustarkian never-never lands that more often drew his attention.[24]

In his dedication to romantic poetry, Scollard found literary kinship with a younger man, Thomas S. Jones, Jr., of Boonville (1882–1932), whose first volume, *Path O'Dreams* appeared in 1905, a year after he graduated from Cornell University, where he was class poet. Although Jones worked with the dramatic staff of the *New York Times* and became editor of Reuter's Cable Service in New York for two years, a heart condition forced his return to Utica and Boonville from 1907 to 1914. There he met both Clinton Scollard, who counseled him in technique, and G. W. Browning, the Clinton publisher who brought out a number of his later books, including five small volumes in 1908 and 1909. In 1910 and 1911 Jones and Scollard collaborated on three more volumes, also published by Browning. In 1914 Jones returned to New York City, although his ties to Oneida County continued to be strong. After much travel in Europe, which resulted in more poetry that received considerable critical praise, he died in 1932 and was buried in Boonville, his native village.

Perhaps as a result of Scollard's influence, Jones was at his poetic best with demanding forms — especially the sonnet. But whereas Scollard was a vague kind of pantheist, Jones cherished organized religion and tradition and consequently had religious heroes — especially the French Jesuits — and concrete religious ideas to express in poetry. *Shadow of the Perfect Rose,* for instance (published posthumously in 1937), contains a number of sonnets that are fine by any standards. Like his friend Scollard, Jones was a bookish man, and often expressed in sonnets his admiration for such historical European figures as Pico della Mirandola, Michelangelo, Copernicus, Galileo, and Pascal, as well as his own English masters, Donne, Herbert, Vaughan, and Crashaw. But he could also look closer to home for his inspirations and produce splendid sonnets about Jacques Cartier, Jean de Bréboeuf, and Isaac Jogues. And in one poem (also a sonnet), "The Unicorn," he reached a height that prompted one competent American critic, R. P. T. Coffin, to compare his work with that of Francis Thompson, the English author of "The Hound of Heaven."[25]

Even before Jones' first volume appeared, another Utican, William Walker Canfield, had discovered a different kind of romantic material that deserved to be recorded. Canfield, who was to become editor of the Utica *Observer-Dispatch,* was one of the first central New Yorkers to collect and transcribe the lore and mythology of the Iroquois. Inspired, no doubt, by Lewis Henry Morgan's seminal *League of the Ho-de-no-sau-nee, or Iroquois* (1851), Canfield spent years gathering his material, which was published in 1902 as *The Legends of the Iroquois, told by "The Cornplanter."* This work appeared at an appropriate time. In 1901 and 1902, Robert W. Chambers of Broadalbin had published two very popular novels, *Cardigan* and *The Maid-at-Arms,* both of which prompted wide interest in the story of the Iroquois. Canfield's work complemented Chambers' and gave further impetus to more careful study of Iroquois life that was to come later in the definitive studies of Arthur C. Parker.

A decade after the appearance of *Legends of the Iroquois,* Canfield put his knowledge of Indian life into a novel, *The White Seneca* (1911), admitting in a foreword that the work was written for "the young, and such adults as have not lost taste for a tale of adventure." The tale is written in the old tradition of the captivity narrative, popular in America since colonial times, and still popular; but it also contains something new — a fictional account of the battle of Oriskany told from the point of view of the Indians who participated in the ambush of Herkimer's army. A year after *The White Seneca,* Canfield produced another Indian work, *At Seneca Castle* (1912), which further dramatized his devotion to study of the Iroquois.[26]

Except for the fiction of Canfield and the continuing volumes of poetry from Scollard and Thomas S. Jones, Jr., little imaginative writing in the form of fiction or poetry came out of Oneida County during the first quarter of the twentieth century. Occasionally, a small volume of verse appeared: Mrs. Clara Griffith Gazzam produced *Port O'Dreams* in 1911; Mrs. Nannie Deaderick Betts' *Flower of the Season* appeared in 1912; Mrs. Annie Crim Leavenworth's *Wild Geese and Other Poems,* in 1921; Mrs. Mary McGavern Combs' *In May and Other Poems,* in 1922; and Margaret Root Garvin produced two volumes separated by several years — *Walled Garden and Other Poems* (1913) and *Peacocks in the Sun* (1925).[27]

Also during these years a group of young men, only temporary residents of the county, passed through Hamilton College en route to notable careers as writers. Samuel Hopkins Adams, whose love affair with central New York was to continue until his death in 1958, graduated from Hamilton in 1891 and went on to write such favorites as *Canal Town* (1944), *Grandfather Stories* (1955), and *Tenderloin* (1959) — all published after a long and great career in magazine journalism. Ezra Pound, considered by some critics to be the most influential poet of the twentieth century, acquired his degree in 1905 and stormed out of the quiet village of Clinton into the most controversial literary career of the twentieth century. Alexander Woolcott, the "Town Crier" of the great days of radio, graduated in 1909; Alec Drummond and Harold W. Thompson, teacher-playwright and folklorist respectively, followed shortly, as did John Van Alstyne Weaver, poet and playwright. Carl Carmer, of the class of 1914, went on to a distinguished career as a folklorist, poet, and folk-historian. All carried with them into the world beyond something of what might be called the Oneida County mystique.

Not until 1929, however, did another born-and-bred Oneida County writer make a real stir in American letters. Walter D. Edmonds was, in his own words, "born in Boonville in the east bedroom" in 1903. After being educated at private New England schools and Harvard, from which he graduated in 1926, Edmonds came home to discover two features of the upstate landscape that few writers had ever noticed before: the Black River and the Erie canals. After publishing several short stories in magazines like *Scribner's* and the *Atlantic Monthly,* he turned to a novel, published in 1929 as *Rome Haul.* Set in the 1850s, *Rome Haul* is, surprisingly enough, the first significant fictional treatment of life on the New York state canals that had all but disappeared before Edmonds discovered them and brought them back to life. A critical as well as a popular success, *Rome Haul* was later made into a play and, still later, into a motion picture entitled *The Farmer Takes a Wife.*

The reception of Edmonds' first novel set the direction for his later career. In 1930 he published *The Big Barn* (reprinted later as *The Magnificent Wilders*), essentially the story of an Oneida County patriarch who wants to establish a strong family tradition that will live after him. Next came *Erie Water* (1933), a panoramic fictional study of the building of New York's Grand Canal. In 1934 came a collection of Edmonds' short stories, *Mostly Canallers,* which contains — according to Edmund Wilson, Edmonds' lifelong friend — some of his best work. In 1936 Edmonds published *Drums Along the Mohawk,* certainly one of the most popular historical novels ever to appear in America. A much longer novel than Frederic's *In the Valley,* Edmonds' *Drums* spans the years 1776–84 and introduces not only fictitious characters but a host of real-life figures with family names that still flourish proudly along the Mohawk — Weavers, Realls, Demooths, Helmers, and Smalls, among others, who fought through Oriskany and beyond until the threat of aristocratic control of the valley was completely destroyed. *Drums Along the Mohawk* was made into a motion picture that was still being shown on television forty years after the novel first appeared.

Edmonds' next work was *Chad Hanna* (1940), which takes the reader on a delightful tour with a circus throughout upstate New York during the 1830s. Traveling in a big circle from Canastota, where the action begins, to the road to Coxsackie Landing, young Chad Hanna and "Huguenines Great and Only International Circus and Equestriole" visit bustling upstate villages that had never been pictured in fiction before. *Chad Hanna* became the third of Edmonds' novels to be transferred to the motion picture screen, starring young Henry Fonda, who had already starred in *The Farmer Takes a Wife* (i.e., *Rome Haul*). Seven years after *Chad Hanna* came two shorter works. One of these, *In the Hands of the Senecas* (1947), is Edmonds' contribution to the perennially fascinating captivity narrative (like Canfield's *The White Seneca*) which recounts the trials and troubles of a white who is captured by Indians. The second, *The Wedding Journey* (also 1947), is a charming story about a wedding trip from Schenectady to Buffalo in 1835 on an Erie Canal packet. Into this short novel, obviously one of the author's own favorites, Edmonds reintroduced characters (or at least names) familiar to readers of his earlier works. The captain of the packet *The Western Lion,* for instance, is Dan Harrow, father of the young hero of the earlier *Rome Haul*; and one of the passengers is Mrs. Lucy Cashdollar of Utica, the central figure in "The Voice of the Archangel," an early Edmonds short story that appeared in the *Atlantic* in January 1928. After these short works, Edmonds produced *The Boyds of Black River* (1953), the story of a family of horse-breeding farmers in the early 1900s. Most of the action of this full-length novel occurs on land directly across the Black River from Edmonds' own home near Boonville; Oneida County readers will relish many scenes, including a breakneck race down Deerfield Hill between a blue-blooded horse and an early Packard automobile (the horse wins). Since *The Boyds of Black River,* Edmonds has devoted his time to nonfiction and children's books (his first juvenile, *The Matchlock Gun* of 1941, won the coveted Newbery Award). *The Musket and the Cross* (1968) is a history of colonial New York and recalls the activities of the French Jesuits in the seventeenth and eighteenth centuries.

In order to be fully appreciated, Edmonds' work—like that of the earlier Cooper and Harold Frederic—is most significant when read in context. Whereas Frederic provides a horizontal picture of Oneida County in the 1870s and 1880s in *Seth's Brother's Wife, The Lawton Girl,* and *The Damnation of Theron Ware,* Edmonds provides a vertical picture of approximately the same area from 1776 to about 1910. From *Drums Along the Mohawk* to *The Boyds of Black River,* Edmonds' fiction provides the reader with a colorful story of the development of upstate New York from Revolutionary times to the early days of the twentieth century. With the exception of Hawthorne and William Faulkner, few American writers have looked so carefully and lovingly at their native soil and the history that has accrued on it.[28]

Rome Haul was published in February, 1929, some nine months before the nation started its unhappy plunge into the Great Depression. During the many economically dismal years that followed, a number of upstate novelists followed Edmonds' lead and looked to their own familiar areas for new values and attitudes to carry them through troublesome times. During the next twenty-five years — that is, well beyond World War II — a great quantity of regional fiction (i.e., fiction in which local setting plays an important part) appeared in upstate New York. Among the "new regionalists," as they came to be called, were several Oneida County writers.

Paul Hoffman's *Seven Yesterdays* (1933) is a semiautobiographical novel about a boyhood and adolescence in the upstate city of "Naples," in "Mohican County." The seven loosely related chapters recall the life (from about 1910 to about 1930) of a German Protestant family, with action in the "Maize Hill" section of the city. With its pictures of German-American characters and traditions and its simple sincerity, Hoffman's novel has, in the words of an admiring *New York Times* reviewer, "a quality of wistful charm and sensitivity rare in contemporary writings."

Five years later, another Utican, Joseph Vogel, produced a novel quite different in most ways from Hoffman's. *Man's Courage* (1938) is a proletarian novel of social protest, set in the Polish section of Utica, here called "Genesee," during the darkest days of the depression. Vogel's work contains vivid and angry pictures of relief administration in the early and mid-1930s. At the end of the novel, Polish-American Adam Wolak, trying to save his family from eviction, is shot to death by a marshal in a brutal confrontation scene. Vogel's book is not, however, an indictment of individuals; it is rather — like much of John Steinbeck's earlier fiction — a protest against a humiliating and frustrating system.[29]

Two less vigorous but much happier novels came from the pen of Consolata Carroll (Sister Mary Consolata) in 1947 and 1949. A native of Rome, Sister Consolata looked back to a pleasant childhood in an Irish Catholic family first in *Pray Love, Remember* (1947) and continued her semiautobiographical work in *I Hear in My Heart* (1949). As in the fiction of earlier Oneida County writers, Sister Consolata's cheerful pictures contain background scenes — including some that center on Rome Free Academy — that many central New Yorkers will recognize and relish.

Less than twenty years later, the Welsh, too, took their place in this series of fictional ethnic or sociological studies of Oneida County's varied population. In 1964 Howard Thomas of Prospect — who had already published a number of valuable volumes of local history, biography, and folklore — produced *The Singing Hills,* a novel about Welsh settlers in the Steuben hills in the 1840s. In this and in a second novel, *The Road to Sixty* (1966), Thomas drew memorable pictures of Welsh-American customs and traditional ceremonies that had found their way from ancient Wales to the rolling hills of northern Oneida County.

Even more recently, Eugene Paul Nassar, a professor at Utica College and lifelong resident of the city, wrote *East Utica* (1971). This evocative prose-poem, set in the city's substantial Lebanese community, reminds

us that still another ethnic group has contributed much to the interesting
variety of Oneida County life. Covering the years 1944–64, Nassar's work
takes the reader along an "infamous, colorful, insulted" Bleecker Street,
into the mills on Broad Street and "the Ah'we," a Lebanese-Syrian coffee
house on Elizabeth Street. It crosses ethnic lines to let the reader hear the
Banda Rosa, Italian musicians "tooting, wiggling, and drumming . . . for
the Madonna and her Son and Santa Rosalia," patron saint of Sicily. All
this is part of a journey that few Americans, even in Oneida County, have
ever made. *East Utica* is, in essence, the story of a sensitive young person
who, though born in the New World, is aware of strong ties to the Old;
who realizes (sadly, at times) that he may be of the last generation of Americans to feel the strong pull of ancient traditions and loyalties; and who
knows that the term "The American Dream" — now in disrepute — derives
much from the vision and values of his immigrant parents and neighbors
who, while they looked to a future, refused to forget a proud past.[30]

Thus four large ethnic groups in the county — the Germans, the Poles,
the Irish, and the Lebanese — produced literary spokesmen who told their
story in competent fiction. Meanwhile, from 1926 on another group of
young men finished their studies at Hamilton College and moved on to
other places and careers that included writing. B. F. Skinner graduated
in 1926 and went on to become not only a world-famed psychologist but
the author of a dystopian novel, *Walden II.* Louis C. Jones, class of 1930,
later the distinguished Director of the New York State Historical Association, stayed close to his ancestral ties along the Mohawk, and produced
two books beloved of all American devotees of ghostlore, *Spooks of the
Valley* (1948) and *Things That Go Bump in the Night* (1959). Howard C.
Hosmer, who graduated in 1933, moved into a career in journalism but
also made a name as a historian of Rochester and Monroe County. Lionel
Wyld, class of 1949, later wrote the widely read *Low Bridge! Folklore and
the Erie Canal* (1962). John T. Nichols II, class of 1962, wrote *The Sterile
Cuckoo,* a novel that contains many scenes familiar to Oneida County
readers; the motion picture version starring Liza Minelli, was filmed in
good part against location backgrounds at Hamilton College and Sylvan
Beach.

Not to be forgotten either are several writers who, although legal
residents of adjoining counties, had strong attachments to Oneida County
that surfaced in their writing. Constance Noyes Robertson, for instance,
belongs properly to Madison County, but Oneida County owes her a debt
of thanks for such novels as *Seek-No-Further* (1938), a fictional account
of life in a community much like the one founded by Mrs. Robertson's
grandfather, John Humphrey Noyes, almost on the border between Madison and Oneida counties. Other novels that came from her pen, like *Salute*

to the Hero (1942), *Fire Bell in the Night* (1944), *The Unterrified* (1946), *Six Weeks in March* (1953), and *Go and Catch a Falling Star* (1957), reflect her continuing interest in upstate history and culture and often carry the reader across the dim border that separates Oneida from her sister counties.

Like Mrs. Robertson, Herman Peterson of Poolville, near the village of Hamilton, was a resident of Madison County. Nevertheless, two of his fast-moving novels are filled with a history in which Oneida County has a part. The first of these, *The Covered Bridge* (1950), is — like Clinton Scollard's earlier *A Knight of the Highway* — a story of the hop-growing country of which Oneida County was once a part. The second, *The Road* (1952), retells the story of the infamous Loomis Gang (Peterson calls them the "Huggins" gang) and their forays from a base in Nine-Mile Swamp. Peterson's account of the "Hugginses" differs from Harriet McDoual Daniels' better known *Nine-Mile Swamp* (1941) because it does not pretend to present history — only romantic fiction about a family of bandits who terrorized central New York throughout much of the nineteenth century.

One of Oneida County's most ardent nonresidential admirers was Edmund Wilson (1895-1972). Born in New Jersey, Wilson grew up to become the most cosmopolitan American writer since Henry James. Early in life, however, he realized that his roots were in Talcottville, a hamlet only a few miles north of Boonville and across the Lewis County border. Wilson's love for Oneida and Lewis counties is reflected in a number of his works — most dramatically, perhaps, in a short prose-poem entitled "Oneida County Fair; Upstate New York" (in his volume entitled *Night Thoughts* 1961) which is actually a description of a Boonville Fair. His final volume, *The Devils and Canon Barham* (1973), contains an essay on Harold Frederic that was originally delivered as a talk at Utica College in 1967. But the richest tribute to Oneida and Lewis counties paid by "The Last American Man of Letters" (as Wilson was described by Harry Levin in the *London Times Literary Supplement* for 11 October 1974), appeared in *Upstate* (1971). "The places in which I feel most at home," he wrote, "are Talcottville, London and Paris." Later, describing the last stage of a trip from Wellfleet on Cape Cod, Wilson wrote:

> At last you emerge into the country of Oneida and Lewis Counties — it was misty, just at sundown and beautiful, the mist lying along the green silky fields, the blurred orange light in the sky . . . it always gives rise in me up here to a kind of lofty and purified thoughts: dignity and beauty of the country which somehow has ennobled the lives of the people and all that old story of their immigration and their living, away from New England, among the hills and the fields and the forests, where they were all alone, but independent — free, flourishing — their human relationships

and labors against the non-human grandeur of the setting—riding along those uphill and downhill roads, a man behind a horse in a buggy, a farm wagon or carriage, under the high heavens, with fluid orange light or dark blue thunder clouds.[31]

Francis Adrian Van der Kemp, riding alone across the same hills in 1794, was also awed by the "non-human grandeur of the setting" and perhaps by the same orange light and blue thunder clouds that Oneidans know so well. He would have approved of Wilson's words; he would have approved also of the efforts of the six generations of Americans who followed him into Oneida County, there to make, on both sides of a great river, their solid contributions to the cultural and intellectual as well as the social growth of what was to become a vast republic.

But good writing in Oneida County was never restricted to novelists, poets, or other belletrists. In addition to its imaginative writers, the county has also produced a remarkable number of perceptive and literate historians whose work—although well recognized in other places—deserves mention in this account. The first formal history of the county, for instance, *Annals and Recollections of Oneida County* (1851), by Pomroy Jones, is still a classic of its kind. Jones (1789–1884), who lived almost a full century in Lairdsville, wrote his invaluable book only sixty-seven years after the first permanent settlements in Oneida County. Prompted, perhaps, by the publication of other county histories like Jeptha R. Simms' *History of Schoharie County* (1845), J. H. V. Clark's *Onondaga* (1849), and Hiram C. Clark's *History of Chenango County* (1850), Jones gathered together notes he had been making since 1838. Then—despite heavy duties "as a member of the County Courts"—he roamed the hills and valleys of Oneida County, one town after another, sometimes on foot, sometimes on horseback, gathering both fact and folklore for his book. What he learned and recorded is still dependable and eminently readable. Especially interesting, perhaps, is the final chapter (30) on the Indians of Oneida County; by the time another county historian appeared, the Indians were gone. But Pomroy Jones had seen them (*Annals* 869), and was able to record, firsthand, their tragedy, as he was also able to record the triumphs of the Whites of Whitestown and of James Dean of Deansboro. *Annals and Recollections* remains a rich source of material for historians and imaginative writers alike.[32]

During the sixty years following the appearance of Jones' book, three more impressive county histories were published. Samuel Durant's *History of Oneida County, 1667–1878* (1878), a by-product of interest stimulated by the centennial celebration, is a massive compendium of narrative, sta-

tistics, documents, biographical sketches, and splendid illustrations, including maps as well as portraits. Daniel E. Wager's *Our County and Its People:
Oneida County* followed in 1896, updating both Jones and Durant and
containing new illustrations and photographs. In 1912 Henry J. Cookinham produced a *History of Oneida County from 1700 to the Present Time*
in two volumes. Volume Two of this work contains about 450 biographical
sketches of Oneida County residents, past and present.

Meanwhile, Dr. Moses M. Bagg—distinguished physician and grandson of one of the earliest settlers in the county—had written *Pioneers of
Utica* (1877) and *Memorial History of Utica* (1892), two valuable works
concerned with the county as well as the city. Ellis H. Roberts, editor-owner
of the Utica *Morning Herald* from 1850 until 1889, also proved himself
to be a capable historian, first with his lengthy, carefully researched address delivered at the Oriskany Centennial Celebration on 6 August 1877;
this address, later reprinted in several places, is still regarded as the most
complete and accurate account of the battle of Oriskany of its time. Roberts later wrote a well-received history of the state, *New York; the Planting and the Growth of the Empire State* (1887) and still later served as
Treasurer of the United States under Presidents McKinley and Theodore
Roosevelt.

After the appearance of Cookinham's work in 1912, however, interest in state and local history diminished somewhat, as news from Europe
became increasingly ominous. Not until well after the end of World War I
did Oneida County historians resume their work—encouraged by intelligent leadership from the New York State Historical Association and the
office of the State Historian. The 150th anniversary of the battle of Oriskany and the relief of Fort Stanwix, for instance, was observed both in
Rome and at the Oriskany battlefield on August 6, 1927. A memorable
celebration—marked by a speech by John Albert Scott, who had recently
published a book-length study entitled *Fort Stanwix and Oriskany,* and
a pageant with verse narrative by Josephine Wilhelm Wickser—sparked
new impetus for local historians.[33]

The first few years of the Great Depression, starting in 1930, brought
this impetus to a temporary halt. By the middle of the decade, however,
historians—national, state, and local—were happily back at work. Federal
and state programs, notably the WPA, made possible the appearance of
much valuable work relating to the history of both state and county. The
regional spirit that had budded first in Edmonds' *Rome Haul* came to full
flower as dismal economic conditions turned Americans, including Oneida
historians, back to the land and basic values that had been lost during
the 1920s. The appearance of the monumental ten-volume *History of the*

State of New York (1933–37), edited by Alexander C. Flick, plus the federal government's encouragement of artists and historians, kept the state and the county culturally alive.

As the depression ground to an end—and even as the nation started to prepare for another traumatic experience, World War II—Oneida County produced a group of historical writers whose works are still cherished. In 1940 Dr. T. Wood Clarke of Utica—later to become President of the Oneida Historical Society—published *The Bloody Mohawk.* A year later, he produced *Emigrés in the Wilderness* (1941), the hitherto untold story of French immigrants who "tried to found French colonies in the wild lands of New York and Pennsylvania." And in 1952 he produced *Utica for a Century and a Half,* especially valuable for its account of the growth of industry in both the county and city.

Also during the 1940s a group of talented writers appeared to explore Oneida County history, folklore, and geography in a number of books still dear to Oneida County readers. David Beetle reported happy experiences in *Along the Oriskany* and *Up Old Forge Way*—informal reports of ramblings through areas that all Oneidans know well. In the late 1940s Thomas C. O'Donnell, a native of Michigan, retired to Boonville and immediately made the land his own in a series of "informal histories" that includes *Snubbing Posts* (1949)—a history of the Black River Canal; *The Sapbush Run*—a history of the Black River and Utica Railroad; *Birth of a River*—a history of the Black River headwaters; and *Tip of the Hill*—a history of Fairfield Academy and its once distinguished Medical College that flourished for decades in the high hills of Herkimer County. Also during the 1950s and beyond, Howard Thomas of Prospect (already mentioned above as a novelist) wrote a series of books stemming from his knowledge of Oneida County history and folklore. These included *Trenton Falls, Yesterday and Today; Marinus Willett,* a biography of the man who was second in command at Fort Stanwix during the siege of 1777; *Boys in Blue from the Adirondack Foothills; Tales from the Adirondack Foothills*; and *Folklore from the Adirondack Foothills.*

Since the end of World War II, historians at both Hamilton and Utica colleges have contributed significantly to our knowledge of both county and state social and intellectual history. Utica College's Harry F. Jackson produced, in 1963, *Scholar in the Wilderness: Francis Adrian Van der Kemp,* a full-length biography of the remarkable Dutch refugee whose career is briefly discussed at the beginning of this essay. In 1962 Walter Pilkington published *Hamilton College 1812/1962,* a history of central New York's oldest college. Finally, this most recent period has seen the emergence of David M. Ellis of Hamilton College as the premier historian of New York State. A native of Utica and lifelong resident of the county, Ellis made his first mark with *Landlords and Farmers in the Hudson-Mohawk Region* (1946), which not only won an award from the American Historical Association but proved so valuable that it was reprinted in 1966, two full decades after its original appearance. In 1957 Ellis served as senior author of *A Short History of New York State*. Widely acclaimed as a model of its kind, this work was revised and updated in 1967 as *A History of New York State,* with Ellis again serving as senior author and editor. In 1969 Ellis wrote *The Saratoga Campaign,* certainly the clearest and most readable account of the series of episodes that resulted in the downfall of John Burgoyne and his British army at Saratoga in 1777. Ellis' authoritative studies of the "Yankee Invasion" of New York and of aspects of Dutch and Welsh life in the state (including Oneida County) have appeared in America's finest historical journals.

And so, since 1784, when Hugh White and his sons dropped their gear and decided to settle what was to become "Whitestown," Oneida County's imaginative writers and historians have worked together. The healthy intellectual, literary, and cultural climate that developed from Boonville on the north to Bridgewater on the south, from Utica on the east to Verona Beach on the west, is a living tribute to the generations of writers and thinkers who shaped it.

Notes

1. *Our County and Its People: Oneida County,* edited by Daniel E. Wager (The Boston History Co., 1896), Pt. I, p. 137. For a list of early newspapers in the county see J. H. French, *Gazetteer of the State of New York* (1860), pp. 459-61.

2. Moses M. Bagg, ed., *Memorial History of Utica, N.Y.* (1892), pp. 164-65, 476-90. See also John Camp Williams, *An Oneida County Printer: William Williams* (Scribner's, 1908).

3. See Helen Lincklaen Fairchild, *Francis Adrian Van der Kemp, 1752-1829, An Autobiography. . . .* (Putnam's, 1903), p. 130. For a full-length biography see Harry F. Jackson, *Scholar in the Wilderness* (Syracuse University Press, 1963). I am indebted to Dr. Jackson's book for factual information in my comments about Van der Kemp.

4. Jackson, p. ix.

5. In John F. Seymour, *Trenton, N.Y.: Its First Settlement. Centennial Address, July 4, 1876* (Utica, 1877), pp. 47-128. The letters are also reprinted in Samuel Durant, *History of Oneida County* (Philadelphia: Everts and Fariss, 1878), pp. 542-77.

6. Charles L. Todd and Russell T. Blackwood, eds. *Language and Value*

(New York: Greenwood Publishing Corp., 1969), p. [165]. Unless otherwise noted, factual information about Alexander Bryan Johnson comes from this volume.

7. Quoted in Johnson's obituary, Utica *Morning Herald,* 12 September 1867. I am indebted to Professor Todd for a copy of this obituary, written by "a gentleman of this city who has enjoyed an acquaintance of half a century with the deceased."

8. Stillman Drake, "Introduction" to *The Meaning of Words* by A. B. Johnson (New York: Greenwood Press, 1969), p. [1]. This book, Johnson's sixth, was originally published by D. Appleton in 1854 and in a second edition in 1862.

9. Drake, "Back from Limbo: the Rediscovery of Alexander Bryan Johnson," in *Language and Value,* p. 14.

10. See *Language and Value,* pp. xl–xlv, for the most complete bibliography of Johnson's published works.

11. David Millar, "Introduction," *The Philosophical Emperor: A Political Experiment* (New York: Greenwood Press, 1968), p. [1]. See also Professor Millar's "A Note on A. B. Johnson's Philosophical Emperor," in *Language and Value,* pp. 221–25.

12. For a more detailed analysis of Johnson's belletristic writing see Thomas F. O'Donnell, "Johnson's Miscellaneous Essays and Fiction" in *Language and Value,* pp. 209–220.

13. Reprinted by Greenwood Press in 1968 were the following (year of original publication in parentheses): *The Philosophical Emperor* (1841); *Religion in Its Relation to the Present Life* (1841); *A Treatise on Banking* (1850); *The Meaning of Words* (1854); *The Physiology of the Senses* (1856); *A Guide to the Right Understanding of Our American Union* (1857); *Deep Sea Soundings . . . : or The Ultimate Analysis of Human Knowledge* (1861).

14. For a more detailed account of Mrs. Whitcher's career and the history of *The Widow Bedott Papers,* see T. F. O'Donnell, "The Return of the Widow Bedott: Mrs. F. M. Whitcher of Whitesboro and Elmira," *New York History* 55 (January 1974): 5–34.

15. See Rufus Wilmot Griswold, ed. *The Female Poets of America* (Philadelphia: Moss, Brother and Co., 1860), pp. 246–49. Poems by Mrs. Eames include "Crowning of Petrarch," "The Death of Pan," "Cleopatra," and a series of technically well-wrought sonnets, both Petrarchan and Shakespearean.

16. See Griswold's *The Female Poets of America,* pp. 241–45 for a brief biographical sketch written while Mrs. Judson was in Burma and for a number of her poems. She also wrote a novel, *Allen Lucas, the Self-Made Man* (1847). The Rev. Adoniram Judson, her husband, is the subject of Honore Willsie Morrow's romance, *The Splendor of God* (1929). For more about Mrs. Judson's career see A. C. Kendrick, *Life and Letters of Mrs. E. C. Judson* (1860).

17. "Celeste: a Romance of Oneida Lake," by J. M. T. Tucker, reprinted in Jones, appeared in *The Roman Citizen* for 24 November 1846, after appearing first in *The American Ladies' Album.*

18. The most complete account of Greene's career is contained in Muriel Block, "Beriah Greene, The Reformer," (unpublished Master's thesis, American

History, Syracuse University, 1935). See also D. Gordon Rohman, *Here's Whites-boro: An Informal History* (New York: Stratford House, 1949), pp. 34–53. T. F. O'Donnell, "The Return of the Widow Bedott," briefly treats Green's career in the context of Mrs. F. M. Whitcher's childhood and adolescence in Whitesboro.

19. The story of Trenton Falls is recounted in three books published at widely separated intervals. The earliest was *Trenton Falls: Picturesque and Descriptive,* edited by N. Parker Willis (New York: N. Orr and Co., 1868); two generations later came Charlotte A. Pitcher's *The Golden Era of Trenton Falls* (Utica: n.p., 1915); and still later, Howard Thomas' *Trenton Falls: Yesterday and Today* (Prospect, N.Y.: Prospect Books, 1951). All three books are profusely illustrated. Charlotte Pitcher's book is especially interesting because it contains excerpts from works by authors, foreign as well as American, recording their reactions to the sight of the series of falls and rapids.

See also Catherine Maria Sedgwick's novel, *Clarence* (1830), a part of which is set against the Trenton Falls area; and Mrs. Caroline Gilman's *Love's Progress,* also about the falls, published anonymously by Harper's in 1840.

20. Works by Frederic still in print and available include *The Damnation of Theron Ware* in paperback (Holt, Rinehart and Winston) and hardback (Harvard University Press); *Seth's Brother's Wife* (Gregg Press); and *Harold Frederic's Stories of York State* (Syracuse University Press, 1966), which contains all of Frederic's Civil War stories and an introduction by Edmund Wilson. A complete edition of his work is in process at the University of Texas at Arlington; the first volumes are scheduled to appear in 1977 or 1978. A definitive biography of Frederic is being written by Robert H. Woodward of San Jose State University. The most complete biography to date is T. F. O'Donnell and H. C. Franchere, *Harold Frederic* (New York: Twayne Publishers, 1961). For a full-length study of Frederic's novels see Austin Briggs, Jr., *The Novels of Harold Frederic* (Cornell University Press, 1969). For a complete listing of all of Frederic's work, including his journalism and commentary on his fiction, see *A Bibliography of Writings By and About Harold Frederic,* compiled by T. F. O'Donnell, Stanton Garner, and R. H. Woodward (Boston: G. K. Hall and Co., 1975). Available also in the Utica Public Library and the Utica College Library are copies of a newsletter, *The Frederic Herald,* published at Utica College, 1967–70.

21. For information about Rose Elizabeth Cleveland I am indebted to Mr. Brian Ure of Holland Patent. For a brief essay on her career see also Howard Thomas, *Tales from the Adirondack Foothills* (Prospect Books, 1962), pp. 125–26. For an amusing anecdote about one of President Cleveland's visits to Holland Patent see Howard Thomas, *Folklore from the Adirondack Foothills* (Prospect Books, 1958), pp. 63–64. See also Allan Nevin's Pulitzer Prize biography, *Grover Cleveland: A Study in Courage* (1933), which contains considerable information about both Rose Cleveland and Harold Frederic.

22. Sawyer's career is outlined briefly in *Dictionary of American Biography.* See also his lengthy obituary in the Utica *Morning Herald,* 30 December 1898, under the headline "Death of a Sage." The Alumni Collection, Hamilton College Library, contains a number of Sawyer's books, as does the library of the Princeton

Theological Seminary. I am indebted to both these libraries for copies of Sawyer's papers. The five epistles from Paul that Sawyer accepted as authentic are Thessalonians I, Galatians, Corinthians I and II, and Romans. See Sawyer, *The Final Theology, Vol. I: Introduction to the New Testament, Historic, Theologic, and Critical* (New York: M. B. Sawyer, 1879), Division I.

23. For a brief sketch of Foster's career see *Dictionary of American Biography*. See also *A Bibliography of the History and Life of Utica* (Compiled by Utica Public Library, 1932), which lists (p. 102) eleven of Foster's books as being in the Utica Public Library in 1932.

24. *The Singing Heart* (1934) contains a memoir of Scollard written by his wife, Jessie B. Rittenhouse. For a list of twenty-nine of his books see *A Bibliography . . . of Utica* (1932), pp. 112–15. Apparently no complete bibliography of his work has been prepared, although the Hamilton College Library has considerable material relating to his career.

25. Jones produced at least sixteen volumes of poetry, many of which are available in various Oneida County libraries. *The Shadow of a Perfect Rose: Collected Poems of T. S. Jones, Jr.* (New York: Farrar and Rinehart, 1937) contains a memoir and notes by John L. Foley. *A Bibliography . . . of Utica* lists (pp. 107–108) thirteen books and several pamphlet collections.

26. Canfield also wrote another novel, *The Spotter: A Romance of the Oil Region* (1907), set in the area between Olean, N.Y. and Bradford, Pa. Biographical material about him is lacking. The account of Oriskany in *The White Seneca* is found in Chapters 22 and 23.

27. Oneida County authors of earlier volumes of poetry include Fanny E. Bacon (1832–81), whose work was posthumously published in *A Reminiscence of Fanny Elizabeth Bacon*; she was the daughter of Congressman William J. Bacon and sister of William Bacon for whom the Adjutant Bacon Corps of Cadets was named. Another single-volume poet was Marc Cook (1854–82), whose "Van-Dyke Brown" *Poems* was published, also posthumously, in 1883, with "Prefatory Words" by Cook's friend, Harold Frederic. The six-page essay was the first of Frederic's work to appear in book form. Charles W. Darling's poetry appeared in pamphlet form in the 1880s; and Channing Moore Huntington (1861–94) produced *Bachelor's Wife and Other Poems* in 1889.

28. Several of Edmonds' novels are still in print. In 1961 Little, Brown and Co. published an omnibus volume entitled *Three Stalwarts,* which contains in their entirety *Drums Along the Mohawk, Rome Haul,* and *Erie Water.* Edmonds' work and career are discussed at some length in Lionel D. Wyld, *Low Bridge! Folklore and the Erie Canal* (Syracuse University Press, 1962). For more recent information, see Richard Benedetto, "Spinner of Yarns Knits Novels of our Rich Regional History," Utica *Observer-Dispatch,* Sunday, July 14, 1975, p. 1B. This interesting interview is accompanied by splendid photographs by Leo Hobaica. Throughout his career, Edmonds' work has been examined in a number of articles. One of the best early ones is Dayton Kohler, "Walter D. Edmonds, Regional Historian," *The English Journal* 27 (January 1938): 1–11. Wyld's *Low Bridge* contains a valuable bibliography of other critical comments about Edmonds. [Editor's note: In 1982

Syracuse University Press published Wyld's book *Walter D. Edmonds, Storyteller.*]

29. Vogel's other novels include *At Madame Bonnard's* and *The Straw Hat.* The latter, published in 1940, is set in an upstate summer resort.

30. Nassar's *East Utica,* with woodcut illustrations by Robert Cimbalo (also of Utica), was published by Munson-Williams-Proctor Institute. It exists also in a somewhat longer version printed previously in bound mimeograph form. [Editor's note: For Utica's Italians, see Helen Barolini, *Umbertina* (1979), available since 1982 as a Bantam book.]

31. Edmund Wilson, *Upstate* (New York: Farrar, Straus and Giroux, 1971), p. 77.

32. Letters and original source material that Jones used in preparing his *Annals and Recollections of Oneida County* have recently been acquired by the Rome Historical Society, 113 West Court St., Rome, N.Y. (For this information I am indebted to Mrs. Virginia Kelly, Oneida County Historian.)

33. See *Souvenir Program: 150th Anniversary of the Battle of Oriskany and the Siege and Relief of Fort Stanwix. Saturday, August 6, 1927 at the Oriskany Battlefield and in the City of Rome.* (no publisher, no date), a 48-page pamphlet.

4 Selective Checklist of Thomas F. O'Donnell's Publications

Books and Editions

Harold Frederic. (Twayne's United States authors series, 3). New York: Twayne, 1961 (with Hoyt C. Franchere).

Back Home in Oneida; Hermon Clarke and His Letters. Syracuse: Syracuse University Press, 1965 (with Harry F. Jackson).

James Kirke Paulding, *The Dutchman's Fireside* (masterworks of literature series). Edited for the modern reader by Thomas F. O'Donnell. New Haven: College & University Press, 1966.

Harold Frederic, *Stories of York State.* Edited by Thomas F. O'Donnell, with an introduction by Edmund Wilson. Syracuse: Syracuse University Press, 1966.

Adriaen van der Donck, *A Description of the New Netherlands.* Edited with an introduction by Thomas F. O'Donnell. Syracuse: Syracuse University Press, 1968.

The Merrill Checklist of Harold Frederic (Charles E. Merrill program in American literature). Columbus, Ohio: C. E. Merrill, 1969.

A Bibliography of Writings By and About Harold Frederic (research bibliographies in American Literature; no. 4). Boston: G. K. Hall, 1975 (with Stanton Garner and Robert H. Woodward).

Harold W. Thompson, *Body, Boots & Britches. Folktales, Ballads, and Speech from Country New York.* Introduction and notes by Thomas F. O'Donnell. Syracuse: Syracuse University Press, 1979 (reprint of the 1939 edition published by Lippincott, Philadelphia).

"The Complete Poems of William Dean Howells." Forthcoming as one of the volumes in "A Selected Edition of W. D. Howells" from Indiana University Press.

Articles

"New York's Role in American Literature, 1650–1865," 55; "Literary History of New York 1650–1865," 56 (map); "New York Literature from Reconstruction to the Great Depression," 57; "Literary History of New York 1866–1928," 58 (map); "New York in Literature: The Renaissance after 1929," 59; "Literary History of New York 1929–1958," 60 (map). In *Richards Atlas of New York State*. Robert J. Rayback, Editor-in-Chief. Phoenix, NY: Frank E. Richards, 1957–59 (maps prepared by Thomas F. O'Donnell, illustrated by Jane Basenfelder).

"Harold Frederic (1856–1898)." *American Literary Realism* 1, 1 (Fall 1967): 39–44.

"More Apologies: The Indian in New York Fiction." *New York Folklore Quarterly* 23, 4 (December 1967): 243–53.

"Frederic in the Mohawk Valley." Occasional Papers from Utica College. Utica: Utica College, 1968. 14 pp.

"The Return of the Widow Bedott: Mrs. F. M. Whitcher of Whitesboro and Elmira." *New York History* 55, 1 (January 1974): 5–34.

"*Koningsmarke*: Paulding vs. Scott in 1823." *American Transcendental Quarterly* 24, 1 (Fall 1974): 10–17.

"Theron Ware, the Irish Picnic, and *Comus*." *American Literature* 46, 4 (January 1975): 528–37.

"Oriskany, 1877: The Centennial and the Birth of Frederic's *In the Valley*." *New York History* 57, 2 (April 1976): 139–64.

"Literary Highlights." In *The History of Oneida County* (Utica: Oneida County, 1977), 73–78.

"Harold Frederic's 'Cordelia and the Moon.' Text, with Comment." *American Literary Realism* 11, 1 (Spring 1978): 34–51.

Miscellaneous

Editor, *The Frederic Herald*. Published three times a year at Utica College, Utica, New York (three volumes of this newsletter appeared between April 1967 and January 1970).

Tom O'Donnell's published notes, reviews, and newspaper articles as well as his papers, lectures, and speeches are too numerous to be even selectively listed here. He also had a creative vein and wrote the words and music for "Samuel Kirkland" (1941), a favorite song of his alma mater,

Hamilton College; "A Dam for Delta" (1957), a one-act play which received honorable mention in the Drummond playwriting contest at Cornell University; and "The Legend of White Eagle" (1959), a monodrama performed at the American Management Association camp at Lake Moraine, Hamilton, New York.

From 1964 to 1969, Tom O'Donnell was a member of the Syracuse University Press Faculty Editorial Committee. For an even longer period, he was a reader and advisor for many manuscripts under consideration by the Press. His contributions to the Press's York State Books are especially noteworthy.

Part II

5 Writers of the Hudson Valley and the Catskills

PERRY D. WESTBROOK

S OON AFTER 1614, the date of the first Dutch trading post near the present site of Albany, the valley of the Hudson River became a favored area of colonization, and the river itself was the chief route of commerce northward from Manhattan. So vital was the river that control of it was a military goal in the French and Indian wars and the American Revolution. But the river had other things to offer. Scenically its valley and adjacent mountains were superbly beautiful. More important for early settlers, the land on either side was fertile, and the forests abounded in furs and timber. These attractions were delightfully apparent in 1609 to Robert Juet, an officer on Henry Hudson's *Half Moon,* during a leisurely exploration far upstream. In his account, "The Third Voyage of Master Henrie Hudson . . . ," in Samuel Purchas' *Hakluytus Posthumus* (1625), Juet wrote of "good ground for Corne and other garden herbs with great store of goodly Oakes, and Wal-nut trees, and Chest-nut trees, Ewe trees, and trees of sweet wood in great abundance, and great store of slate for houses, and other good stones" (369). On the way down the river Juet singled out the spot where Newburgh is now located as "a very pleasant place to build a Towne on," and he thought that the nearby Highlands might contain "some metall or minerall" (371). If the river was a disappointment as a passage to the Orient, it promised well for future colonization and commercial exploitation.

The Dutch were quick to act on these promises. Within the next twenty years, towns and villages as well as trading posts were established along the river, either under the strict control of the Dutch West India Company, or as somewhat independent patroonships, like that of Kiliaen Van Rensselaer. As encouragement for immigration, glowing accounts of the transatlantic territories were circulated in Holland. For example, Jacob Steendam, a merchant of New Amsterdam, writing in florid Dutch verse, described the river lands as flowing in milk and honey. "A very Eden" (65), he cried, after listing every fish, fowl, and beast, and every plant and species of tree in the colony, and lauding its air, water, and soil. After the English seized New Netherland, in 1664, the efforts to attract settlers continued, as evidenced in a promotional tract titled *A Brief Description of New York* (1670), in which the author, Daniel Denton, excitedly calls attention to the Hudson Valley for being "as good Corn-land as the World afford, enough to entertain hundreds of families" (13).

Writings such as these produced results, but not the ones envisaged by their authors. The immediate response was not so much from families wishing to settle on small holdings as from investors seeking extensive tracts to be held as patroonships or manors. Thus many farmers perforce held their land under lease rather than in fee simple. This system of tenure persisted until the 1840s, and the rebellion by which the farmers finally ridded themselves of it was the subject of James Fenimore Cooper's *Littlepage* trilogy, Henry Christman's *Tin Horns and Calico* (1945), and a dramatic chapter in Carl Carmer's *The Hudson* (1939).

Yet by no means all the farmers in the Hudson Valley were leaseholders. The first work of real literary merit dealing with the region, St. John de Crèvecoeur's *Letters from an American Farmer* (1782), presents a very different picture of the farmer's lot in Orange County. This book and another by Crèvecoeur, *Sketches of Eighteenth Century America,* consisting of letters probably intended for the 1782 volume but excluded from it perhaps for political reasons, contain an account of their author's success and at least temporary happiness on land to which he was able to acquire full ownership. Michel-Guillaume Jean de Crèvecoeur (as he was baptized) was born in 1735 in Caen, France. After attending a Jesuit college, he spent some time with relatives in Salisbury, England, where he became proficient in English. At about the age of twenty he sailed for Quebec, joining Montcalm's army as a surveyor and cartographer. After the French defeat, he found his way to New York, where he took the name James Hector St. John and became a naturalized citizen. For a number of years Crèvecoeur wandered through the North American colonies engaging in various occupations. He gives an account of his travels and observations in *Journey into Northern Pennsylvania and the State of New York* (published in French in 1801, in English in 1964). Eventually he settled into his favorite way of life, that of a farmer, first on rented land in Ulster County and later on land that he purchased in Orange County a few miles west of Newburgh. In 1769 he married.

During the following decade he wrote most of his *Letters* and

Sketches. On the title page of *Letters* he described himself as "a Farmer in Pennsylvania," but this bit of disguise is to be ignored. His first years at Pine Hill, as he called his farm, were a time of deep personal fulfillment. He tilled his land, lived at peace with his neighbors, found time to observe nature and record his observations. But these years quickly passed. Crèvecoeur believed that the English colonies were justly governed and that life in them was the best to be found anywhere in the world. As the Revolution approached and after hostilities began, he was increasingly at odds with his neighbors. By 1779 his situation had become so precarious that he decided to return to France for a while. On his way he stopped in England and arranged for the publication there of his letters, later going on to France. On his return to New York in 1783 as French consul, he learned that his wife was dead and that his house at Pine Hill had been burned by Indians, though his children were safe. In poor health, he returned to France in 1785 but two years later was back in New York. In 1790 he left America permanently. He died in France in 1813.

Our present concern is with Crèvecoeur's years in Orange County. During this time he realized a dream of peaceful rural existence, farming the land, studying the birds, the beasts, and the insects, as well as human behavior, and enjoying a closely knit family life. "I am but a feller of trees, a cultivator of land," he wrote in *Letters* (206). But as we have seen, he was much more, and most importantly today he was a writer — the first of any consequence in New York State and one of the few of true talent in all of eighteenth-century America. Moreover, he was typical, in many of his interests, of the writers who were to follow him in the Hudson Valley. During the 1770s his chief concern, as expressed in the *Letters,* was with establishing a home for himself and his family — a preoccupation we shall find among such authors as Washington Irving, Nathaniel Parker Willis, and John Burroughs. In Crèvecoeur's case the home was to be a working farm. Like Jefferson, he thought that agriculture was the most enduring foundation for a stable society, and he repeatedly praised farm life for its joys and rewards. But its satisfactions, he found, were fully realizable only under a benignly disposed government.

"Where," Crèvecoeur asked, "is that station which can confer a more substantial system of felicity than that of the American farmer, possessing freedom of action, freedom of thoughts, ruled by a mode of government which requires little from us?" (*Letters* 118). This felicity stems largely from the farmer's ownership of his land. "The instant I enter on my own land," Crèvecoeur wrote, "the bright idea of property, of exclusive right, of independence exalt [*sic*] my mind. Precious soil, I say to myself, by what singular custom of law is it that thou wast made to constitute the riches of the freeholder?" (*Letters* 20). Elsewhere Crèvecoeur points out that corollary to ownership of land and equally important to a farmer's success and happiness is a large measure of self-sufficiency in producing food and other necessaries. "The philosopher's stone of an American farmer," he advised, "is to do everything within his own family; to trouble his neighbors by borrowing as little as possible; and to abstain from buying European commodities. He that follows this golden rule and has a good wife is almost sure of succeeding" (*Sketches* 104).

Crèvecoeur's enthusiastic account of his farm at Pine Hill vividly illustrates his claims for rural life, but his case may have been somewhat special. His feelings about his happy lot are expressed in a watercolor painting he did of his farm. This rather primitively executed picture shows, as background, his house in a setting of fields and hills. In the foreground is a grove where Crèvecoeur and his wife are seated, watching their slave ploughing a meadow. On the plough in an improvised seat beneath an umbrella rides Crèvecoeur's four-year-old son — the purpose being, as Crèvecoeur tells us in his *Letters,* to accustom the little boy to rural chores. But the scene suggests that Crèvecoeur enjoyed a greater material prosperity than most farmers. However, he provides in his books case histories of men, many of them immigrants, who starting with nothing gradually established themselves on their own land, the most memorable such case being that of Andrew the Hebridean as told in Letter III of the *Letters.* The immigrants were able to accomplish this, Crèvecoeur explains, through a combination of their own determined efforts, the help of their neighbors, and, not least, the absence of an oppressive government and heavy taxes. But the road to this sort of fulfillment was not easy. To get started, most farmers incurred debts that took years of unceasing toil to repay.

Though Crèvecoeur has been accused of sentimentality in his views of farm life, he in no way minimizes its difficulties. Felling a forest, draining a swamp, building a house and barns require skill and endurance. "The common casualties of nature" (*Letters* 58) may frustrate the most tireless efforts. But perhaps the greatest danger to a farmer's well-being is his fellow men — the same neighbors, possibly, who helped him clear his fields and raise his barn. Crèvecoeur's own rural idyl was shattered by hatreds generated by civil strife. In "The Distresses of a Frontier Man" (*Letters*) and in "The Man of Sorrows" and "The American Belisarius" (*Sketches*), as well as in other writings, he describes the ruination visited upon families not in sympathy with the revolt against Britain. With neighbors pitted against neighbors, suspicion, betrayal, and hate blighted once peaceful communities. As the war progressed, Indian raids such as those at Wyoming Valley and Cherry Valley, both of which Crèvecoeur describes in *Sketches,* devastated the countryside.

Yet Crèvecoeur retained his glowing vision of the promise of America as voiced in those of his *Letters* which were written before the Revolution. At the center of this vision was the emergence of a "new man" (39) in a new world flourishing under a mild colonial rule, as he thought, and later under the equally mild laws of the republic. This new man, limned in the most famous Letter, "What Is an American?", is to a large extent a product of the new environment. "Men are like plants," Crèvecoeur wrote. "The goodness and flavour of the fruit proceeds from the peculiar soil and exposition (*sic*) in which they grow. We are nothing but what we derive from the air we breathe, the climate we inhabit, the government we obey, the system of religion we profess, and the nature of our employment" (40). But the new man, the American, is also genetically new. Crèvecoeur was an early proponent of the melting pot theory. With the exception of New England, where the population was overwhelmingly of English stock, he found Americans to be a mixture of "English, Scotch, Irish, French, Dutch, Germans, and Swedes. . . . Individuals of all nations are melted into a new race of men, whose labours and posterity will one day cause great changes in the world" (37–39). Crèvecoeur, himself a New Yorker, did not need to look far for examples of this American amalgam. Settled in the eastern part of the colony were Dutch, English, French Huguenots (in Westchester and Orange counties), and Palatine Germans (in Columbia County and in the Schoharie and Mohawk valleys). These and groups with other cultural origins became scattered over the region and by intermarriage created the "new race." Though similar demographic findings would be valid for all the middle and to some extent the southern colonies, Crèvecoeur's essay had special accuracy in regard to New York. In rural regions what unified persons so diverse in their origins was the common goal held by all — the goal of bettering their worldly situations through ownership and tillage of land. To achieve this they were willing to help one another in spite of differences in backgrounds. Traditional prejudices and enmities wilted as neighborly cooperation flourished, and quite naturally intermarriage steadily worked to eradicate ethnic divisions.

Crèvecoeur was a keen student not only of human affairs but also of outdoor nature — an interest in which he again anticipates other Hudson Valley writers like Burroughs and Willis. Among his *Letters* and *Sketches* we find such titles as "On Snakes; and On Humming Birds," "An Ant-Hill Town," and "A Snow Storm as It Affects the American Farmer." Crèvecoeur was also very much aware of the effects of human presence on nature. The clearing of fields and the draining of marshes for hard-working families were fully acceptable to him. Yet, he pointed out, these necessary practices also dried up the streams powering the mills in which the farmers' grain was ground. "Man is a huge monster," he wrote in *Sketches,* "who devours everything and will suffer nothing to live in peace in his neighborhood" (117); as examples, he cited the slaughter of black-birds and the destruction of beavers, "the philosophers of the animals; the gentlest, the most humble, the most harmless" (*Journey* 126) — a spectacle that caused him unashamedly to weep. Also, he pleaded for the preservation of some of the virgin forest — "these beautiful cedars, these gigantic pines, these venerable hemlocks, these godlike oaks, which human industry could never replace" (*Journey* 121). Like so many of the New York writers who followed him, Crèvecoeur had an almost religious reverence for the beauty and grandeur of nature at the same time that he studied the uses to which human beings must put nature for their survival. He was a romantic as well as a practical farmer. Like Emerson and Burroughs he saw nature not only as "commodity" (that is, as a supplier of humanity's physical needs) but also as a source of moral, esthetic, and spiritual instruction and values. The spectacular aspects of nature — the sublime, in the language of the romantic poets — impressed him deeply, as is evident from his description in *Journey* (114-27) of sailing up the Hudson from New York to New Windsor: the flights of his prose, even in English translation, rival the most rhapsodic effusions on Hudson River scenery that were to appear during the nineteenth century.

Washington Irving

Most of Irving's writing was on subjects and scenes far removed from New York, especially upstate New York. Only a few pages of the Knickerbocker *History* are within the scope of the present study. Four other volumes — *The Sketch Book, Bracebridge Hall, Tales of a Traveller,* and *Wolfert's Roost* — along with a number of periodical pieces contain the writings to be considered here. The material of the bulk of Irving's works is either drawn from his travels and residence in England and the continent of Europe or deals with such subjects as Columbus, Mohammed, the American West, or the history of Spain. Yet today, in America at least, his reputation rests almost entirely on his New York State writings, and especially those associated with the Hudson Valley.

"I thank God I was born on the banks of the Hudson!" Irving wrote in 1839. "I think it an invaluable advantage to be born and brought up in the neighborhood of some grand and noble object in nature; a river, a lake, or a mountain. We make a friendship with it, we in a manner ally ourselves with it for life" ("Letter" 103). Irving's first acquaintance with the river was at Manhattan, his birthplace, where at an early age he already exhibited "a rambling propensity," wandering about the island, much of which was then rural, visiting "every spot where a murder or a robbery had been committed or a ghost seen" (*Sketch Book* 8). Already he was unknowingly amassing material and impressions that would serve him in such stories and sketches as "Dolph Heyliger," "Wolfert Webber," "Hellgate," and "The Adventure of the Black Fisherman."

At the age of fifteen he visited his friend James Kirke Paulding in Tarrytown on the Tappan Zee some twenty-five miles upriver. Here the two boys wandered inland to Sleepy Hollow, inhabited then "by families which had existed there from the earliest times, and which, by frequent intermarriage, had become so interwoven as to make a kind of natural commonwealth" ("Sleepy Hollow" 105). The church there was especially fascinating. The pulpit, from which Dutch was still spoken, the communion table, the weathercock, and even the brick in the walls had been brought from Holland; and the gravestones behind the church were inscribed in Dutch. The farmers of the Hollow, more like Rip Van Winkle than the prosperous Van Tassels in "The Legend of Sleepy Hollow," preferred hunting and fishing to tilling the soil. The region abounded in stories of the Revolution, especially about the capture of the spy John André, and there were tales of witches, ghosts, and a phantom boat on the Tappan Zee. Writing his *Sketch Book* some twenty years later, Irving returned in imagination to Sleepy Hollow, drawing a rich literary harvest from memories of its atmosphere and lore. Later still, in 1835, he returned to the area to live, buying an old Dutch cottage that he remembered from his boyhood and converting it almost unrecognizably into the home he named Sunnyside. In a sketch, "Wolfert's Roost," he described the original cottage and gave its history, drawing again on his lifelong knowledge of the real and legendary history of the region and adding embellishments from his own imagination.

Irving first sailed up the Hudson to Albany in 1800 — he was then seventeen years old — on his way to visit two married sisters in Johnstown. He sailed on a sloop captained by a Dutch native of Albany, whose slaves served as crew. Irving was spellbound as he passed for the first time through the Highlands and "gazed with wonder and admiration at cliffs impending far above . . . , crowned with forests, with eagles sailing and screaming around them; or listened to the unseen stream dashing down precipices; or beheld rock, and tree, and cloud, and sky reflected in the glassy stream of the water" ("A Voyage" 345). At night, as the vessel lay at anchor beneath the mountains, Irving thrilled with the wonder and mystery of the darkness and listened to the cry of the whippoorwills and the splash of leaping sturgeons. But above all, his imagination was stirred by the Catskill Mountains. "As we slowly floated along," he wrote, "I lay on the deck and watched [the mountains] through a long summer's day; undergoing a thousand mutations under the magical effects of atmosphere" ("A Voyage" 345). From then on the Catskills were to Irving "the fairy region of the Hudson" ("The Catskill Mountains" 163–64). On board the sloop was an old Indian trader who regaled the youth with legends associated with landmarks along the river — "Spuyten Devil Creek, The Tappan Sea [sic], The Devil's Dans-Kammer, and other hobgoblin places. The Catskill Mountains especially called forth a host of fanciful traditions" ("The Catskill Mountains" 164). The voyage left him with memories that lasted throughout his life.

In 1803 Irving sailed up the Hudson en route to Montreal with Mr. and Mrs. Hoffman (Irving was studying law with Mr. Hoffman and was in love with his daughter Matilda). They stopped at Ballston Springs and Saratoga, watering places that were already becoming popular. Later Irving wrote a satirical piece, "Style at Ballston," for *Salmagundi* (1807–1808). Irving preferred writing to the study of law. During 1802 and 1803, under the pseudonym of Jonathan Oldstyle, Gent., he wrote a series of satirical sketches on New York society and the theatre that were published in his brother Peter's newspaper, the *Chronicle*. Several years later he collaborated with his brothers and James Kirke Paulding in writing the *Salmagundi* papers, also satirical comments on the manners and politics of the times. Shortly afterwards, Irving began his first major work, Diedrich Knickerbocker's *History of New York* (1809).

In April 1809, Irving suffered a crushing blow in the death of Matilda Hoffman, whom he had hoped to marry. In his grief he fled up the Hudson to the home of a friend, Judge William Van Ness, in the quintessentially Dutch town of Kinderhook, fifteen miles south of Albany. Here Irving struggled during May and June to allay his sorrow by completing the *History*. But there were lighter moments as well. Living part of the time at the Van Ness farmhouse was Jesse Merwin, the teacher in the school attended by the judge's children. Merwin, who served later as the model for Ichabod Crane, was described by Irving as "pleasant good-natured . . . with native, unimproved shrewdness and considerable humor" (*Letters* 1:263). Also among Irving's acquaintances in Kinderhook were two other supposed originals of characters in "The Legend of Sleepy Hollow": Katrina Van Alen, who lived in an old Dutch house near the Van Ness home and may have been the original of Katrina Van Tassel, and Brom Van Alstyne, perhaps the original of Brom Bones.[1]

In August and September 1810, Irving visited Captain Frederick Philipse in his "Castle," as Irving called it, across the river from West Point. As always the Highlands impressed him with their rugged beauty. Irving, who later adopted the pen name Geoffrey Crayon, had aspired to become a painter, had associated with artists, and indeed had considerable artistic talent of his own, wrote the word "sketch" over some of the descriptions in his journal at this time. Though he had composed word pictures of Italian landscapes, he did his first of American scenes during the 1810 visit with Captain Philipse. Some of these anticipate descriptive passages in "Rip Van Winkle" — and Irving may well have had them in mind when he wrote that story. Another — a description of a brook near his host's dwelling — is clearly echoed in *The Sketch Book* in "The Angler." The prose in these journal entries, however, is not in finished form. Rather, it consists of notes, impressions, like a painter's tentative drawing. Irving's intention was obviously pictorial, as the following reveals, even though in one instance it appeals to the sense of hearing:

> Fine clear day — view from top of old magazine <of> on Constitution Island opposite W Point. Highlands like bold side Scenes — one bluff beyond another — open country in the distance. Shawang[unk] mountains terminate the view up the river. New Windsor & Newburgh in distance — <beautiful> pure transparent atmosphere — river far below me — sound of cowbells from a little fresh pasture in a nook of the shore opposite shaded with large trees . . . (*Journals* 2:14).

The panoramic spread of the scene, the combining of the pastoral with the pristine ruggedness of the Highlands, the sweep of the river terminating in the distant mountains, and the human presence (the villages) constitute a preview of what the Hudson River School of painters were to do on their canvases a decade or two later. In fact, some of Irving's painter friends avowed that they had learned from his example.[2]

Irving's first book to win acclaim at home and abroad was *The History of New York* "by Diedrich Knickerbocker." This book was originally planned as a joint undertaking with Irving's brother Peter, and was intended to be a parody of a species of pompous history-writing in fashion at the time. But Peter soon dropped out, his influence being felt mainly in Book I, and Irving continued the work not only as a parody but also as a good-natured satire on politics and manners. The book deals only to a limited, but by no means negligible, extent with upstate New York. To begin with, the character of Diedrich Knickerbocker, the whimsical old Dutch antiquarian, who is presented as author of the *History,* belongs to the whole Hudson Valley, indeed to the entire state, though he was a native of New York City. So quickly and decisively did the old gentleman endear himself with the public that his name soon became synonymous with the Dutch tradition of the area; and — as Irving reported in "The Author's Apology," which was written in 1848 and included in a new edition of the *History*—Knickerbocker became "a 'household word' and was used to give the home stamp to everything recommended for popular acceptation, such as Knickerbocker societies; Knickerbocker insurance companies; Knickerbocker omnibuses; Knickerbocker steamboats; Knickerbocker bread; and Knickerbocker ice; and when," Irving wrote, "I find New-Yorkers of Dutch descent priding themselves upon being 'genuine Knickerbockers,' I please myself with the persuasion that I have struck the right chord" (xiii–xiv).

In an "Account of the Author," as expanded in later editions of the *History,* Irving describes Knickerbocker as traveling along the shores of the Hudson from Haverstraw to Schaghticoke, the latter being the "residence of his relations" (18).[3] Along the way he lingered on the shores of the Tappan Zee and in Esopus and Albany, always pursuing his researches. Irving, knowing the value of Knickerbocker to himself as author, quotes him in "Postscripts" to "Rip Van Winkle" and "The Legend of Sleepy Hollow," and resurrects him years later in sketches such as "Sleepy Hollow" and "Wolfert's Roost," written for the *Knickerbocker Magazine*. Thus Knickerbocker has become identified with the whole Hudson Valley, the core of the old Dutch territory.

As for the *History* itself, Irving announced that its "main object . . . was to embody the traditions of our city in an amusing form, to illustrate its local humors, customs, and peculiarities; to clothe home scenes and places and familiar names with those imaginative and whimsical associations so seldom met with in our new country . . . " (xiii). The key words are "imaginative" and "associations." Irving was a romantic after the manner of Walter Scott, whom he greatly admired. To this type of romantic, a locality—especially a scenic one—needed some sort of association, whether historical, legendary, or mythical, to give it more than mere aesthetic interest. The aesthetic appeal, in fact, would be enhanced by the associations. A recurring complaint of American writers in the nineteenth century —among them Cooper, Hawthorne, and Henry James—was the nation's lack of a past that would provide such associations in the form of ruins, superstitions, and the like. Some American authors, of course, tried to make do with Indian lore, but this was not what Americans of European descent really desired. All these writers, however, were quick to praise American mountains, lakes, and rivers, and the Hudson Valley got its share, and more, of the praise.

New York City, upon which most of the *History* focused, did fortunately have its rather dimly remembered Dutch past. So also did the Hudson River north to Albany. In several places in the *History* Irving focuses closely on the upper reaches of the river, though he deals rather perfunctorily with Henry Hudson's voyage northward from Manhattan. The first place that upriver material appears is in Book III, Chapter V, and it is based roughly on historical fact. It is an account of Kiliaen Van Rensselaer's patroonship and his, or his agent's, high-handed actions in defiance of the government at New Amsterdam. Claiming "to hold separate jurisdiction independent of the colonial authorities" (172), Van Rensselaer had a fort erected on Bearn Island a few miles downriver from Fort Aurania, as the settlement on the present site of Albany was called. Later, in Book IV, Chapters X and XII, Irving recounts how a garrison of ruffians from the nearby Helderberg Mountains fired on the official government vessel as it returned from a routine visit to Fort Aurania. The feud, Irving writes, eventually cooled, but he manages to relate it to later troubles of the Van Rensselaers in collecting their feudal rents. In the mid-nineteenth century "the bully boys of the Helderberg" (249) were being particularly troublesome and, according to Irving, gave to the Patroon's agents the same reply—a thumbing of the nose—that the commandant at Bearn Island had given to Antony Van Corlaer when, as emissary of the governor, he had ordered the fort to be vacated.[4]

Chapter IV, Book VI, of the *History* describes "Peter Stuyvesant's Voyage up the Hudson, and the Wonders and Delights of That Renowned River." Stuyvesant's purpose in the voyage was to enlist militiamen to meet the growing threats from the English and the Yankees. But Irving's purpose was obviously to celebrate the scenery along the way. Indeed, this is one of the earliest panegyrics on the beauties of the river. Yet the style tends to be mock-heroic. The governor's ship is described in language that parodies Shakespeare's description of the royal barge in *Antony and Cleopatra*. In his treatment of natural scenery, however, Irving at times almost abandons the mock-heroic tone. He obviously sincerely admires the scenes he is depicting. Here is a typical passage:

> Thus rarely decorated, in style befitting the puissant potentate of the Manhattoes, did the galley of Peter Stuyvesant launch forth upon the bosom of the lordly Hudson, which, as it rolled its broad waves to the ocean, seemed to pause for a while and swell with pride, as if conscious of the illustrious burthen it sustained.
>
> But trust me, gentlefolk, far other was the scene presented to the contemplation of the crew from that which may be witnessed at this degenerate day. Wildness and savage beauty reigned on the borders of this mighty river—the hand of cultivation had not as yet laid low the dark forest, and tamed the features of the landscape—nor had the frequent sail of commerce broken in on the profound and awful solitude of ages. Here and there might be seen a rude wigwam perched among the cliffs of the mountains with its curling column of smoke mounting in the transparent atmosphere—but so loftily situated that the whoopings of the savage children, gamboling on the margin of dizzy heights, fell almost as faintly on the ear as do the notes of the lark . . . (330–31).

As Irving brings the ship to the Highlands, his enthusiasm rises. He now revels in recalling the Indian legends associated with the region, and he elaborates a legend of his own, that of the naming of Anthony's Nose, a prominent mountain at the southern entrance to the Highlands, after the nose of Antony Van Corlaer, the Trumpeter. Irving ends his narration with an account of the fright of Stuyvesant's crew as they pass the *Duyvil's Dans-Kamer* (*sic*) some six miles north of present Newburgh. Here the Indians traditionally held their war dances and other rites, which the Dutch sailors attributed to Satan.

Word sketches of scenery, accounts of old legends, a style that is sometimes ironic, sometimes lyric, but always fluent and lucid — these are the characteristics of Irving's prose in the *History,* and in varying degrees they are found in most of his later writing about New York State.

The intention of the *History* — "to clothe home scenes and places and familiar names with . . . imaginative and whimsical associations" (xiii) — informs the two most famous of Irving's stories, "Rip Van Winkle" and "The Legend of Sleepy Hollow," which appeared in *The Sketch Book* (1819-20). "To me," Irving wrote, "the Hudson is full of storied associations, connected as it is with some of the happiest portions of my life" ("A Voyage" 345). Much that need not be repeated has been written concerning the sources of the central episodes in "Rip Van Winkle" and "The Legend of Sleepy Hollow" in the folklore of Europe, especially that of Germany.[5] Irving's travels in Europe had whetted his already keen interest in folklore and local legends. Urged by Walter Scott, he had begun to study German to gain access to the rich store of folk material in that language. In his day Irving was severely criticized — even accused of plagiarism — for his reliance on other writers, and later he wrote in self-defence that he "considered popular traditions of the kind [that he used] as fair foundations for authors of fiction to build on" (*Bracebridge Hall* 247n). But the German and other legends were really not the foundations of Irving's Hudson River stories. The true foundations were his memories of the people, places, and tales that he had known since boyhood. The German influences were incidental. As Thomas Wentworth Higginson wrote, "It was not Irving who invested the Hudson with Romance, but the river that inspired Irving" (132). The romance had long been there — in the scenery and in stories about the towns and inlets and mountains along the shores. The New York folklorist Harold W. Thompson, when asked to comment on the extent of Irving's dependence on European legends, replied that answers were not easy but added: "You must remember also that the scenery of the Hudson obviously demands a phantom ship [see Irving's "Dolph Heyliger"] and a headless horseman. . . . No German folktale fully explains 'The Legend of Sleepy Hollow'; you must see Kinderhook as it is and imagine Tarrytown as it was. We can show you the Van Tassel house built in 1736 . . ." (118–19).

At any rate, whatever his sources, Irving did accomplish one of his purposes with "Rip Van Winkle" and "The Legend of Sleepy Hollow," not to mention his other river writings. Though the Hudson had traditions connected with almost every locality along its banks, these were not known to a nationwide, or even a statewide, public. After the appearance of *The Sketch Book,* the river and the Catskills entered the national imagination, indeed the imagination of the English-speaking world and, in translation, that of many other nations. As one critic has said, "Irving's magic wand indeed turned the Catskills . . . into fairy mountains. After Irving had settled Henry Hudson and his crew in the wilds of the Catskill Mountains and had made Ichabod Crane at home in the cove of Sleepy Hollow, there never again could be any thought of 'uncouth' mountains, and the 'howling wilderness' of the seventeenth century was discarded forever" (Huth 38). So firmly, in fact, did "Rip Van Winkle" grasp the popular imagination that Irving, during a stay with Paulding at the famous Catskill Mountain House in 1832, had what must have been the strange experience of visiting "the waterfall, the glen, etc., that are pointed out as the veritable haunts of Rip Van Winkle" (*Letters* 2:709).

A strong appeal of "Rip Van Winkle" and "The Legend of Sleepy Hollow" was that Irving peopled them with believable rustic characters, who not only were actors in a folktale but were also tellers of folktales themselves. Both Rip and Ichabod Crane, as well as supporting characters, are inveterate yarn-spinners. They are believers in the truth of exactly the kind of stories Irving was telling. But more important, they were real people — villagers, farmers, a country schoolmaster, a tavern keeper. Indeed in the case of Ichabod certainly, probably in the case of Katrina Van Tassel and Brom Bones, and very likely others, they were sketched from living models. And if these tales did banish the concept of a "howling wilderness" along the Hudson, it was partly because they were set in long-inhabited communities in farmland suggestive of the English countryside that Irving regarded as being pervaded by a "moral feeling . . . associated in the mind with ideas of order, of quiet, of sober well established principles, of hoary usage and reverend custom" (*Sketch Book* 54). The Dutch villages of the Hudson Valley gave Irving this feeling, and his "fairy region" of the Catskills and the "spell bound" Sleepy Hollow are interesting to the reader largely because there are in them true-to-life human beings to sense and to give voice to these intimations of the supernatural.

The presentation of the supernatural without such people as foils would have been an aesthetic disaster, as is demonstrated in Joseph Rodman Drake's "The Culprit Fay." Drake was a New York City physician who wrote mediocre satirical verse but who gave evidence of talent in this one poem. Nathaniel Parker Willis referred to it as "the most imaginative poetry our country has yet committed to immortality" (*Rural Letters* 201). In all its more than six hundred lines Drake made use of the four-stress metre found in Coleridge's "Christabel." The result is fluent, sometimes trite, sometimes truly lyric narrative verse. The great drawback is the clash between the poem's setting and its subject. The setting is the Hudson Highlands, or specifically Cronest (Crow's Nest) Mountain near West Point, and the time is a summer night. In the first stanza Drake was successful in recreating the atmosphere of the place and time, but he made a serious error in peopling the scene with supernatural beings entirely inappropriate to the locality. One experiences a sense of the absurd as Drake herds into the landscape troupes of fays, ouphes, imps, fairies, elves, and sylphs. Nor does the action of the poem improve matters. The Culprit Fay of the title has committed the sin of loving a mortal maiden and in expiation is sent forth to accomplish several difficult deeds, one of which necessitates a trip to the Milky Way. When the poem was published it was ridiculed by Poe but praised by many. Whether Drake intended to provide an "association" that would enhance the Highland scenery is not certain. But it is doubtful if many travelers along the river call to mind "The Culprit Fay" at all. The story simply does not attach itself to the locale, as Rip and the ghosts of Henry Hudson's crew attach themselves to the Catskills. The reason for the disparity is clear. Rip was a believably all-too-human Dutch villager, and Hudson, of course, had been associated with the scene for more than two hundred years. As for Sleepy Hollow, the love of Ichabod for Katrina, unlike that of a fay for a mortal girl, was commonplace and credible; and the story of the headless Hessian was historically suitable for upper Westchester County, as indeed were the other legends circulating there and recounted by the local inhabitants. Drake, who seems to have been influenced by the German poet Christoph Martin Wieland's *Oberon,* scenes in Shakespeare's *Midsummer Night's Dream,* and Shelley's "Queen Mab," obviously transported his ouphes and elves from Europe. Irving, too, borrowed from European sources but not at the expense of dehumanizing his stories. One does not wish to denigrate Drake's poem, which indeed has its stylistic merits. But a contrast with "Rip Van Winkle" and "The Legend of Sleepy Hollow" helps to account for Irving's greater and more lasting appeal.

Over the years Irving's two great Hudson River stories have proved to be more than providers of associations for the localities in which they are laid. Both were immediately esteemed on their publication and became an inspiration for younger American writers, especially Longfellow and Hawthorne. Irving's lifelong friend and collaborator on the *Salmagundi* papers, James Kirke Paulding, closely imitated "The Legend of Sleepy Hollow" in his story "Cobus Yerkes," also laid in the Tarrytown neighborhood. This tale, comic in tone, records an incident in which a drunken Dutchman imagines that he is being chased by a black bulldog which he believes in the "devil incarnate." As in Irving's story, Paulding's rustic and somewhat eccentric and comic characters are credibly drawn, and he supplies interesting local color with references to such actual places as the Sawmill River, Buttermilk Hall, and Raven Rock, where a woman's ghost shrieks at night.

Hawthorne, perhaps, most closely echoes Irving, though how consciously is impossible to say. Hawthorne's ideas about the romance as a literary genre apply to Irving's best fiction as readily as to his own. Hawthorne's basic concept, stated in the Preface to *The House of the Seven Gables* (1851), was that a romance must be psychologically realistic – must not "swerve aside from the truth of the human heart" – but it may "claim a certain latitude, both as to its fashion and material." The romance writer, moreover, is at liberty to "manage his atmospherical medium as to bring out or mellow the lights and deepen and enrich the shadows of the picture" (1), which is precisely what Irving does in his word pictures of mountain and pastoral scenes. Hawthorne regarded literary romance as occupying a "neutral territory, somewhere between the real world and fairy-land, where the Actual and the Imaginary may meet, and each imbue itself with the nature of the other." Conducive to romantic writing, Hawthorne thought, is that dreamy state one falls into "late at night . . . in a familiar room" before a "somewhat dim coal-fire," with moonlight "white upon the carpet. . . . Glancing at the looking-glass, we behold – deep within its haunted verge – the smouldering glow of the half-extinguished anthracite, the white moonbeams on the floor, and a repetition of all the gleam and shadow of the picture, with one remove farther from the actual, and nearer to the imaginative" (*Scarlet Letter* 35–36).

Irving in his writing repeatedly mentions his propensity for "daydreaming . . . losing [himself] in reveries . . ." (*Sketch Book* 12). This mood came upon him often while sailing on sea or river. Recalling his first voyage up the Hudson, he wrote, "The Kaatskill Mountains had the most witching effect upon my boyish imagination" ("Voyage" 345). The river and its valley were to Irving the equivalent of Hawthorne's moonlit and firelit parlor, and the surface of the river, like Hawthorne's haunted mirror, conferred a magical quality upon reality. Rip Van Winkle sees the sloops reflected in the river before his long sleep, and a similar reference to reflections occurs in "The Legend of Sleepy Hollow" (*Sketch Book* 286). As early as 1810 Irving, visiting the Highlands, wrote: "Sloops at a distance on the glassy surface seem as if suspended in the air – The clear reflection of the sky on the water makes it appear as if you saw under the hills and beheld the Sky beyond them."[6]

Irving thus appealed directly to the romantic literary tastes of his time by adding an aura of the unreal, the supernatural, to the scenery of the Hudson Valley. In "Rip Van Winkle" he does this by telling a story inexplicable by reason. In "The Legend of Sleepy Hollow," though the climactic event is explained rationally, the many ghostly tales extant in and about the Hollow make it a haunted place. "Dolph Heyliger" is a straightforward ghost story which does not attach itself strongly to any one locality, but the folk legend of "The Phantom Ship," included in the story, and the descriptions of wild Highland scenes provide "associations" in Irving's characteristic manner. Accordingly, at a time when the reading public desired fiction with a spicing of the unearthly and the uncanny, Irving found a ready audience. That he leavened his fiction with humor and a gentle irony and, unlike Poe, avoided serving up a fare of unrelieved terror seems further to have endeared him to his readers.

Twentieth-century literary criticism has sought, and perhaps found, other dimensions in "Rip Van Winkle" and "The Legend of Sleepy Hollow." For example, Philip Young notes how deeply the story is imbedded in the American imagination. He reminds us that there have been at least five dramatizations of it, one of them the adaptation by Joseph Jefferson and Dion Boucicault, which played almost continuously for a generation after the Civil War, with Jefferson himself cast as Rip. Hart Crane in *The Bridge,* Young points out, regarded Rip as "the muse of memory" (551) and, in a letter to Otto Kahn, referred to Rip as "'the guardian angel' of the journey into the past" (Crane 250). For Rip the past is far superior to the present he returns to, and the appeal of the story and the play, after the devastation of the Civil War, may be that it touched a widespread, though perhaps unconscious, nostalgia for a supposedly idyllic time.

Nostalgia for a bygone era — which certainly is present in "Rip Van Winkle" — implies conservatism, a reluctance to accept change; this reluctance is manifest in much of Irving's work, especially in his essays and tales of the Hudson region. Sleepy Hollow is a place where time has come to a standstill, and this is its chief attraction to Irving. The village in "Rip Van Winkle" before the Revolution was in a similar state of repose. In both cases the inertia is attributed to the propensity of Dutch countryfolk for attachment to a long-established way of life. Irving does not scorn this attitude, though he can be ironical about it; rather he regards it as evidence of stability and orderliness, which are symbolized in the neat Dutch villages and fruitful farms, just as the carefully groomed English countryside suggested moral strengths.

Thus Irving seems to regret changes and intrusions that threaten the peace and stability of the old Dutch culture. In the *History* the worst intrusions came from the New Englanders who contested Dutch rights on the Connecticut River and later, with their lust for migration, infiltrated Dutch territory nearer the Hudson, and finally hand in hand with the British seized all of New Netherland. The Yankees represented restlessness and materialism, not contentment with things as they are or willingness to remain long in one place. Rip, when he returns from his long sleep, finds his village almost unrecognizable. When he visits the inn where he once had enjoyed many peaceful hours, he finds the old building has vanished. "A large rickety wooden structure stood in its place, with great gaping windows, some of them broken and mended with old hats and petticoats" (*Sketch Book* 37). Before the door a liberty pole replaces the shade tree under which the Dutch farmers used to smoke and gossip. The proprietor is no longer the placid Nicholas Vedder. In his stead is the Yankee Jonathan Doolittle. Above all the very character of the townspeople has changed; in the talk at the inn door there is now "a busy, bustling, disputacious tone . . . instead of the accustomed phlegm and drowsy tranquility" (*Sketch Book* 37), and someone is delivering a political harangue. The transformation, in fact, is very much like that which Crèvecoeur found occurring in once peaceful, neighborly Orange County as the Revolution aproached. A new spirit has taken over in Rip's village, and it is a Yankee spirit — contentious, grasping, restless. Yet it would be a mistake to ascribe to Irving an ethnic aversion to Yankees. After all he was Scottish and English by descent. His dislike is directed against the new commercial and political spirit of the age — a spirit associated with Yankees but readily enough assimilated by the Dutch. Irving did not share Cooper's hostility to New Englanders. He deals with them satirically — as he does with the Dutch — but his is not an angry satire.

Ichabod Crane is a case in point. Ichabod is from Connecticut, but at the beginning of "The Legend of Sleepy Hollow" he is not very much unlike the Dutch farmers among whom he lives as schoolteacher. Like them, he is content with his lot, is superstitious, a teller of grisly tales. Indeed he compares very advantageously with the Dutch bully, Brom Bones. Yet Ichabod is quickly seduced not only by a longing for the buxom Katrina, but for her future wealth as heiress of her father's farm, and he has grandiose visions of using that wealth in profitable real estate schemes somewhere in the West, where in Yankee fashion he and Katrina and their children would migrate. And in fact Ichabod does prosper materially after his discomfiture by Brom Bones, for we learn that at one time or another he has been a lawyer, a politician, a journalist, a justice. But he is not presented as evil; he does not suffer from any supposed hereditary Yankee depravity. At worst, he succumbed to the materialistic, grasping spirit of the times.

"The Legend of Sleepy Hollow" is not to be taken as moralistic, or if so, only on a very low key. Irving, in transmitting the manuscript to his brother Ebenezer for publication in the United States, described it as "a random thing, suggested by recollections of scenes and stories about Tarrytown. The story is a mere whimsical bond to connect descriptions of scenes, customs, manners, etc." (Pierre Irving 1:335). This statement might apply, to a lesser degree, to "Rip Van Winkle," but "customs, manners, etc." include much; certainly they do not exclude implied commentary on the spirit of the age.

James Kirke Paulding

Much of Irving's writing, we have seen, was touched by nostalgia for the old Dutch culture of the Hudson Valley. James Kirke Paulding, Irving's lifelong friend and brother-in-law and fellow collaborator on the *Salmagundi* papers, felt an even keener awareness of the passing of the old way of life, perhaps because, unlike Irving, he was himself of Dutch descent. In his accounting for the change, however, Paulding was more specific and more plausible than Irving. Both deplored the blight of materialism and associated its ills with the Yankees, but Paulding saw the main source of the evil in industrialization with its mechanizing of production and its dehumanizing of the men and women who operated or depended on the machines.

Paulding was born in Dutchess County back from the river in 1778, but he grew up in Tarrytown, where his father was a merchant. Here, it will be recalled, Irving at the age of fifteen visited him; and the two, squirrel guns in hand, explored the nearby countryside. In the story "Cobus Yerkes," already mentioned, Paulding uses the Tarrytown area as a setting, as he also does in his novel *The Old Continental* (1846), the chief event in which is the capture of André by, among others, John Paulding, a distant kinsman of the novelist. In an essay reprinted in this volume, Thomas F. O'Donnell discusses Paulding's career and gives due attention to his writings, especially to his fine novel *The Dutchman's Fireside* (1831), which deals with the pre-Revolutionary Dutch upper class in Albany. Another work of Paulding's, however, needs attention, for it reveals very clearly its author's views on the changing times. This is the satirical *The New*

Mirror for Travellers; and Guide to the Springs (1828), purposing to be a handbook for persons journeying from New York to Albany by steamboat and thence overland to Saratoga. The volume is an odd concoction. The central idea in it is that a "steamboat is a composition of horrors, such as modern ingenuity, stimulated by paper money, stock companies, and I know not what could produce" (55), and Paulding especially condemns the fast Albany boats which, racing one another, sometimes explode with great loss of life. The steamboat symbolizes the evils that Paulding sees, and foresees, in a mechanized civilization (consistently, he opposed the use of steam power in the United States navy). His major concern was with the havoc industrialization was wreaking on the old agrarian and patriarchal way of life as he had known it. In an account in *The New Mirror* (147–54) dealing with a Squire Van Gaasbeeck of New Paltz, Paulding relates how the old order was progressively undermined, first by a modern textile factory, which relieved the farm wives of the task of weaving; next by the steamboat, which enabled the women to spend their newly acquired leisure for shopping sprees in New York; and finally mortgages and paper money, which lured the farmers into ruinous debts. Van Gaasbeeck is ruined by this process, and his final comment on his plight is: "The spirit of the age together with the march of public improvement finished me at last" (154).

More deplorable to Paulding than the steamboat and all it represented was the machinelike quality of the passengers aboard the vessel. They must be directed even as to how they should feel about the scenery. "We now approach the Highlands," the author writes, "and advise the reader to shut himself up in the cabin and peruse the following pages attentively, as it is our intention to give a sketch of this fine scenery, so infinitely superior to the reality, that Nature will not be able to recognise herself in our picture" (*Mirror* 114-15). Paulding then launches into the stereotyped verbosity of guidebooks. Yet he has a great admiration for the river scenery, especially the Catskills, which he describes with genuine enthusiasm, and he is an admirer of the Hudson River paintings of Thomas Cole and Guy Wall.

Paulding includes in *The New Mirror* much of the history and legendary lore connected with localities along the river—some of it as excerpts from the twenty volumes of a fictitious Nicholas Nicodemus Janson, a magistrate of Coxsackie, who is a rather colorless imitation of Diedrich Knickerbocker. The city of Albany evoked some of Paulding's most biting satire—though he surely is presenting Albany as a typical, rather than a special, case of the deteriorating quality of life in his day. Speaking through Alderman Janson, Paulding contrasts the earlier "patriarchal" society of the city "with the empty, vapid, mean, and selfish pageantry of the present time, which satiates itself with the paltry variety of display, and stoops to all the dirty drudgery of brokerage and speculation, to gather wealth, only to excite the gaping wonder, or secret envy of vulgar rivals. By St. Nicholas, the patron of good fellows, but the march of human intellect is sometimes like a crab, backwards" (165). In making this contrast between the past and present, Paulding doubtless was drawing his knowledge of old Albany from Anne MacVicar Grant's *Memoirs of an American Lady* (1808), a classic source of information about life and manners in the city in the late colonial period.

From Albany *The Mirror* follows a route northward through Troy and Ballston, finally reaching the Mecca of the world of fashion, Saratoga Springs, where the "vapid, mean, and selfish pageantry of display . . . , and paltry variety of display" castigated in Albany sink to a nadir of vulgarity. One of the first to write extensively about Saratoga, Paulding is also one of the most mordantly satirical. For an admirer of the old Dutch culture, Saratoga was a gallery of horrors, just as the steamboat was "a composition of horrors."[7]

James Fenimore Cooper

Paulding's feelings about the way of life in old Albany and the whole Hudson Valley were strengthened by the fact that his family had once been a part of that life. His nostalgia was for things that were very real to him, and in *The Dutchman's Fireside,* with indispensable help from Anne Grant's *Memoirs of an American Lady,* he set about recreating that lost world of his ancestors. James Fenimore Cooper, relying even more heavily on Grant's book, attempted a recreation of the same scene and social order in *Satanstoe,* the first of the three novels comprising the Littlepage Manuscripts. Actually Cooper's novel is laid in a broader scene than is Paulding's. The action of *Satanstoe* begins in Westchester County and Manhattan but soon moves northward as far as Fort Ticonderoga and Washington County, with Albany — Anne Grant's Albany — the most painstakingly presented setting. In detail he describes the customs and manners of the Albany Dutch — the sledding on State Street, the sleighriding on the frozen Hudson, the pranks of the young men, the impact of British army officers on the staid ways of the town, and the dominating social and political prestige of Madame Schuyler, the lady of Grant's *Memoirs.* Like many of Cooper's novels — *The Pioneers* (1823), for example — *Satanstoe* is valuable as social history as well as entertainment.[8]

Unlike *The Dutchman's Fireside, Satanstoe* and the other two Little-page novels were written to convey a very definite political message. Cooper, a large landowner himself, was writing in support of the even larger land-owners, or patroons, of the Hudson Valley in the "Rent Wars" of the mid-1840s that resulted from the refusal of farmers to pay what amounted to feudal dues on the land they had cultivated for many years. Thus *Satanstoe* has as one of its functions the depiction of the risks, both physical and financial, incurred by the landholding families, whether Dutch or English, in acquiring, settling, and converting to useful ends large tracts of wilderness. The Littlepages buy and survey such a tract (a similar under-taking is described by Grant), and almost at once a greedy and shrewd Yankee from Danbury, Connecticut, intrudes, legally but self-servingly, when he gets a lease on a choice mill site; for in Cooper's view New Englanders were the chief troublemakers in the rent disputes. In the second and third volumes of the Littlepage trilogy—*The Chainbearers* (1845) and *The Redskins* (1846)—the novelist traces the problems that Littlepages of later generations have with their lands, their tenants, and squatters. But these two novels are so unabashedly propagandist that they are virtually unread and unreadable today. They lack almost everything—especially pre-occupation with customs and manners—that makes *Satanstoe* one of Cooper's most interesting books.

Nathaniel Parker Willis

An author who wrote of the Hudson Valley and its people with a notable degree of realism was Nathaniel Parker Willis (1806–1867). Born in Port-land, Maine, and educated at the Boston Latin School and Yale College, Willis started his literary career as an editor and a free-lance writer in Boston, and at the age of twenty-one published a volume of verse; but he soon moved to New York, where he collaborated with George P. Morris in editing the *New York Mirror,* a weekly focusing on literature, the arts, and society news. Soon Willis was in Europe and Asia Minor, whence he dispatched to the *Mirror* letters about his travels and the many prominent persons he met. These letters were published in three volumes titled *Pen-cillings by the Way* (1835–44). Back in New York in 1836 after four years abroad, he wrote and published two romantic tragedies, *Bianca Visconti* (1837) and *Tortesa the Usurer* (1839), and continued writing and publish-ing travel sketches and poetry.

Carl Carmer has called Willis a "dude poet" (247). The designation

is not entirely correct. Willis was not only a travel writer and a rather mediocre poet and dramatist. He also wrote short stories and a novel, *Paul
Fane* (1857) — fiction [whose] "characters, settings, and lightness of touch"
led Van Wyck Brooks to regard him as "a precursor of [Henry] James"
or "the Scott Fitzgerald of the belles of Saratoga" (346). Yet the epithet
"dude" is partly deserved. Willis dressed like a dandy and reveled in his
mixing in the world of fashion — of which he might be called the laureate.
But there were other sides to Willis' character. He was on friendly terms
with many of the authors of his time and was generous in furthering the
careers of some of them — for example, James Russell Lowell, Bayard Taylor, and Edgar Allan Poe.

On his return from his first sojourn abroad, Willis bought a small
farm in Tioga County, New York, near the junction of Owego Creek with
the Susquehanna River — a location remote from urban fashion for one who
is solely a dude. Naming his farm Glenmary and devoting himself to im-
proving its beauty and fertility, Willis wrote about his life there in a series
of dispatches to the *Mirror,* which were later collected and published under the title *Rural Letters* (1849). His residence on the Susquehanna was
terminated in 1842 when business pressures required his presence in New
York. In 1850, suffering from tuberculosis, he took up residence on the
west bank of the Hudson just north of the Highlands, a location recommended by his physician for the supposed dryness of the air there in comparison to that of the seaboard. He named his new house Idlewild because it was on a piece of wild land that was idle, that is, uncultivated.
For the next seventeen years till his death in 1867 this was his home, and
from it he contributed to his and George P. Morris' weekly, *The Home
Journal,* a sufficient number of letters to fill two volumes, *Out-Doors at
Idlewild; or, the Shaping of a Home on the Banks of the Hudson* (1855)
and *The Convalescent* (1859). These two books contain the bulk and
perhaps the most significant of his writings on the Hudson and adjacent
areas.

Before his purchase of Glenmary in Tioga County, Willis had made
a journey that took him to the Mohawk, the Chenango, and the Susquehanna rivers, as well as the Hudson, and he wrote a comparison of them
in an article titled "The Four Rivers" included in *Rural Letters.* After the
inevitable praise of the Hudson scenery and speculation as to the degree
of awe felt by Hendrick Hudson as he passed through the Highlands, he
concludes that, though no rivers are "more desirable to see, there are sweeter
rivers to live upon" (200), and thus he chose the Susquehanna. He points
out the preeminence of the Hudson as a tourist attraction but refrains from
describing the voyage from New York to Albany, "for it is doomed to be
re-written, and we will not swell the multitude of describers" (202). Nor

does he make the usual and, to him, futile comparison with the Rhine; most attempts to do so, he thinks, are failures.

But there is no mistaking Willis' fascination with the Hudson Valley, as evidenced in a book, *American Scenery; or, Land, Lake, and River: Illustrations of Transatlantic Nature* (1840), in which he wrote the descriptive material for a collection of 121 steel plate drawings by the British artist William H. Bartlett. Of these drawings fully one-fourth are of scenes along or near the Hudson, not including a number near New York City or in the vicinity of Lake George. Unlike much of Willis' work, which gives evidence of haste or carelessness, *American Scenery* is carefully written and researched. One commentator has called the book " a vast storehouse of association-enhanced landscape" (Callow 168); and indeed Irving's intention, as stated in the *History,* of providing historical and other associations for familiar names and places is Willis' also. "In the letter-press," he writes, "it has been the author's aim to assemble as much as possible of that part of the American story which history has not yet found leisure to put into form, and which romance and poetry have not yet appropriated — the legendary traditions and anecdotes, events of the trying time of the Revolution, Indian history, etc., etc." (v–vi).

Two or three examples will illustrate Willis' procedure. For the drawing of Saratoga Lake, he alludes briefly to General Burgoyne's campaigns, mentions the proximity of the fashionable springs and the custom of visitors there to fish on the lake. He then relates an anecdote of a "belle" who falls overboard while fishing and earns herself "the sobriquet of the diving belle" (27), and finishes with a rather humorous Indian legend. For the drawing of Undercliff, the home of George Morris near Cold Spring on the Hudson, Willis starts the description in more florid language than is his habit, commenting on the "magic" (an Irvingesque word untypical of Willis) that moonlight lends to the scene. He then mentions a few facts about Morris and quotes from Morris' poems, including the only one known today, "The Oak," which begins, "Woodman spare that tree" (232–37). In many of his comments on other drawings, Willis quotes from appropriate writers, sometimes to establish a historical association, sometimes to set a mood, as with the drawing "The Catterskill Fall, from Below," for which he quotes all of William Cullen Bryant's narrative poem on the subject.

The sociable Willis believed that landscapes are enhanced by a human presence, either historical, or of the present — old buildings, a village, or persons. Commenting on a walk he had taken at Trenton Falls near Utica, Willis wrote: "Considering the amount of . . . pleasure which one feels in a walk up the ravine at Trenton, it is remarkable how little one finds to say about it, the day after. Is it that mere scenery without history is enjoyable without being suggestive?" (*Rural Letters* 348). And elsewhere, concerning his landscaping at Idlewild, he wrote: "The figures in a landscape are half its beauty. 'Grounds' are embellished by groups, and by waving dresses and moving forms, to a degree a painter well understands" (*Out-Doors* 156).

Like many people of his day — and ours, too — Willis thought that nature had much to teach us and could aid in curing our spiritual and physical ills. But he did not share with the mystical romanticists and the transcendentalists the conviction that God is immanent in nature. He could, however, have sympathized with Cooper's Natty Bumppo in *The Pioneers* as Natty sat on the escarpment of the Catskills — at the spot where the famous Catskill Mountain House was later built — and, as he viewed "all creation," experienced a surge of religious insight (297–300). These were feelings and insights felt by the painters Thomas Cole and Asher Durand and by the poet Bryant, and Willis would agree with Bryant that "the groves were God's first temples" (67). As he knew it at Idlewild, nature to Willis was a cathedral: "The Hudson a broad aisle, the Highlands a thunder choir and gallery, black rock a pulpit, and a blue dome over all — and lo! Nature, in her surplice of summer, ready to preach a sermon!" (*Out-Doors* 28).

But Willis' affinity with nature was not primarily religious. Like the painters and his fellow writers he was ready to be awed by the "sublimity" (a favorite word in romantic nature writing) of mountain panoramas, especially in combination with rivers and lakes. Also like them, he was easily pleased by a pastoral scene — nature modified by human effort — or by a combination of the sublime and the pastoral or landscaped. Such a combination is what he sought to achieve at Idlewild with its mountain setting, its forests, and its cascading streams, and many pages of his *Out-Doors at Idlewild* and *The Convalescent* recount his labors in "beautifying scenery." Thus we find him laying out walls, bridging brooks, planting trees, and fussing over the design of a gate for his long driveway. In this "creation of [natural] beauty," as Willis called it, he worked along with his laborers. "Nature wild, in contrast with nature improved" (212), both forms of nature being enhanced in the process — such was the principle on which Willis stood.

The principle had been formulated and practiced by Willis' neighbor in nearby Newburgh, Andrew Jackson Downing. The son of a nurseryman of the region, Downing had married into the Hudson Valley aristocracy, had become interested in landscaping and rural architecture, and had established himself as an arbiter in those arts, not only in the valley but nationwide. His practice was booming and lucrative along the river as the wealthy constructed their mansions and landscaped their estates, and he was enjoying brisk sales of his books — for example, *A Treatise on the Theory and Practice of Landscape Gardening, Adapted to North Amer-*

ica: with a View to the Improvement of Country Residences . . . with Re-marks on Rural Architecture (1841), a title which in itself summarizes its author's interests.

Thus, in addition to painting and writing, a third art began to exert an influence along the river. Earlier the painters and the authors tacitly collaborated in celebrating and recording the beauties of the region, as is typified in Asher Durand's famous painting *Kindred Spirits,* depicting Bryant the poet and Cole the painter standing on a ledge amidst the sublimities of the Catskills. Downing, in full sympathy with the artists and writers, considered it his mission to ensure that the beauty that inspired them was enhanced rather than blemished by the intrusion of more and more human habitations. *Out-Doors at Idlewild* serves almost as a handbook for achieving Downing's goals.

But *Out-Doors at Idlewild* contains much more. Willis begins with a lengthy description of the Highland Terrace, on which his home was located. He lavishly praises the natural beauty and salubrious climate of the Terrace and discusses its future in the light of its easy accessibility to New York by steamboat and railroads on each side of the river. He provides sociological information—the movement of farmers inland as real estate values on the river increased, the rather primitive life of the inhabitants of the nearby hills, the influx of summer boarders. He records the history of the region, retells local legends, and includes believably drawn character sketches of some of his neighbors. As an observer of natural events like floods, landslides, the changing seasons, and the break-up of the river ice, Willis anticipates the writings of John Burroughs, and some of his comments are reminiscent of Thoreau. For instance, after telling how a landslide swept away a neighbor's house, he adds: "We should look to see what we build on" (*Out-Doors* 341).

Out-Doors at Idlewild and its sequel *The Convalescent* constitute a detailed account of a family's life in the Hudson Valley, and as such they are valuable both as natural history and as a social record. But Willis always remained a man of the world. Predictably he delighted in sharing and observing fashionable life in the watering places. Above all he wrote about Saratoga Springs, where the rich and socially prominent and the social climbers from all over the nation congregated in the summer, some actually to follow the cure, many others to enjoy the glamour of the place. Paulding wrote satirically about Saratoga in his *New Mirror.* Willis wrote less satirically, at times conveying a sense of his own pleasure in the amenities and intrigues of life there. In *American Scenery* several of the drawings and accompanying letter-press are on Saratoga subjects—Barhdt's Lake, Saratoga Lake, and Congress Hall, the spa's most prestigious hotel. The first two recount some of the diversions available for visitors. The last describes the way of life in the vast hotel and, though brief, does so with an accuracy of detail — even including an analysis of the chemical composition of the curative water — worthy of a social historian, which indeed Willis was.

Saratoga figures in some of Willis' other writings, including several short stories in *Dashes of Life with a Free Pencil* (1845). Among these are "Larks in Vacation," "The Injured Look," and "The Ghost Ball at Congress Hall," the last being a strong evocation of atmosphere, poignant in its autumnal lament for faded beauty. Even Edna Ferber's *Saratoga Trunk* (1941), impressive as it is as fictional social history, lacks the immediacy and the poignancy of Willis' writing about Saratoga.

John Burroughs

Willis, though he could write about the farmers and mountain folk of Orange County with sympathy and truthfulness, was in his Hudson Valley writings primarily a spokesman for the well-to-do disporting themselves at Congress Hall or luxuriating in their villas along the river. In this respect he was very different from another and better writer, John Burroughs (1837–1921), who also, like Willis at Idlewild, built a home on the Hudson. Burroughs was born on a hill farm near Roxbury in the western Catskills, the seventh of ten children. His parents were hard-working farm folk whose life was a ceaseless struggle with rocky soil and a climate in which snow might lie on the ground for half the year or more. For this farm, or the "Old Home" as he called it, Burroughs never outgrew "a homesickness which home [itself] could not cure" (Barrus 196). Farming was in Burroughs' blood, and in addition to his writing and other activities he found time throughout his life to cultivate and harvest a crop, whether of grapes or berries or celery.

The farm where Burroughs grew up was almost bookless, and aside from attendance at district schools his childhood was intellectually barren. In 1854 he launched into a life away from home. He taught in country schools in New York, New Jersey, and Illinois, and managed to study for a few terms in academies in Cooperstown and Ashland, New York. In 1857 he married a farmer's daughter from Ulster County, and in 1862 he briefly studied medicine with a doctor in his wife's hometown of Tongore. During these years, too, he had tried his hand at writing, had published some prose bits, and in 1860 experienced the heady triumph of having an essay accepted by James Russell Lowell, editor of the *Atlantic Monthly*. The essay, titled "Expression," indirectly owed much to Emerson in style and thought, and Lowell at first suspected plagiarism. The *Atlantic* acceptance marked the beginning of a literary career that lasted sixty years and produced an accumulation that filled twenty-three volumes, in addition to much uncollected material.

During the latter part of the Civil War, Burroughs was in Washington, D.C., as a clerk in the Treasury Department. In Washington he met Walt Whitman—the start of a long friendship during which Burroughs wrote two books interpreting Whitman's verse. One of them, *Notes on Walt Whitman as Poet and Person* (1867) was the first book Burroughs published and the second by any one championing Whitman. Burroughs' next book, a collection of essays under the title *Wake-Robin,* appeared in 1871. Soon after, he left Washington, having received an appointment as a bank examiner in New York State, and during the next two years he built, largely with his own hands, a solid, comfortable stone house high on the bank of the Hudson at West Park. Riverby, as he named it, was his home until his death, though he had a woodland cabin, Slabsides, a mile back from the river, to which he could retire for study and writing. In the last thirteen years of his life he spent summers in an old house named Woodchuck Lodge adjacent to the ancestral farm at Roxbury. Thus by heritage, birth, and residence Burroughs belonged to the Catskills and the mid-Hudson Valley, and those regions, really a single one, provided him with most of the material he needed for his nature writing, for which he was best known.

Burroughs has been acclaimed as one of the three outstanding American writers on nature, along with Thoreau and John Muir. This is a fair assessment, for Burroughs was an expert field naturalist, primarily an ornithologist but deeply interested in other branches of natural science such as geology and general biology. His format was the essay, and his style was simple, lucid, unadorned, highly readable, and appealing to the educated but scientifically inexpert readership for which he wrote. One cannot summarize the content of his work on these subjects, but it included his observations of birds and animals and the weather and such human occupations as ice-cutting on the Hudson; and it contained accounts of personal experiences, for example a boat trip down the East Branch of the Delaware River and a hike up Slide Mountain in the Catskills. No other writer has approached Burroughs' achievement in recording the natural history and geographical features of the region he took as his domain. Willis' writing at Idlewild bore some resemblance to Burroughs' insofar as Willis was interested in the weather and wildlife and the geography of the Highland Terrace, but a greater interest for Willis lay in the history and the legends and the people of the vicinity. Burroughs had little or no interest in folklore or history. Thus he differed markedly from the other authors so far considered, with the possible exception of Crèvecoeur, who was an amateur naturalist and a careful recorder of what he saw in the fields and forests near his farm and in places he visited.

A naturalist and outdoorsman, Burroughs was also a conservationist — one of the earliest in New York State, though we have seen that Crèvecoeur had some serious misgivings about human devastation of the environment. In an essay in *The Summit of the Years* (1913) Burroughs wrote: "A riotous, wasteful, and destructive spirit has been turned loose upon this continent, and it has used the weapons which physical science has placed in its hands in a brutal, devil-may-care sort of way, with the result that a nature fertile and bountiful, but never kind and sympathetic, has been outraged and disfigured and impoverished, rather than mellowed and subdued and humanized" (67). He also complained of "howling locomotives . . . pouring out their huge volumes of fetid carbon" (66) on the tracks on both sides of the river, differing here from Willis, who hailed the railroads as instrumental in making the river accessible to visitors and commuters to and from the city. Unhappy with the mushrooming of industry, Burroughs was of the opinion that "a great manufacturing town is hideous, and life in it is usually hideous" (67). Science, he conceded, could be used beneficially for humanity without destroying the earth's beauty, but thus far, particularly in America, it had been employed mainly for selfish ends which often ignored the question of what was best for the environment.

Burroughs' thinking on nature was not limited to concern for conservation. His attitudes were much more complex, but they rest upon three basic assumptions. First, nature is bountiful; if she is not misused, she can supply all the physical commodities that humanity needs. Second, humanity's survival and well-being depend upon its living in harmony with nature. Third, we must understand nature, her laws and limitations, if we are to reap her benefits.

The gifts of nature are not only for the body, Burroughs insists, but for the spirit as well. Burroughs, it must be remembered, was a disciple of Emerson and an ardent admirer of Whitman. Their mode of thought, transcendentalism, met his own spiritual needs; and he eagerly adopted it, for he had early rejected the rather crude Calvinism of his father's Old School Baptist faith. Transcendentalism, insofar as it can be defined, is a monism which sees divinity as spirit pervading all things — the infinite manifested in the finite. In *Time and Change* (1912) Burroughs clearly states his transcendentalist outlook: "When we come to see that the celestial and the terrestrial are one, that time and eternity are one, that mind and matter are one, that death and life are one, that there is and can be nothing not inherent in Nature, then we can no longer look for or expect a far-off unknown God" (246-47). Between this belief and science Burroughs, like

Emerson and Whitman, saw no conflict. Science, when it contributes to an understanding of nature, is supportive of transcendentalism, though science as a mere accumulation of meaningless facts can be of little spiritual significance. Nature, Emerson taught, is a teacher of the mind and the soul, and Burroughs agreed. Thus his observations in the fields and forests, like Thoreau's, were important as aids in the perception of spirit underlying life and matter. Burroughs insisted that we see nature as she really is, not as certain sentimentalists claimed to see her. He had no patience with "nature fakers," as he called popular writers like Ernest Thompson Seton who attributed to animals human qualities that animals simply do not have. Though Burroughs marveled as much as any one at the ways of nature, he refused to stray from what he saw as facts. Similarly, though the river and mountain landscapes in which he lived were a joy and inspiration to him, he wrote about them with restraint. The rhapsodic outpourings of some of the earlier writers in the presence of Hudson and Catskill "sublimities" were foreign to Burroughs' pen. He could write feelingly of the graceful, sweeping lines of his native hills, but he also explained these contours geologically.

Burroughs' philosophical turn of mind led him to other authors whose thought was congenial to him. As a result he wrote a considerable body of literary criticism on writers like Carlyle, Emerson, Thoreau, and, of course, Whitman, and on literature in general, especially in its relation to nature. Much of his criticism is perceptive and worth reading today. His greatest contribution, he thought, was in his interpretations of Whitman, on whose acceptance as a world poet Burroughs piqued himself as an important influence.

In his lifetime Burroughs enjoyed a popularity which is now diminished but far from extinct. His writing attracted the attention of the general reading public as well as of figures like the amateur naturalist, Theodore Roosevelt, who became his good friend. Some of his writings were adopted for reading in schools across the nation; thus generations of children learned about nature from him. Among other naturalists and nature writers of his time and later — for example, Edwin Way Teale — he was respected both for his scientific knowledge and for his literary skill.

Herman Melville

Three of America's major novelists — Herman Melville, Henry James, and Edith Wharton — had connections with the Hudson Valley one way or another, though all were born in New York City. Of the three, however, only Edith Wharton used the valley at all extensively as a setting for fiction.

Melville had deep Albany roots. His mother, a native of the city, was a Gansevoort, a leading Dutch family of the upper Hudson, and his grandfather, General Peter Gansevoort, had won fame for his successful defense of Fort Stanwix against the British in 1777. During his childhood Melville accompanied his mother on long visits to Albany; and after his father, a New Englander, failed in business, the family moved permanently to Albany. There Melville attended the Albany Academy briefly, tried his hand at various jobs, and did a bit of writing for local newspapers. In the meanwhile the father had died, and the family was left dependent on the mother's relatives. Eventually poverty forced the family to move to cheaper quarters in Lansingburgh, several miles north of Troy. Soon after, Melville went to sea, first as a sailor on a merchantman and later as a whaler. In his writings Melville drew remarkably little from his Dutch background and what must have been an intimate knowledge of Albany, its people, and its ways.

The Albany writer Alice Kenney, however, has made an exhaustive study of Melville in relation to the Dutch tradition of the Hudson and has come up with some plausible conclusions and surmises. In an article, "Herman Melville and the Dutch Tradition," she points out that Melville, while in Albany, heard Dutch spoken by his mother and her family. While he probably did not speak it himself, he may have been influenced by the Dutch propensity for "extravagant rhetoric" (287), as exemplified in much of Melville's writing, especially in *Mardi* (1849) and *Pierre* (1852). Further, Kenney suggests that in *Mardi* there is a "striking resemblance between the Yillah story . . . and one of the very few Dutch dialect folk tales that have been collected" (391) in New York State. The tale relates an incident supposedly occurring on the Normanskill, a stream a mile or so downriver from Albany. It involves a Lorelei, or water maiden, and a youth, and may well have been heard by Melville. Also, Kenney finds vestiges of the Dutch tradition in the points of view and attitudes of some of the characters in *Mardi*.

Less speculative perhaps is Melville's apparent drawing from his own experiences or observations in the opening chapters of *Redburn* (1849), describing the youthful hero's departure from his pleasant home on the Hudson and his unpleasant trip down the river by steamboat to New York. In *Pierre* Melville's awareness of his Hudson Valley Dutch heritage emerges very succinctly. Early in the novel he describes the vast domains of the patroons — "far-descended Dutch meadows [that] lie steeped in a Hindoo-ish haze" (10) — and asserts that he is describing these estates "to establish the richly aristocratic condition of Master Pierre Glendinning" (11), the chief character in the novel and heir to an estate like the one Melville has just described. Kenney has much to say about *Pierre* in her book *The Gansevoorts of Albany* (1969). The Glendinnings in the novel resemble, Kenney thinks, the landed gentry of the lower Hudson—like the Van Cortlandts, with whom the Melvilles were acquainted. She also notes a resemblance of certain characters in the novel to members of Melville's family. For example, the haughty Mrs. Glendinning, with her pride of birth, bears a likeness to Melville's mother. Other parallels might exist between Lucy and the wife of Melville's brother or perhaps Melville's own wife, and Isabel and one of Melville's cousins. Pierre's ancestry resembles Melville's very closely. Pierre's grandfather, Pierre Glendinning, was famous for having successfully defended a fort, as was Melville's grandfather, Peter Gansevoort (note the initials of each); and Pierre's father and Melville's both died when their sons were about twelve years old. Indeed, the adolescent Pierre may reflect Melville's own self-image as a youth.

Yet despite these similarities of characters in the novel to members of Melville's own family and the dithyramb to "ancient and magnificent Dutch manors at the North" (10), the Glendinnings are not even Dutch and their "manor" is situated unmistakably in the Berkshires near Pittsfield, where Melville had spent much time as a boy and was living when he wrote the novel. The point is worth noting—this disguising of the very heritage he was so freely drawing from—but it does not alter the fact that the near feudal way of life of the Glendinnings is modeled on that of the Hudson Valley patroons.

Pierre, though seriously blemished as a literary work, is Melville's most notable evocation of the Dutch tradition. Several ephemeral items— two poems and a brief story—drawing from this tradition remain to be mentioned. The story, "The Happy Failure" (1854), Kenney says, is laid at Melville's Uncle Herman's estate at Gansevoort, New York, just north of Saratoga. It recounts the cheerful resignation with which an old man, modeled on Uncle Herman, accepts failure of an invention he has labored on for years. Some critics believe that the story reflects Melville's own attempts to come to terms with his declining reputation as a writer.

One of the poems, "A Dutch Christmas up the Hudson in the Time of the Patroons" (1891), is a pleasant account of the customs of a passing era. The other poem, "Rip Van Winkle's Lilac" (1891), is preceded by a prose introduction in which Melville takes some liberties with Irving's tale. Rip on returning from his sleep finds his ruined house overspread by a lilac bush in full bloom, which he had planted years before as a peace offering to his wife. Some time before Rip's reappearance, an artist, struck by the picturesqueness of the old house and the lilac, sets up his easel to paint it. Soon "a gaunt hatchet-faced stony-eyed individual, with a gray sort of salted complexion like that of a dried codfish" (*Poems* 287), accosts the artist, upbraids him for painting such a shabby subject, and recommends for his brush a shiny new church perched bleakly on a nearby hill. The artist rejects the suggestion, considering the church "a cadaver" (287). The poem and the prose introduction make the point that Rip's life was not a total failure. Like Melville, now in eclipse as an author, Rip has contributed some beauty to the world. The hatchet-faced man is suggestive of the Yankees who shattered the tranquillity of Rip's village in Irving's story. Thus, in addition to its autobiographical undertones, Melville's piece reasserts Irving's misgivings about progress and an uncritical admiration for the new.

Edith Wharton and Henry James

Nathaniel Parker Willis in *Out-Doors at Idlewild* commented on the great estates that lined the Hudson's eastern shore, which from early times had been "a garden of Dutch aristocracy," or the "Knickerbocracy" (375–76), as he called it. Originally these estates had been manors controlling huge tracts of land. As time went on they became simply rich persons' country seats, for much of the land was lost after the antirent agitations. And joining the Dutch along the river were other wealthy families who built elaborate mansions, which they occupied perhaps only part of the year, their main residences being in the city. Many of these newcomers, of course, were not of Dutch descent: among their motives in coming, the search for social prestige was not the least.

The outstanding recorder of life among these families was Edith Wharton (1862–1937), who was born into the New York City elite and was acquainted since childhood with families who owned the river estates. In two of her novels, *The House of Mirth* (1905) and *Hudson River Bracketed* (1929), she deals with the way of life she had observed. In the first of these, only part of the action takes place upstate, in the villa of an affluent New York City couple, Gus and Judy Trenor. The activities of the Trenors and their friends, both in town and in the country, are described with an exactitude flavored with sharp satire. With the exception of the heroine, Lily Bart, and the rather ineffective Lawrence Selden, who is half-heartedly in love with Lily, the characters whom Wharton brings together in house parties on the Hudson are a collection of boobs, bounders, social climbers, and schemers of one sort or another. Their pastimes consist of gambling, gossiping, backbiting, keeping up appearances, and self-promotion. Though actually quite young, Lily Bart, a decent person, is a bit too old to achieve the brilliant marriage which since babyhood she has been trained to regard as the only worthwhile goal in a young woman's life. Her efforts and the connivings of her so-called friends fail to land an eligible, that is, wealthy, man, though her scruples about virtually selling herself for money cause her to miss several chances. Lily is handicapped by having values, however vague, which prevent her from playing the hypocrite or totally conforming to society's rather sleazy standards. In the end, impoverished, she dies from an overdose of sleeping medicine, taken not suicidally but in a desperate effort to get a respite from unbearable weariness. Commenting on the novel years later, Wharton wrote: "a frivolous society can acquire dramatic significance only through what its frivolity destroys. Its tragic implication lies in its power of debasing people and ideals" (*Backward Glance* 207). *The House of Mirth* does attain tragic stature in its unrelenting dissection of a high society that is not only frivolous but at times downright evil.

Hudson River Bracketed deals with a very different sort of people from the triflers and destroyers in *The House of Mirth* who use their river villas as one of their several playgrounds. In *Hudson River Bracketed,* Wharton examines a way of life rooted in an enduring and honorable tradition. The title of the novel is taken from Andrew Jackson Downing's classification of architectural styles for rural American houses. All these styles are derived from Europe with the exception of "Hudson River bracketed," which is indigenous to the United States. To Wharton this architecture represents a worthwhile tradition and a decent set of values. In the novel there is a house, the Willows, that is a fine example of the bracketed style, and Wharton describes its exterior and interior in loving detail (57-70). The most obvious exterior features are ornate brackets supporting roofs and balconies and an overall irregularity produced by a tower, arched windows, and urns on each side of the front steps. Wharton gives the description through the eyes of a midwestern boy who has come east to the banks of the Hudson to recuperate from a severe illness and is staying with poor relations. This youth, Vance Weston, often visits the Willows, which has long been unoccupied. A young woman, Halo Spear, who lives with her family in their ancestral Dutch house nearby, befriends Vance and helps him understand the tradition of which the Willows and she and her family are the products.

The Willows makes Vance aware of "the novelty of permanence" (132) in America; it is a door "into the illimitable windings of the past" (154), for among other things it contains many old books. The Willows serves in the story as a leitmotif representing an older, firmer culture as compared with that of the Midwest or that of New York City. "This is the Past — if only I could get back into it" (333), Vance exclaims. But he does get back into it, with the help of Halo, and as a result he begins to realize his potential as a writer, which he had always wished to be. The Willows "symbolized continuity, that great nutritive element of which no one had ever told him, of which neither Art nor Nature had been able to speak to him, since nothing in his training had prepared him for their teaching" (498). Vance does flourish as a writer finally, thanks to the new presence in his life of a sense of the past.

   Hudson River Bracketed is a strong book thematically, though in its plot, which for present purposes may be ignored, it has weaknesses. Wharton is obviously examining facets of her own patrician and privileged past, and she clearly has deep associations with the scenes she describes. As is almost inevitable, apparently, with any writer concerned with the Hudson Valley, she on occasion in this novel, as well as in *The House of Mirth,* releases spates of purple prose in efforts to reproduce the landscape as she sees it, and her success in so doing ranks with that of the best.

   Wharton's friend and to some extent her mentor, Henry James, (1843–1916), lived most of his life abroad, especially in England, because he felt that America lacked associations (in Irving's sense of the word). In 1904 he returned to America for a lengthy visit, an account of which he published in *The American Scene* (1907). During his extensive journeying up and down the nation he rediscovered the Hudson Valley. Entering New York State by train from the West, he had "the absurdest sense of meeting again a ripe old civilization and traveling through a country that showed the mark of established manners" (147). Apparently this sense seemed less absurd as the train progressed eastward. By the time it was passing through "antique Albany" (147), where his father had been born and grown up and where James had often visited as a child, he looked on the scene "as through the glaze of all-but-filial tears" (148). As the train sped southward, he "saw the river shine, as a great romantic stream" (148). The landscape "was veiled, for the most part, in a mist of premature spring heat, an atmosphere draping it indeed in luminous mystery . . . " (149). Riding in his Pullman car, James was experiencing something very close to young Irving's sense of the magic and fairy quality of the river scenery on his first voyage to Albany a hundred years before. To Irving the magic was enhanced by tales and legends associated with localities along the way. James, too, saw the passing scene through "a shimmer of association that still refuses to be reduced to terms; some sense of legend, of aboriginal mystery, with a still earlier past for its dim background and the insistent idea of the river as above all romantic for its warrant" (154). James wonders whether the paintings of the Hudson River School and the tale of Rip Van Winkle may have contributed to this feeling. A short time after this train ride, James went upriver again to West Point, where he marveled in a quite orthodox manner over the beauties of the Highlands, but more poignant were his comments on his visit, during the same trip, to Washington Irving's Sunnyside — a glimpse into "the little American past" (155). Like James, Irving was a New Yorker; he too at an early age had known the river; and he too had lived long abroad and done much of his writing about foreign places and people. Such thoughts may have hovered in James' mind as he wrote a beautifully impressionistic and evocative account of his visit to the home of Irving's old age. Irving, it seems, was James' chief association with the river.

James in his fiction made little use of his knowledge of upstate New York, and in this he resembled Melville. Yet several of his major fictional characters hail from upstate; and in the case of Isabel Archer, heroine of *The Portrait of a Lady* (1881), he goes to considerable pains to sketch her Albany background. He presents the mores and social milieu of the city at some length; for, in contrast to the surroundings into which he later places Isabel, they are important in explaining why she acts as she does. But James' most impressive contribution to the literature of upstate New York is in the chapter in *The American Scene*. There he reveals with the insight and sensitivity that characterize his best writing the qualities, evasive but nonetheless very real, that are unique to the Hudson River Valley and have generated the uniqueness of its literature.

Notes

1. Moreover, Irving may have used the Van Alen house as a model for the Van Tassel homestead. For the Kinderhook sources for Irving see Stanley T. Williams, *Life of Washington Irving* 1:109, 408n, 429n.

2. Williams 1:123. For the "formula" for Hudson River School painting see Howard Mumford Jones, "James Fenimore Cooper and the Hudson River School," *Magazine of Art* 45 (1952):243–51. In the "sketch" just quoted and in others, as well as in his finished works, Irving anticipates the painters in following many aspects of this formula. Jones uses as examples some scenes from Fenimore Cooper's works. Sometimes the artists used scenes from literary works as subjects for their paintings. Occasionally the painters were able to improve on the literary original. Such was the case with Cole's illustration for Gulian C. Verplanck's "Gelyna," a sentimental tale of Albany and Abercromby's disastrous expedition against Fort Ticonderoga. Cole's rendering of a wild mountain scene with storm clouds overhead and two human figures — one dead, the other alive — diminished by the vastness of the landscape conveys a sense of tragedy totally lacking in the mawkishly sentimental story.

3. In fact, a Judge Herman Knickerbocker did reside in Schaghticoke, and Irving visited him there in 1832 (*Letters* 2: 772–73).

4. Actually it was Van Rensselaer's agent who defied the government; the Patroon remained in Holland, never setting foot on his vast holdings. Bearn Island is now named Barren Island, a corruption of the Dutch *Beeren,* meaning bears. In garrisoning the fort with Helderbergers, Irving was taking liberties with historical fact, probably for the purpose of satirizing events in the so-called rent wars of upstate New York. No white people were settled in the Helderbergs in the seventeenth century. Irving's remarks about the Helderbergers were absent from earlier editions of the *History.* They were added in the 1848 edition, several years after the rent wars came to a head.

5. For useful studies of Irving's use of foreign sources, see J. B. Thompson, "The Genesis of the Rip Van Winkle Legend," *Harper's New Monthly Magazine* 67 (1883): 612–22, and Henry A. Pochmann, "Irving's German Sources in the *Sketch Book,"* *Studies in Philology* 27 (1930): 477–507.

6. Irving, *Journals* 2:16. For further discussion of Irving, Hawthorne, and the romantic imagination, see Haskell S. Springer, "Creative Contradictions in Irving," *American Transcendental Quarterly* 5 (1970): 14–18.

7. See Louis D. Owens, "James K. Paulding and the Foundations of American Realism," *Bulletin of the New York Public Library* 79 (1976): 40–50, for a discussion of Paulding's attitude toward the industrial and commercial development of the country. Writing of Albany at about the same time as Paulding, Gulian C. Verplanck (in several introductory paragraphs to "Gelyna, a Tale of Albany and Ticonderoga") praised the contemporary (c. 1830) city for its "agreeable variety of society and manners." It was not a place of clod-hopping, sturgeon-eating burgomasters or "seventeen-petticoated beauties" but rather a scene in which might "be found talent and learning, and accomplishment and beauty." In all respects Verplanck found Albany to be far superior to such European provincial towns as York or Tours (303–304).

8. For a full and specific account of what Paulding and Cooper owed to Anne Grant see Dorothy Dondore, "The Debt of Two Dyed-in-the Wool Americans to Mrs. Grant's *Memoirs*: Cooper's *Satanstoe* and Paulding's *The Dutchman's Fireside,"* *American Quarterly* 12 (1940): 52–58. See Thomas F. O'Donnell's "Introduction" to *The Dutchman's Fireside* for comments on Paulding's debt to Mrs. Grant.

Works Cited

Barrus, Clara. *Our Friend John Burroughs.* Boston: Houghton Mifflin, 1914.

Brooks, Van Wyck. *The World of Washington Irving.* 1944; rpt. Cleveland: World, 1946.

Bryant, William Cullen. *Poems.* London: Oxford University Press, 1914.

Burroughs, John. *Notes on Walt Whitman as Poet and Person.* New York: American News, 1867.

———. *The Summit of the Years.* Boston: Houghton Mifflin, 1913.

———. *Time and Change.* Boston: Houghton Mifflin, 1912.

———. *Wake-Robin.* Boston: Hurd and Houghton, 1871.

Callow, James T. *Kindred Spirits: Knickerbocker Writers and American Painters.* Chapel Hill: University of North Carolina Press, 1967.

Carmer, Carl. *The Hudson.* New York: Farrar and Rinehart, 1939.

Cooper, James Fenimore. *The Pioneers.* New York: Holt, Rinehart, and Winston, 1959.

———. *Satanstoe.* Lincoln: University of Nebraska Press, 1962.

Crane, Hart. *Complete Poems and Selected Letters and Prose.* Edited by Brom Weber. Garden City, N.Y.: Doubleday, 1966.

Crèvecoeur, Michel-Guillaume St. Jean de. *Journey into Northern Pennsylvania and the State of New York.* Ann Arbor: University of Michigan Press, 1964.

———. [J. Hector St. John de]. *Letters from an American Farmer.* New York: Dutton, 1957.

———. [St. John de]. *Sketches of Eighteenth Century America.* Edited by Henri Bourdin et al. New Haven: Yale University Press, 1925.

Denton, Daniel. *A Brief Description of New York.* 1670; rpt. Harrison, N.Y.: Harbor Hill Books, 1966.

Dondore, Dorothy. "The Debt of Two Dyed-in-the Wool Americans to Mrs. Grant's *Memoirs*: Cooper's *Satanstoe* and Paulding's *The Dutchman's Fireside.*" *American Quarterly* 12 (1940): 52–58.

Grant, Anne. *Memoirs of an American Lady, with Sketches of Manners and Scenery in America, as They Existed Previous to the Revolution.* New York: Appleton, 1846.

Hawthorne, Nathaniel. *The House of the Seven Gables.* Edited by William Charvat et al. Columbus: Ohio State University Press, 1965.

———. *The Scarlet Letter.* Edited by William Charvat et al. Columbus: Ohio State University Press, 1962.

Higginson, Thomas Wentworth. *Longfellow.* Boston: Houghton Mifflin, 1902.

Huth, Hans. *Nature and the American: Three Centuries of Changing Attitudes.* Berkeley: University of California Press, 1957.

Irving, Pierre. *Life and Letters of Washington Irving.* New York: Putnam, 1882–84. Vol. 1.

Irving, Washington, *Bracebridge Hall or the Humourists.* Edited by Herbert F. Smith. Boston: Twayne, 1977.

———. "The Catskill Mountains." In *Miscellaneous Writings, 1803–1859.* Edited by Wayne R. Kime. Boston: Twayne, 1981, 2: 163–67.

———. "A Chronicle of Wolfert's Roost." *Knickerbocker Magazine* 13 (1839): 317–28.

———. *A History of New York from the Beginning of the World to the End of the Dutch Dynasty,* by Diedrich Knickerbocker. New York: Putnam, 1857.

————. *Journals and Notebooks, 2, 1807–1822.* Edited by Walter A. Reichart and Lillian Schlissel. Boston: Twayne, 1981.

————. "Letter of 'Geoffrey Crayon' to the Editor of the *Knickerbocker Magazine.*" In *Miscellaneous Writings, 1803–1859.* Edited by Wayne R. Kime. Boston: Twayne, 1981, 2: 100–104.

————. *Letters, 1, 1802–1823.* Edited by Ralph M. Aderman et al. Boston: Twayne, 1978.

————. *Letters, 2, 1823–1838.* Edited by Ralph M. Aderman et al. Boston: Twayne, 1979.

————. *Miscellaneous Writings, 1803–1859.* 2 vols. Edited by Wayne R. Kime. Boston: Twayne, 1981.

————. *The Sketch Book of Geoffrey Crayon, Gent.* Edited by Haskell Springer. Boston: Twayne, 1978.

————. "Sleepy Hollow." In *Miscellaneous Writings.* Edited by Wayne R. Kime. Boston: Twayne, 1981, 2: 104–113.

————. *Tales of a Traveller.* New York: Putnam, 1857.

————. ["A Voyage up the Hudson River in 1800"]. In *Miscellaneous Writings.* Edited by Wayne R. Kime. Boston: Twayne, 1981, 2: 344–45.

————. *Wolfert's Roost.* Edited by Roberta Rosenberg. Boston: Twayne, 1979.

James, Henry. *The American Scene.* Edited by W. H. Auden. New York: Scribner's, 1946.

————. *The Portrait of a Lady.* New York: Modern Library, 1961.

Jones, Howard Mumford. "James Fenimore Cooper and the Hudson River School." *Magazine of Art* 45 (1952): 243–51.

Juet, Robert. "The Third Voyage of Master Henrie Hudson . . . ." In Samuel Purchas, *Hakluytus Posthumus.* 1625; rpt. New York: AMS Press, 1965, 13:333–74.

Kenney, Alice. *The Gansevoorts of Albany.* Syracuse: Syracuse University Press, 1969.

————. "Herman Melville and the Dutch Tradition." *Bulletin of the New York Public Library* 79 (1976): 286–99.

Melville, Herman. *Collected Poems.* Edited by Howard P. Vincent. Chicago: Packard, 1942.

————. *Mardi and the Voyage Thither.* London: Constable, 1922.

————. *Pierre or, The Ambiguities.* New York: Hendricks House, 1962.

————. *Redburn: His First Voyage.* Garden City, N.Y.: Doubleday, 1957.

Owens, Louis D. "James K. Paulding and the Foundations of American Realism." *Bulletin of the New York Public Library* 79 (1976): 40–50.

Paulding, James Kirke. "Cobus Yerkes." In *Minor Knickerbockers.* Edited by Kendall B. Taft. New York: American Book, 1947, pp. 42–52.

————. *The Dutchman's Fireside.* Edited by Thomas F. O'Donnell. New Haven: College and University Press, 1966.

————. *The New Mirror for Travellers: and Guide to the Springs.* New York: Carvill, 1828.

Pochmann, Henry A. "Irving's German Sources in the *Sketch Book.*" *Studies in Philology* 27 (1930): 477–507.

———. "Irving's German Tour and Its Influence on His Tales." *PMLA* 45 (1930): 1150–87.

Springer, Haskell S. "Creative Contradictions in Irving." *American Transcendental Quarterly* 5 (1970): 14–18.

Steendam, Jacob. "The Praise of New Netherland." In *Anthology of New Netherland*. Edited and translated by Edwin C. Murphy. 1865; rpt. New York: Garrett, 1970.

Thompson, Harold W. *Body, Boots & Britches*. Philadelphia: Lippincott, 1940; rpt. Syracuse: Syracuse University Press, 1979.

Thompson, J. B. "The Genesis of the Rip Van Winkle Legend." *Harper's New Monthly Magazine* 67 (1883): 617–22.

Verplanck, Gulian C. "Gelyna, a Tale of Albany and Ticonderoga." *The Talisman for MDCCCXXX*. New York: Elam Bliss, 1828, pp. 302–35.

Wharton, Edith. *A Backward Glance*. New York: Appleton-Century, 1934.

———. *The House of Mirth*. New York: Scribner's, 1905.

———. *Hudson River Bracketed*. New York: Appleton, 1929.

Williams, Stanley T. *Life of Washington Irving*. 2 vols. New York: Oxford University Press, 1935.

Willis, Nathaniel Parker. *American Scenery; or Land, Lake and River: Illustrations of Transatlantic Nature*. 1840; rpt. Barre, Mass.: Reprint Society, 1971.

———. *The Convalescent*. New York: Scribner, 1859.

———. *Dashes at Life with a Free Pencil*. 1845; rpt. New York: Garrett, 1969.

———. *Out-Doors at Idlewild; or, The Shaping of a Home on the Banks of the Hudson*. New York: Scribner, 1855.

———. *Rural Letters*. New York: Baker and Scribner, 1849.

Young, Philip. "Fallen from Time: The Mythic Rip Van Winkle." *Kenyon Review* 22 (1960): 547–73.

The Meaning of the Indians and Their Land in Cooper's *The Last of the Mohicans*

6

FRANK BERGMANN

SUMMARIZING THE ACHIEVEMENT of Upstate's greatest writers of the nineteenth century, Thomas F. O'Donnell served up an epigram: "After Cooper, upstate New York could be seen; after Frederic, it could be understood" (57 c.4). Tom meant this in a strictly regional sense; he knew, of course, that Cooper not only painted surfaces but also probed depths. Frederic's Upstate was a region developed enough to be capable of being understood. The Upstate of Cooper's Leatherstocking tales was, by contrast, a wilderness pockmarked by a few white settlements, military outposts more often than not; there was not much there to be understood in Frederic's way. Generally, Frederic's Upstate is therefore actual; Cooper, however, consistently invests his Upstate with symbolic meaning, and nowhere more so than in *The Last of the Mohicans* (1826). In his "Historical Introduction" to the novel in the Cooper Edition, James Franklin Beard analyzes the Glens Falls as the book's major, far-reaching metaphor.[1] The movement of the falls' waters is, however, opposite to that which the narrative — after wending its way convolutedly from Fort Edward through and past the falls to Fort William Henry in the book's first half — takes in the second half. The narrative leads into the wilderness beyond the Horican; this wilderness constitutes a second major metaphor whose symbolic force equals that of Glens Falls.

Beard's introduction does Cooper's readers another major service: gently but firmly it refocuses their eyes from the mythic readings scholars of the past several decades have favored to the Indian matter at the heart of the novel. From the first, Cooper has come under attack for holding a brief for the Indians, with the strictures generally masking themselves as challenge to his historicity; Lewis Cass's terse "'the last of the Mohegans' is an Indian of the school of Mr. Heckewelder, and not of the school of nature" may stand for them all.[2] Harsh criticism of Cooper's art surfaces just as early, though the most infamous example is Mark Twain's "Fenimore Cooper's Literary Offenses" of 1895. Today, Cooper's plots are still widely considered to be "tiresome" or "makeshift," although very recently some energetic efforts have been made to show that Cooper's presumed artistic weaknesses may in fact be his greatest strengths.[3] I believe that in *The Last of the Mohicans* Cooper says more about the race problem than most critics have conceded, and that he does so with greater art than has generally been acknowledged. Central to my view is the consideration of how Cooper ties together the three concerns given separately in condensed form on the novel's title page: "The Last of the Mohicans; A Narrative of 1757. 'Mislike me not, for my complexion, The shadowed livery of the burnished sun.'" The book's major message is the historical lesson inherent in the disastrous race conflict, a lesson for both Cooper's time and ours; the "narrative" is a more effective and carefully constructed vehicle for Cooper's message than the scoffers would have us believe; and the motto from Shakespeare's *The Merchant of Venice* is more than a pious sentiment engraved upon a stately burial monument.

Most of the charges against Cooper as artist seem to me based on a discernibly Aristotelian definition of plot, which is tacitly assumed by critics as a given and which Cooper is then shown as violating. Handbook definitions, however cautious and intelligent, tend to encompass too much, such as this one when it speaks of plot as "a planned series of interrelated actions progressing, because of the interplay of one force upon another, through a struggle of opposing forces to a climax and a *dénouement*" and of its function as translating "character into action."[4] The outlines of Attic tragedy are too clearly visible here, and little is made of the scarcity of novels in Aristotle's time and of the absence of a universally accepted theory of the novel in ours. Since Cooper has appealed to generations of readers at home and abroad as storyteller, we profit more by considering E. M. Forster's discussion of "story" and "plot" as two of the several aspects of the novel.

Forster's discussion is unpretending. Story "is a narrative of events arranged in their time sequence" (47); it asks, "and then?" (130) Plot springs from the story and is a higher aspect, since it is based on causality, requires memory and intelligence, and offers surprise and mystery; it asks, "why?" (130) Story is a low aspect of the novel because it is based on curiosity only. Nevertheless, Forster — as some recent theorists of the novel forget — is quite emphatic about the importance of story (if the story was unimportant, why would Forster have spent on it one of his lectures that comprise *Aspects of the Novel*?): "the fundamental aspect of the novel is its story-telling aspect" (44), and, no matter how barren aesthetically and morally that aspect may be, "we have much to learn from it" (48).[5] Without a story there can be no novel; Forster insists that Gertrude Stein, who attempted to do away with time and therefore with story, failed "because as soon as fiction is completely delivered from time it cannot express anything at all" (67). Worse: "The time-sequence cannot be destroyed without carrying in its ruin all that should have taken its place; the novel that would express values only becomes unintelligible and therefore valueless" (68). And, of course, remains unread.

Unread by whom? A further critical fallacy, the harder to guard against the more sophisticated theoretical discourse becomes, is the inevitable assumption that the novelist writes for the literary critic who makes his living writing books about books. Forster, however, identifies four audiences: the true scholar, who is rare and therefore not discussed in detail (22); the pseudo-scholar—ubiquitous in the civil service and in the academy—who sits before him at Cambridge and with whom he not only jokingly identifies (23–28, 45); the modern equivalent of the caveman, who is interested in the story as entertainment only (44–45); and the ideal reader, who "is quite good-tempered and vague, and probably driving a motorbus at the same time and paying no more attention to literature than it merits" (44). This reader, and his attitude toward the novel, Forster respects and admires (45). The bus-man is in that "state in which," Helen Vendler says, "the text works on us, not we on it" (344). To find the proper corrective to the resigned condescension toward the story which Forster says he shares—"Yes—oh, dear, yes—the novel tells a story" (45)—Cooper scholars too might remember the days before they became critics, might attempt to regain what Vendler calls "that early attitude of entire receptivity and plasticity and innocence before the text" (344). Cooper, I submit, wrote *The Last of the Mohicans* for the bus-man in all of us, and so "it kind of tells a story, so to speak" (*Aspects* 44).

Cooper designs his story to make the reader give him a hearing; above the story, the plot transmits the values. Outside is the sugar coating, inside the medicine. The apparent problems of the story of *The Last of the Mohicans* have often been ridiculed,[6] and indeed, where is the logic in the girls' desire to join their father at such an inopportune time? They would be much safer in Albany or New York. But we are already asking "why?", which means that we are picking up the plot even as we follow the story. After all, the girls' father might die, and so we have no right to call them imprudent or stupid. If go then they must, at such a time, they would appear to be safest amidst the contingent that marches the high road from Edward to William Henry between sunup and sundown. Duncan Heyward, however, wants to make time and further errs in feeling that Magua is a trustworthy guide. The girls are not properly outfitted: they wear riding veils instead of Allagash hats, slippers instead of Herman Survivors. We worry. Twice during the first half of the book does the story reach a climax, both times linking fear for life with fear for virtue. After Cora has persuaded Leatherstocking, Chingachgook, and Uncas not to await everyone's death at Glens Falls but to run for help, she wants Duncan to join the three. He refuses, because of his military honor — how could he possibly show himself to Munro without the girls? — and because of the likelihood of having to save the girls from "evils worse than death" (80) by killing them before the Mingoes can defile them. Magua's proposal to Cora somewhat later makes death for the party imminent because of Cora's refusal to become his squaw. The daring rescue by Leatherstocking and the two Mohicans, Magua's escape, the tight moment at the old blockhouse, the scene with the French sentinel, and finally the dangerous confusion outside William Henry are further spine-tingling episodes along the simple story line of getting the two girls to their father. The experienced reader knows, of course, that nothing will go really wrong with the girls this early in the book; a glance at the many pages yet to come assures him. At William Henry, the story's expected resolution is briefly unveiled; the girls have joined their father not just to be with him but so that he may promise one of them to Duncan. We may be disappointed that Alice is the one rather than Cora, but precisely because Cooper gives the story this turn do we stay with it. We sense that the deeper implications of Cora's racial background will be addressed beyond Duncan's sidestepping, but the story takes yet another turn: what will become of Cora and whether we will see the wedding of Duncan and Alice must yield for the time being to the negotiations for the fort's surrender and to the massacre, that is, to the largely historical "narrative of 1757."

It has often been noted that Cooper doubles his story, that the book's center marks the shift from two daughters in search of their father to "the father in quest of his children" (183). There are, nevertheless, major differences between the book's two halves. The initial journey from Edward to William Henry is clearly delimited: twelve miles or so along the road, somewhat more by the forest paths. The journey into the wilderness beyond the Horican, however, is open-ended; whereas the father's whereabouts are known at the outset of the first half, the daughters are we know not where at the beginning of the second half. Not only do we face an away match, so to speak, we do not even know where the opponent's ballpark is. Leatherstocking remarks grimly that by now the girls may be in the wilds of Canada (189). It is this open-endedness which changes the entire character of the book: in the first half, the story leads us to a white men's fort and the plot makes us think about a white men's war; in the second half, the story leads us into the land of the Indians and the plot makes us think about their lives.

In the first half of the book, cultural comparisons are rare and oblique. The most shocking incident before the massacre is not anything Magua does but instead Chingachgook's murder of the French sentinel. Duncan's presence of mind and Cora's sympathy, as well as their French, get the party past the danger of detection and detention. Then the presumably good (because he helps the girls) Chingachgook kills the sentinel and takes his scalp. Even Leatherstocking is shocked; then he explains rather lamely that it is a worthy deed for an Indian, no matter how reprehensible it would have been for a white man. Yet just before, Leatherstocking relates with almost ghoulish relish an earlier massacre for which he was responsible and in which totally unsuspecting French troops were not made prisoners but instead butchered and dumped into the same Bloody Pond that received Chingachgook's victim, with the only difference being that their scalps were still on their heads. Chingachgook's deed and the terrible slaughter of William Henry's British garrison by Montcalm's Indian allies eclipse the earlier massacre in the reader's mind. The conclusion that the whites are capable of being as savage as the Indians reaches the reader almost subconsciously; since it requires precisely that memory which the story in its onward rush seeks to disable, it is a — high — function of plot achieved virtually in opposition against the very story that generates it.

The novel's second half presents this sort of comparison directly in the story and reserves to the plot even more complex matters. The travel pattern in the second half makes the story into a mechanism of discovery: an object or circumstance encountered along the way becomes itself an insight, frequently explained by Leatherstocking as an answer to a question barely broached in the first half. For example, the fear that Cora and Alice might be raped at Glens Falls is lifted when they are not: whatever might have happened does not happen because Magua happens to have other plans. In the second half we are told that it was not Magua's plans that made the difference but Indian custom of never violating captive women. Munro has been worrying himself sick; he wants his "babes" (209) returned to him "spotless" (223). He and Duncan worry because they know that white warfare — "shame be it to our colour" (215), says Leatherstocking — has at all times given plenty of evidence that whites consider captive women fair game, evidence that World War II and Vietnam have done nothing to weaken.

Leatherstocking becomes in the second half an interpreter not only of Indian languages but more importantly of Indian customs. Nor does Cooper make his case for Indian civilization by Uncas alone, whom the romantic requirements of the story cast as the epitome of the noble savage; Chingachgook and even the bad (because they do not help the girls) Indians are enlisted. Cooper has the reader observe the warm relationship between Chingachgook and Uncas, the son's instant obedience when the father wishes to end their conversation and go to sleep, the musicality of the Indian language (no bloodcurdling yells or cavemen's grunts here), and the high standards of Indian debate (which Cooper recommends as a model for whites — and who, considering the deplorable lack of decorum in many of today's parliaments in western Europe, including the British, would disagree?). The rape matter, the Indians' not hurting a "non-composser" (224), Leatherstocking's stern lecture to David Gamut on the Indians' — even the Mingoes' — worshiping not idols but "the true and living God" (226) are further lessons for Leatherstocking's white companions and Cooper's readers. The bad Indians, we observe, have rules as strict as those of baseball; Reed-That-Bends looks, so to speak, at three pitches and therefore strikes out: he has dishonored his tribe by cowardice thrice and is therefore summarily executed. Tamenund's Delawares prize justice and go to some length to establish it; they also obey the Indian law of hospitality so scrupulously that the reader thinks immediately of the Christian notion of turning the other cheek.

Most significantly, Cooper makes the anxiety of the white travelers before the uncharted wilderness across the Horican express the anxiety of the white reader before the unfamiliar culture. Duncan and Munro must enter this wilderness to reclaim daughters and bride; the reader must learn about Indian culture to reclaim a vital part of his past. Neither party is qualified; Duncan and Munro must be guided by Leatherstocking and the two Mohicans, the reader by Cooper. The guilt of having lost the girls motivates the two officers; the guilt of having dispossessed and decimated the Indians should motivate the white American reader. Cooper's job is the more difficult of the two: his reader does not wish to go. Hence, the wilderness beyond the Horican becomes the book's second major metaphor, a symbol for the white man's attitude toward Indian life and history in general:

> The party had landed on the border of a region that is, even to this day, less known to the inhabitants of the states, than the deserts of Arabia, or the steppes of Tartary. It was the sterile and rugged district, which separates the tributaries of Champlain from those of the Hudson, the Mohawk, and of the St. Lawrence. Since the period of our tale, the active spirit of the country has surrounded it with a belt of rich and thriving settlements, though none but the hunter or the savage is ever known, even now, to penetrate its wild recesses (212).

Here and in several of his footnotes of 1831, Cooper makes clear that the locales of the novel's first half — Lake George, Glens Falls, Ballston Spa, all in the southeastern foothills of the Adirondacks — have by 1826 been appropriated by the white man, but the Adirondacks proper have not been. "Sterile" and "rugged," they cannot be made over into a garden, but even travelers do not visit them. It is most revealing that Cooper does not set Rome or Paris against the Adirondacks but foreign wildernesses instead. The Adirondacks thus are the metaphor for the past one wishes to deny by ignoring it, even while one professes to have an open, exploring mind. They are the blot on the landscapes of the map as well as of the soul. Out of sight, out of mind; in our time, he who visits Auschwitz or Hiroshima is more likely to think about the holocaust than he who spends his vacation exploring Nullarbor Plain or Queen Maud Land, not to mention lounging on the Riviera.

"If it was not for death and marriage I do not know how the average novelist would conclude" (143), says Forster. Uncas and Magua must die, for in 1826 the Eastern Indians are, for all practical purposes, dead. Duncan and Alice must marry, or else most readers hostile to Cooper's teaching will not finish the book. But there is more than death and marriage at the end; they are the winding up of the story, which for this purpose briefly reverts to its erstwhile level. It is the plot which, in taking up the title motto, inquires after the sense of the ending.

Cora bears the full weight of that motto: "Mislike me not, for my complexion, The shadowed livery of the burnished sun." From the beginning, she is the dark lady, no matter how white she may appear, though she seems much better off than Mark Twain's Roxy of *Pudd'nhead Wilson,* for her speech matches her beauty, and she is no slave. She likes Duncan but is too noble to cut in on her half-sister Alice. Uncas and Magua find her attractive, although they see her as white, since Cora's background is revealed only to Duncan, at William Henry, in the privacy of Munro's quarters. From the first, she judges persons by anything but their complexions. She defends Magua against Alice: "'Should we distrust the man, because his manners are not our manners, and that his skin is dark!' coldly asked Cora" (21); she says "dark," not "red"! Magua should of course have been distrusted for the likelihood of wanting revenge for the whipping Munro subjected him to. Later, she commends Duncan for his assessment of noble-looking Uncas: "'Now Major Heyward speaks, as Major Heyward should,' said Cora; 'who, that looks at this creature of nature, remembers the shades of his skin!'" (53) When she rejects Magua's deal — to free the others by becoming his squaw — she conceals "her powerful disgust" (104), which arises primarily from his calculating vengeance. That she has little to hope for becomes clear to the reader in Duncan's interview with Munro when Duncan conceals his prejudice against her blackness by a lie and an encomium of Alice.

Cooper does not solve the complexities of Cora's mixed blood. When she speaks to Tamenund of how "'the curse of my ancestors has fallen heavily on their child!'" (305) and Tamenund replies with a spirited condemnation of white racial prejudice, the matter is not pursued any further ("'but why — it is not permitted us to inquire!'" says Cora), and nobody is the wiser. To Magua, her blackness would scarcely have made a difference; what counts for him is that she is Munro's daughter, and her duties as a squaw would have been no different than those of the blacks Magua describes in his speech to the Delawares, "'to work for ever'" (300). Uncas, Cora's match in nobility of spirit, could not have cared either, though their "future prospects" (344) are denied by Leatherstocking anyway and would have greatly unsettled "the self-command of both Heyward and Munro" (344) who, unlike Uncas and Leatherstocking, know that Cora is not pure white.

In not explicitly exploring the ramifications of the racial problem posed by Cora's background, Cooper clearly considers the attitude of his reader. His immediate goal is a revision of his contemporaries' view — kept alive by the memory of Jane McCrea — of the Indians as unmitigated savages; that goal can be achieved without the detailing of Cora's mixed background (or, better yet, entirely without Cora, since her beauty and death call to mind Jane McCrea's).[7] But Cora and her problem are in the book, which therefore has a goal beyond the immediate one. Cooper's activating the Shakespeare motto is not a matter of story but a subtle enriching of plot; it requires the reader's memory and intelligence of which Forster speaks, although it may also well be comprehended intuitively by the busman's unpretending good nature and decency of character. Except — and because of — Bassanio, Shakespeare's Portia dislikes all suitors *a priori.* She then finds acceptable reasons for disliking them in their shortcomings: who would really wish her a drunkard for a husband? We do not know much about the Prince of Morocco. He is a bit blustering, but apparently he has the record to back it up. We do not know why he courts Portia, nor does it greatly matter, since he chooses the wrong casket anyway. What matters is Portia's reaction. She mislikes him because of his complexion, not because of any character deficiencies. When he honors the stipulations and leaves quickly, like a gentleman, Portia comments: "A gentle riddance. Draw the curtains, go. / Let all of his complexion choose me so."[8]

One is tempted to equate Morocco with Uncas, Portia with Cora — but Morocco is black, not red. His lines are on Cooper's title page because in Cooper's day as in ours, the blacks — unlike the Indians — are alive and numerous. The motto and Cora's being part black in a world that sees the white man triumph over the redskins can have but one message: let us not do unto the blacks as we have done unto the Indians. Hence, the reaffirmation of Leatherstocking's friendship for Chingachgook at the end of *The Last of the Mohicans* becomes the symbol of mutual racial acceptance, an acceptance which today's "black is beautiful" echoes in calling for not a problematic merging but a rightful coexistence. Stripped of their dogmatic use, the lines from Psalm 133 which David Gamut sings at the book's beginning might, more fitting than Tamenund's cyclic epitaph, dismiss the congregation of Cooper's readers at the book's end: "How good it is, O see, / And how it pleaseth well, / Together, e'en in unity, / For brethren so to dwell" (26). That Tamenund's lines do close the book tells us that Cooper is well aware of the realities of history indeed; nevertheless, that awareness does not fetter his imagination. In his Introduction of 1831, Cooper writes that "the business of a writer of fiction is to approach, as near as his powers will allow, to poetry" (7). E. M. Forster, we remember, locates the "spongy tract" that is the novel between "the opposing ranges of Poetry and of History" (17–18). In moving away from the historical "narrative of 1757" in the second half of *The Last of the Mohicans,* Cooper aspires to poetry and asks for a world more tolerant and more humane than he knew his was and he suspected ours would be.

Notes

1. Albany: State University of New York Press, 1983, p. xxii (all references to the novel in my text are to this edition). Many of Professor Beard's insights first appeared in his Afterword to the Signet Classic edition of the novel (New York: New American Library, 1962); it is there that they first met me and changed my thinking about Cooper's landscapes. In a less specific way I am equally indebted to the balance and general good sense of the late William Charvat's Introduction to the Riverside edition (Boston: Houghton Mifflin, 1958).

2. H. Daniel Peck's *A World by Itself. The Pastoral Moment in Cooper's Fiction* (New Haven: Yale University Press, 1977), for example, includes a searching discussion of the landscape in *The Last of the Mohicans,* but I cannot follow him to the mythic "eternal feminine" (122). For Cass, see James Grossman, *James Fenimore Cooper* (New York: Sloane, 1949), p. 47.

3. For Mark Twain's and other attacks see Warren S. Walker, *Leatherstocking and the Critics* (Chicago: Scott, Foresman, 1965). Negative on Cooper's plots are, among many others, R. W. B. Lewis, *The American Adam* (Chicago: Univer-

sity of Chicago Press, 1955), p. 100, and Blake Nevius, *Cooper's Landscapes* (Berkeley: University of California Press, 1976), p. vii. The most spirited defense of Cooper's art is Jane P. Tompkins, "No Apologies for the Iroquois: A New Way to Read the Leatherstocking Novels," *Criticism* 23 (1981): 24–41.

4. The quotations are from William Flint Thrall et al., *A Handbook to Literature* (New York: Odyssey, 1960), pp. 356, 358. C. Hugh Holman's third edition (1972) gives a much more differentiated entry on "Plot" and adds a new one on "Story."

5. My discussion summarizes and paraphrases parts of Chapters 1, 2, and 5 of *Aspects of the Novel*. Miriam Allott, *Novelists on the Novel* (New York: Columbia University Press, 1959) neglects to heed Forster's definition of audience (161) and therefore quite erroneously speaks of his "contempt for the 'story'" (176). Robert L. Caserio, *Plot, Story, and the Novel* (Princeton: Princeton University Press, 1979) ignores Forster's clarification by using the terms plot and story "interchangeably" (4) and charges Forster with being hostile to plot, not realizing that in the section in question, Forster summarizes not his own attitude but that of André Gide (and playfully at that). Forster himself dislikes finely spun definitions and is perhaps for that reason not too popular with critics. "For me," he writes, "the 'whole intricate question of method' resolves itself not into formulæ but into the power of the writer to bounce the reader into accepting what he says" (119).

6. A fine example is Leslie A. Fiedler, *Love and Death in the American Novel,* revised edition (New York: Dell, 1967), p. 205. Fiedler's indispensable discussion of the novel explores the race problem and the title motto (197–209), but his interest in the theme of "the pure marriage of males" (211) leads him onward before he has done full justice to these.

7. For the murder of Jane McCrea, see the note on Vanderlyn's painting (xi) and the reproduction of the painting (Plate 1, following xviii) in the Cooper Edition.

8. II.vii.78–79. The act opens with Morocco's "Mislike me not" lines: II.i.1–2. — II.vii.41–42 ("The Hyrcanian deserts and the vasty wilds / Of wide Arabia . . .") may have prompted Cooper's "deserts of Arabia" and "steppes of Tartary."

Works Cited

Cooper, James Fenimore. *The Last of the Mohicans; A Narrative of 1757.* Albany: State University of New York Press, 1983 (the Cooper Edition).

Forster, E. M. *Aspects of the Novel.* New York: Harcourt, Brace, 1927.

O'Donnell, Thomas F. "New York Literature: From Reconstruction to the Great Depression." In *Richards Atlas of New York State.* Phoenix, N.Y.: Frank E. Richards, 1957–59.

Shakespeare, William. *The Merchant of Venice.* In *The Complete Works.* Edited by G. B. Harrison. New York: Harcourt, Brace, 1961, pp. 579-612.

Thrall, William Flint, and Hibbard, Addison. *A Handbook to Literature.* Revised and enlarged by C. Hugh Holman. New York: Odyssey, 1960.

Vendler, Helen. "Presidential Address 1980." *PMLA* 96.3 (May 1981): 344-50.

7   The Other Harold Frederic

STANTON GARNER

I F THE MOHAWK VALLEY of upstate New York has produced an important literary figure, that figure must be Harold Frederic, the "country boy of genius," as he has been called. Frederic was endowed with the requisite talents, and by the time of his death those talents had manifested themselves in a substantial body of fiction. Perhaps in his eight novels and in his shorter works he achieved that importance, or perhaps he did not: after many years of considering the matter, the arbiters of literary rank remain undecided. Fashion has discovered Frederic and discarded him, only to rediscover and to rediscard him again, with the result that his reputation has always been in a state of becoming, never in a settled state of being.

We are at fault in the way we have approached Frederic's works, I believe, and it is this that has prevented us from dealing with them with proper decisiveness. The fault is this: because of our persistent need to categorize authors, to confine the works of each to a single group or school or movement or mode, we have tended to misunderstand and to punish versatility.

And versatile Harold Frederic was, to the point that the variety of his works is bewildering. For example, although his first novel was in the then new and exciting vein of regional realism, full of local color and nasal upstate dialect, in order to find time to write it he had to interrupt his decade-long attempt to write an historical romance. And though he continued for some time to produce regional works, he also tried his hand at sentimentalism, satire, romance, and futurism, and had he not failed in the attempt he might have become a dramatist-poet as well. When criticism labels him a regionalist, therefore, and treats his other kinds of works as aberrations, it is limiting him unduly and inhibiting the kind of intelligent consideration that would permit a genuinely informed re-evaluation of his achievement.

Though he was indeed a boy of genius, Frederic was hardly a country boy, unless Utica, New York, at the time a city of twenty thousand souls, can be thought of as "country." There Frederic was born on August 19, 1856, and there as a child he witnessed the local consequences of the Civil War and learned the ways of a small city and, with his piscatorial grandmother, of the fishing streams of the surrounding countryside. There, eventually, he became a teenaged photograph retoucher until, in an attempt to employ his pencil more creatively, he traveled to Boston in order to make his way as a graphic artist. Then, having learned the ways of a large American city and also the folly of his attempt to sketch his way to fame and fortune, he returned to Utica and entered journalism.

It was then that Frederic demonstrated his genius. By the age of twenty-four he had become the editor of the Utica *Observer* and an important figure in the affairs of the city; by twenty-six he was editor of the late Thurlow Weed's *Evening Journal* in Albany, New York, where he became a figure of importance in state affairs through his political endorsement of and friendship with Grover Cleveland. It seemed at that point as though Frederic's horizons and influence might continue to expand indefinitely.

What was it that Frederic could not do, once he set about it? He was quick of mind, energetic, and forceful of personality, a trait that most people forgave because of his underlying warmth and kindness and because of his ability to entrance those about him with the brilliance and humor of his discourse. He had a way, too, of going straight to the heart of matters, and thus he was able to channel his energies directly toward the accomplishment of his purposes.

Cleveland understood his young friend's ability: he wanted Frederic to enter politics, and Frederic himself assumed that had he done so he could have become president. He was admired in the world of journalism as well. After the triumph of his dismissal as editor of the *Evening Journal* in 1884, a triumph in the sense that as a punishment for his editorial independence it made him a journalistic hero of the moment, Frederic was offered editorships in Chicago and New York. But he decided against politics or the control of a metropolitan newspaper and instead became the London correspondent for the *New York Times*. The reason is not difficult to find: he wanted to write literature.

Ever since Joseph Conrad characterized him villainously as "a notable journalist (who had written some novels)," it has been assumed that Frederic indulged in the writing of fiction as an avocation, that he was in the main a newspaperman. But that assumption does not accord with

what we know. During his first days on the Utica *Observer* he had written
tentative short stories, and as early as 1877 he had determined to write
a novel about the Mohawk Valley during the Revolutionary War. Only a
year before his departure for England he had lamented (rather lavishly)
to the writer Benjamin P. Blood that he had recently had a quarrel with
his muse. "I discovered that I had no style," he wrote. "In the rapier practice and single-stick exercise of politics I had forgotten the lute-playing
art of romance. My hand had lost its cunning, the fantasies had fled from
my brain." In mid-1884 he desired to recapture the cunning and to woo
back the fantasies. By that time, too, he had made plans for several novels
set in the Mohawk Valley in contemporary times, and he had that work
to do. He was ready to commence as soon as he had settled into the routine of his London duties.

No, Frederic's success as a foreign correspondent, brilliant even when
he was wrong about the affairs of the world, has obscured the fact that he
went to England not for that but rather to achieve sufficient independence
from routine to become a literary artist. "I dream of the day when I can
command a living by honest work in good humane literature, as the an-
chorite dreams of the day when he shall exchange his hair-shirt for the
white robe," he had written Blood. Frederic did not expect to spend the
rest of his life working for the *Times,* though in fact he did. At first he
hoped that he could quickly earn enough money as a novelist to allow him
to return to America in triumph; later, when events had demonstrated the
impossibility of this dream, he asked President Cleveland for the Liver-
pool consulship that Nathaniel Hawthorne had occupied, intimating that
he might eventually become the equal of Hawthorne. In the end, he seems
to have reconciled himself to the fact that his finances would never permit
him to escape his weekly news cable, but in his own mind he was always
a literary figure sustaining himself through journalism, not a journalist
writing literature.

Frederic must have set to work on his first novel almost immediately
after he had familiarized himself with his new duties and surroundings,
because it was finished in twenty months and in thirty it was running as
the first novel to be serialized in the new *Scribner's Magazine.* However,
it was not the romance but, instead, the first of his series of contemporary
regional stories, *Seth's Brother's Wife.* He wrote that work first, he maintained with his tongue in or near his cheek, in order to practice book-length
fiction in preparation for the romance. However, *Seth* is not by any means
a student exercise but is, rather, one of the contemporary works he had
planned before he left Albany. It is much taken up with Mohawk Valley
politics, some devoted to journalism, and, shockingly, its plot includes the
near-seduction of the protagonist by his sister-in-law. *The Lawton Girl,*

the second of the series, deals mostly with industrial turmoil and financial piracy in the valley, and its shocking aspect is the fact that one of its principal characters is a former prostitute intent upon regaining her respectability. The Civil War tales emanated at least in part from Frederic's memories of life at home during that war, the political divisions amongst the civilians, the impact of modern war on people whose received values were those of an earlier era, the tears and joys that resulted from the publication of the casualty lists with their inclusions and omissions, and the mangled survivors of war and the coffins that commenced to arrive in the towns and on the farms as the war lengthened. *The Damnation of Theron Ware,* or, more properly, *Illumination,* is the last of these regional works, though it is something more, a story of upper New York State religion and of the impact on a poorly educated minister of the crosscurrents of modernism that threaten his beliefs. That novel has its shocking elements, too, including a glimpse of the bed of a liberal-minded red-headed beauty.

This body of literature, published between 1887 and 1896, is somewhat larger than the sum of its parts. Most of the stories are linked together through their invariable setting in the fictional "Dearborn County," through common characters whom, unobtrusively, they share, and through the way in which their thematic concerns often dovetail. Thus *The Copperhead* treats of the politial intolerance between neighbors during the Civil War and of the violent means through which tolerance is restored, while "The War Widow" treats of the social intolerance within a single family and of the double tragedy of war through which that intolerance is all but erased. The later *Damnation* deals, in part, with traditional American intolerance toward the Irish, toward Roman Catholics, and toward Irish Roman Catholics.

Taken singly, the works are uneven, ranging from the extraordinary achievement of *The Damnation* to the relative failure of *The Lawton Girl.* But taken together, they "do" upper New York State, as W. D. Howells liked to put it, very well, and together they make up a coherent treatise on the scenery, the life, and the manners of the region and its populace in that era.

Many of these stories are well conceived and well executed from beginning to end. But even when Frederic's synthesizing imagination was not working well enough to fashion a novelistic structure through which parts cohere into a whole, the parts are, at least, well done. In fact, Frederic's grand gift as a raconteur resulted in a plenitude of memorable scenes and bits of scenes. Thus while the dialect notations of *Seth* are annoying— though no more so than are those of O. W. Holmes in *Elsie Venner*—and the plot resolution smacks of the improbable, the novel remains memorable. There are few things in fiction more delightful, though it is done in an impish spirit, than the country funeral that makes up Chapter Five, and there are few moments of dramatic action anywhere that are more excruciating than is the scene in which Seth Fairchild is taunted by his brother for his foolish susceptibility to the wiles of the brother's wife.

Similarly, if there is one image in all fiction that succeeds in rendering visible the bereavement that the families in the North experienced during the Civil War, it is Aunt Susan's loom:

> "If this war goes on much longer," commented my Aunt, "Every carpet in Dearborn County'll be as blue as a whetstone."
> . . . For two years now the balls of rags had contained an increasing proportion of pale blue woollen strips, as the men of the county round about came home from the South, or bought cheap garments from the second-hand dealers in Tecumseh. All other colors had died out. There was only this light blue, and the black of bombazine or worsted mourning into which the news in each week's papers forced one or another of the neighboring families. . . . The loom spun out only long, depressing rolls of black and blue.

At his best, Frederic was a fine stylist, a compliment that cannot be paid to some of his better-known contemporaries, such as Henry Blake Fuller: in the ease and fluency of his language Frederic belongs in the camp of Mark Twain. Sister Soulsby, whose characterization is one of the treasures found in *The Damnation,* is akin in conception to the King and the Duke of *Huckleberry Finn,* but in her dialogue she is somewhat better realized. We tend to think of Twain's drifters in terms of the rascality of their actions, such as their attempt to make a few dollars by betraying the slave Jim back into servitude, or in terms of their outrageous notions of drama. But the brilliance of Sister Soulsby resides largely in her language, in the soft flow of her hypnotic phrases as they present us with a cascade of arresting folk metaphors. In fact, throughout Frederic's works his mastery of dialogue gives a high degree of psychological validity to his characters that their actions alone could hardly convey.

As a realist, then, and as a specifically regional realist, if there is another kind, Frederic's achievement is memorable. And that is one of the principal reasons why Thomas F. O'Donnell, who loved the Mohawk Valley as an adolescent loves his automobile, was attracted to Frederic. Tom enjoyed strolling among the grimy brick buildings of Utica that Frederic had seen new and fresh, and his ears rejoiced in listening to the speech of the natives of the valley for echoes of that twang that Frederic had heard, too, and recorded. Tom read Frederic as though he were translating a message in code from a fellow conspirator, or more properly, as though he

were receiving clues in a treasure hunt. Tom followed those clues, locating
Frederic's birthplace in Utica, finding the real Catholic church that served
as a model for Frederic's fictional one, and roaming the Trenton Assembly
Park where, in Frederic's imagination, Theron Ware had preached. Yet Tom
was a critical enthusiast: Frederic could not have won him over with mediocre or insincere work, and Tom's admiration is an important testi-
monial to the genuineness of Frederic's achievement as a Mohawk Valley
regionalist.[1]

When Tom and I disagreed about Frederic, which was not very often,
it was because his loyalty could not completely tolerate my occasional in-
fidelity to his beloved valley. Tom never slighted Frederic's *other* fiction;
he always gave it the importance that, in his eyes, it deserved. But deep
in his heart, a term that I use advisedly, he preferred to meet Frederic on
the common ground that they shared on the banks of the Mohawk. Like
Stephen Crane, Tom felt that Frederic had abandoned his true audience
when he shifted the *mise en scène* of his works to England.

For my part, I do not believe that Frederic intended to be unfaithful
to the soil in which his past was rooted when he moved beyond it in his
fiction. He had given it what he believed to be his finest effort in his earlier works, but especially so in *In the Valley,* the Revolutionary War romance that in his own mind he compared to William Makepeace Thack-
eray's *Henry Esmond. In the Valley,* linked to his other regional fiction
not only by its setting but also because of the fact that some important
characters of *The Lawton Girl* are descendents of its protagonist, fell short
of being the masterpiece that Frederic meant it to be by surprisingly little.
It has much merit. It is factually true to history, its characters are representative, believable, and complex, and its plot is both interesting dramatically and significant metaphorically. It eludes success for the single reason
that it is stylistically awkward. It is ironic that the magnificence of Frederic's intention, which was to do homage to his subject rather than to en-
dow his story with life, prevented him from writing with the ease, the self-
assurance, and the vigor that in other works were his greatest fictional assets.

However, to the end of his life Frederic believed that *In the Valley*
was his magnum opus. In his heart he had dedicated it to the rude farmers
and villagers of Dutch and German origin, who, in 1777, had through the
sacrifice of blood, flesh, and bone prevented the forces of European mon-
archy from cutting the colonies in two. Although the book failed to gain
him the American laureateship that he believed he deserved, it continued
long after his death to be one of his most popular novels.

Despite the impressive achievement of his earlier career, Frederic did
not remain a regionalist. His life was a succession of phases during which
his vision expanded from the local boundaries of his youth to the global

vistas of his middle age, and his interests expanded with his vision. It was inevitable that as these changes occurred his fiction would reflect them.

The works of other authors have changed similarly, sometimes with similarly unfortunate effects on their popularity. Take the case of Herman Melville, for example. He was a realist of a sort in his first two novels, *Typee* and *Omoo,* supposedly recording genuine events as he had actually experienced them. The opening chapers of *Mardi,* too, concerned as they were with ordinary life aboard a whaling ship, were admired by his readers and reviewers, as were *Redburn* and *White-Jacket,* also supposedly accurate records of the author's own adventures. But the main body of *Mardi,* in which allegory becomes dominant, was rejected by Melville's readers, and the unfavorable reception of *Moby-Dick, Pierre,* and his other later works, none of which were "realistic," ended his career as a public man of letters. Yet it is these later works, more mature than his more documentary fiction, that have seized the imagination of modern readers.

In Melville's case it was his "metaphysics" that doomed his later works to unpopularity in their own time; in Frederic's case it was the abandonment of his native region as the setting of his novels that has caused his later works to be dismissed as frivolous in intent, as fiction designed to delight shopgirls, and has also, one is tempted to conclude, discouraged many critics and literary historians who pretend to know Frederic's fiction thoroughly from ever reading them. In the age of Theodore Roosevelt it was unpatriotic of Americans like Henry James to write about England, and Frederic's "English" novels have suffered from that odium.

If we are to profit from our fortunate distance from this sort of Teddiesque xenophobia, we must do it, in this case, by looking at these later works with fresh eyes. Abandoning easy formulations and meaningless comparisons between Frederic's Mohawk Valley fiction and his "English" novels, we must ask ourselves not why he abandoned his mother country but what he was about and what he achieved.

In late 1890, just after the publication of *In the Valley* and at about the same time that he began *The Damnation of Theron Ware,* Frederic wrote a short story in a style that he had never before attempted and that he never attempted again. "The Song of the Swamp-Robin" is, unashamedly and unsuccessfully, an imitation of a Hawthorne tale. Although this story little deserves to be remembered for any other reason, it marks the beginning of the later phase of Frederic's work. This phase took some years to mature, and in the meantime he had his Civil War tales to write. Yet it is interesting to speculate that had *The Damnation of Theron Ware* been completed on schedule 1892 rather than in 1895, it might have been a novel of pure regionalism rather than the magnificent fusion of types that it is.

Earlier, I stated that *The Damnation* is the last work of Frederic's regionalist phase, but now I will also claim that it is the first of those later novels which I will call, for want of a better term, romances. At this point in criticism it is unnecessary to note how much this work owes to *The Scarlet Letter,* "Young Goodman Brown," "Rappaccini's Daughter," and some other Hawthorne works. What I do claim is that the elements of romance that Frederic appropriated are not used in *The Damnation* gratuitously, that is, for the sole purpose of honorific reference to Hawthorne, and that they are not, as has been asserted, immiscible with the elements of realism.[2] As to the latter, the borrowings are so modified and adapted that they are at no point obtrusive; in fact, it has required skilled readers to identify them. As to the former, Frederic estimated well the exact dimension of significance that they would add to his work and he used them to that end.

To explain a bit, hopefully without simplifying the matter too much, it has been argued that realism deals with societal issues, while romance deals with moral issues, and consequently that the two are mutually exclusive. Perhaps that is true in a way, but it is also true that societal issues have their moral elements, and that moral questions may be moot unless they are linked to the functioning of the social mechanism. Thus the political fraud of Albert Fairchild in *Seth's Brother's Wife* is wrong in the sense that it subverts the political mechanism through which representatives of the community are properly selected — a social wrong, I take it — but Seth's inability to combat the scheme stems from his lust for Albert's wife — a moral wrong. Thus as early as Frederic's first novel, the social and moral elements are interdependent. The melding of realism and romance in *The Damnation* simply allows Frederic to assert this relationship or interaction more effectively than he had previously been able to do.

The problem that Theron Ware confronts is how to prosper in his ministry in the face of low salary and troublesome parishioners. That is a social problem, true enough, as his mentor, Sister Soulsby, well knows. To solve this problem, she teaches him to do as she does in her revivals, to offer the best possible entertainment to his parishioners, since reduced to social considerations alone the ceremonies of both debt-raiser and clergyman are essentially entertainments. But the first chapter of the book has, in the manner of romance, displayed symbolically the several generations of Methodist clergymen arranged in descending order of moral earnestness, with the aged evangelists at the top and with Theron's contemporaries on the bottom. Therefore, Theron's quest for creature comfort and other forms of self-gratification must be understood in the context of the loss of piety and godly vocation among his kind. To some of those about him, to his wife and to his one sympathetic church trustee, his social problems exist in the larger moral context.

Because under the tutelage of Sister Soulsby Theron comes to see his three new sophisticated friends, Celia Madden, Father Forbes, and Ledsmar, in social terms, he is blinded to whatever moral considerations may motivate them. Celia, the attractive aesthete, has money enough, he supposes, to practice lewdness without constraint; Forbes, the philosophical skeptic, uses the Catholic church as a place of concealment within which he can gratify his appetite or appetites, Theron imagines; and Ledsmar, the scientist, gathers data on the private lives of his friends as well as on his flowers, reptiles, and Oriental servants, Theron believes. Yet his understanding is faulty: when they reject him, as they all do, they do so for essentially moral reasons.

It is this mixture of realism and romance that makes the ending of the story so rich and so provocative. What can a young American Adam do when he has allowed himself to descend from the freshness of innocence and of loyalty to his creed and his marriage to the barkeeper level of mean suspicion and intentions? If he seeks to change the course of his life by moving to Seattle and taking up a different occupation, what problems will he really solve? Sister Soulsby believes, or appears to believe, that he can solve them all that way, but Theron's wife knows better. She understands that her marriage has, in effect, been annulled, and that the success of Theron on the West Coast will be, at best, a material success, and that it will be his alone, not the success of husband and wife together. Her future, unfortunately, will depend upon his moral character.

In this alloy of realism and romance through which he was enabled to write simultaneously of social matters and of their moral implications, Frederic achieved a unique success. Having done so, he paused to write a series of four medieval Irish tales that, though admirable, are off to one side of the main stream of his development. They are beautifully crafted, a tribute to the Irish and to the Ireland that he had come to love since he had first become acquainted with the Irish cause in Utica, and since perhaps no more than a dozen living persons have ever read them all I will list their names here: "The Path of Murtogh," "The Truce of the Bishop," "In the Shadow of Gabriel," and "The Wooing of Teige." Fine work, as I have said, but done with the left hand.

Frederic's next major effort was *Gloria Mundi,* a novel that, taken by itself, falls considerably short of complete literary success. However, when taken together with the work that followed it, *The Market-Place,* it is of considerable interest. Apparently, the two were originally intended to be a single story and were separated because the material proved to be too long and too complex for a single work. Whatever the case may be, the closer *Gloria Mundi* is brought to *The Market-Place,* the better it is as a work of art.

Although the plot is of the lost-heir variety, in which a poor French

schoolteacher named Christian Tower is discovered to be the rightful Duke
of Glastonbury, this discovery occurs at the beginning of the book so that
the reader can become acquainted with the state of the hereditary English
aristocracy along with the new Duke. And a miserable state it is. The formerly great barbarians, who, clothed in armor and brandishing broad-
swords, once dominated the land and once pinched their wealth out of
the labors of their serfs, are now little more noble than the hounds who
are their best-loved companions. Their women are used up and they themselves frequent the most vulgar and debased London "entertainments."

These aristocrats subsist on the alms of the wealthy merchant-Jew
branch of the Tower family, who are also the intellectuals of the story. They
have hopes that the new Duke will follow their lead in an experiment in
bringing feudal order, welfare, and discipline back to the land and its people,
but in the end Christian has the power to renew nothing. He can only make
a Duchess of a young socialist and, beyond that, permit the heavy inertia
of history to propel him year by year toward his grave.

Such a marriage and such resignation to tradition set the stage per-
fectly for *The Market-Place,* though they hardly provide an adequate resolution for *Gloria Mundi.* One asks, "What will become of this land and
of this world, now that the formerly powerful have lost their power?" What
will take place is the rise of Joel Stormont Thorpe. The society over which
the moribund dukes and earls of the realm can no longer preside is the
society on which Thorpe, the new aristocrat, will feed. He is a brilliantly
conceived character, seemingly torpid, heavy, single of purpose, ruthless,
and a portfolio of psychological complexes and brute lusts. He is an En-
glishman, but he belongs so little to any single culture that he is sometimes
mistaken for an American. Thorpe is Thorpe, as the world will learn.

Thorpe begins as nobody, but the successful Thorpe is everyone, the
man of the hour, the worker of schemes, the coming Cromwell, the man
on horseback. The irony of his success is that it is the success of nothing.
Of the property on which the stock promotion that brings him wealth rests,
there is actually nothing. Of real stock sales there are essentially none. From
his enemies, the "Jews," he buys nonexistent stock, and what they deliver
in return is not stock or property but that ultimate abstraction, money.
Thorpe bilks an aristocrat and in the process proves that he is nothing,
and when he murders a nobody named Tavender he does so through the
offices of another nobody he has created, General Kervick. Out of this
nullity and from the sea of faceless Londoners comes the new somebody,
Thorpe.

The story of Thorpe's campaign for riches is gripping for the reader
who makes the small effort required to understand his manipulations, and
it is not at all difficult to find oneself standing on his side and cheering

him on toward success. For Thorpe is, at least, a moving object, a living organism, set against the background of decay and defeat of *Gloria Mundi*. When he wins his fortune, his first impulse is to buy with his purse the station and the privilege that he has been denied by inheritance. Thus he assembles by bits and pieces, in the fashion of Faulkner's Thomas Sutpen, the paraphernalia of aristocratic status. An estate can be purchased and staffed, and a mistress for it can be arranged, too—Edith Cressage, the nobody whose title is not real who Christian Tower had jilted in *Gloria Mundi*. If one does not inherit a Glastonbury, he can, with enough money, create one.

But by doing that Thorpe is retreating into the century that has passed, where he does not belong, not advancing into the century to come, where he does belong, for he is clearly a twentieth-century man. The substance for which he has mistakenly yearned was a nineteenth-century ideal, whereas his triumph, as a twentieth-century man, must be a triumph over nothingness in which he speaks the creative Word over the vastness of modern chaos. Having achieved the means of power, money, Thorpe must abandon the substance that bores and belittles him: giving up the goal of establishing himself as a member of the rural gentry, he seeks instead the vacuum of political struggle. The thrill, the achievement, is not to own but to control, to wreck Jews, to pillage, to bribe, to seize, and to destroy—to gain power and more power and to control masses and more masses. Kings and their retinues will pass, but dictators will endure, and first among them will be Thorpe; at his side will be Edith, who is stifled by the substance of land and buildings and servants and stimulated by the blank visions of rapine to come. She is to Thorpe as Eva Braun may have been to Adolf Hitler, and one can even imagine her making hideous lampshades. Celia Madden, the red-haired temptress of *Theron Ware*, returns here to eulogize Thorpe: "crime was his true vocation."

Frederic died on October 19, 1898, before either of these last two works had been published. He was at the height of his powers and of his reputation. What might have been his fame and his achievement had he lived longer it is useless to speculate, and we can judge him as an author only on the basis of what he did write.

Decent people were shocked to find out that Frederic had kept two households and two sets of children, and their shock was validated when they found out that he had left both families in near poverty. Then they were shocked once again when his mistress and a healer were brought to court for Christian Science improprieties connected with his death. After he was gone his enemies enjoyed belittling his works, and careless literary historians made a point of saying, without taking the trouble to ascertain the truth, that he composed his fiction rapidly and carelessly. These things contributed to the neglect of his works that has been one of the notable critical blunders of our century.

But those errors were made long ago. Eighty-five years after the publication of his last book we must assess Frederic on new, totally literary grounds — what did he write, and how well did he write it? And this is the end point of what I have been saying. We have enjoyed Frederic as a regionalist, praising much of what he wrote up to and including *The Damnation* and then stopping. But Frederic was much more than this. As a Mohawk Valley writer he looked first at the region of his birth and young manhood and he celebrated it, well and at length. But eventually he looked beyond those narrow confines and, adding a pinch of Hawthorne to his Howells, he looked into the soul of America, in the person of the American innocent whose innocence destroyed him. Then he looked farther still, to the ancient European cradle out of which his culture had risen, and he wrote *Gloria Mundi* as a testament to its senility and impotence. And finally, his vision copious and his artistry firm, he looked into the future, not to the future of America or of England alone, but to the future of the West and of mankind, and there he saw the ominous face of Thorpe.

My original purpose in writing this essay was to discuss Frederic the regionalist of the Mohawk Valley. But it seems to me that that is the writer whom we already know, and perhaps for the moment it is useful to set him to one side. We do neither him nor the Mohawk Valley he loved so much any disservice when we admit that he continued to grow beyond his native soil in his fiction, just as any adventurous writer might do, whatever his place of birth. And when we follow Frederic to this unexplored destination, we find that his literary achievement was greater than what we had been led to believe, that in addition to the regionalist we know there was another Harold Frederic whose vision grew much broader. We must look at these two Frederics together if we are to locate the "country" boy of genius.

Notes

1. For many years Thomas F. O'Donnell was the dean of Frederic scholars. For several of those years he published, edited, wrote for, and distributed a delightful little journal entitled *The Frederic Herald*. Genial and witty, the journal informed readers that the house in which Frederic was born was still standing at 324 South Street, Utica, that the original of the Catholic church, St. John's, was still standing in downtown Utica, but that the original of Theron Ware's Methodist

church had been torn down to make room for a parking lot. The *Herald* was issued from April 1967 to January 1970. A few of his other contributions to Frederic scholarship were the book he co-authored with Hoyt C. Franchere, *Harold Frederic,* Twayne's U. S. Authors Series, No. 3 (New York, 1961) and an edition of Frederic's Civil War fiction, *Harold Frederic's Stories of York State,* introduction by Edmund Wilson (Syracuse, N.Y., 1966).

2. George W. Johnson, "Harold Frederic's Young Goodman Ware: The Ambiguities of a Realistic Romance," *Modern Fiction Studies* 8:361–74. Johnson concludes that *Theron Ware* is "more complicated than complex, a flawed monument to an endeavor audacious, artful, and American."

8   North Country Voices

KATE H. WINTER

I N THE NORTHERN COUNTIES of New York State, some folks still tell this antique anecdote. Though variations echo periodically in the give-and-take of North Country talk, the version most well known is that recounted by Irving Bacheller, the upcountry farm boy turned literary man. As he told it, the exchange between a downstate visitor and a North Country farmer takes place as both contemplate the steep, rocky hillside of the latter's farm:

> "How did you get the seed to stick in the side of that mountain?" the visitor asked.
> "Shot it in with a musket."
> "Is that a fact?"
> "Nope! It's conversation" (Samuels 17).

The luxury of talk has always been valued by the people in the upper regions of the state. The voices of the settlers in the first decades of the nineteenth century sounded against the dead quiet of the remote wilderness. Families scattered on the plateau that arches along the shores of Lake Ontario and the St. Lawrence River to the foothills of the dense Adirondacks. In a dismal and dangerous interior, many ached for the talk that a chance meeting or a trading expedition might furnish. Conversation, whether twisted into epigrammatic terseness or spun out to leisurely tale-telling, provided relief from the awful quiet that isolation, fear and struggle bound them in.

For the most part, the early northern Yorkers were Yankees moving

over from Vermont, across the northern passage beside the St. Lawrence
or through the Adirondacks, down the Black River Valley, until they met
the settlers coming up from Connecticut through the Oneida and Onondaga regions. A young farmer, perhaps eager for bounty land after the
Revolution, would plunge across Lake Champlain and make his way along
the foothills of the mountains until he found a congenial location. The
crescent of low land that buffers the waters from the mountains seemed
to provide rich soil and ample space. Having staked his claim, the Yankee
would return to Vermont to gather his mother, sisters, wife, and children,
brothers with their families, and perhaps some livestock, frequently returning to the homestead in winter when it was easiest to transport their loads
on the frozen surfaces of lake and land. Sometimes they never returned
to the spot originally chosen, settling instead along the way where the wagon
broke down, a cow freshened, or a member of the family was buried. Families began to clear the land and knit small settlements of kin, but beyond
the margins of their homesteads were the threatening wilderness, the silence of long winters so harsh that the Indians retreated to the mountains
each autumn, and the brooding quiet.

Against the silence they had the pleasure and comfort of talk. With
few books, libraries, schools, teachers or preachers before mid-century, the
rich promise of words might have been lost except for the exuberance and
vigor of Yankee speech. Hungry for the sustaining sound of others' voices,
the settlers cultivated conversation in diverse forms, relishing the virtuos-
ity of a good yarn-spinner as much as a good gossip. Little written literature was produced there before the Civil War, but as roads were constructed,
debating societies and church circles were settings for a good deal of chatter and palaver. These hardy pioneers saw themselves as a special, self-
sufficient group, isolated by choice and chance, chosen out of New England
to be the New Yorkers. Separated as they were from the German, Dutch,
and English in the southern territories, and untouched by the migration
of the post-Civil War era, the North Country folk retained much of their
New England character, yet they saw themselves as a singular kind of crit-
ter. One of Bacheller's characters describes them:

> Many of them have the blood of those who came over in the *Mayflower*.
> The forefathers of many fought to put America on the map. Up here
> there's a big colony of good blood, shut off from the rest of the world
> by mountains and wilderness in the south and the water boundary of an
> alien land in the north. East of us there are timbered mountains and a
> great lake is west of us. We stay at home. Our amusement is mostly read-
> ing and it's good reading—Longfellow, Tennyson, Dickens, Thackeray,
> Emerson. Money has not corrupted us. No great quantity of it ever gets

here. We have not much need of it. . . . Still we're a happy, contented lot of people (*Winds of God* 289–90).

Out of the North Country there almost simultaneously rose two very different literary voices to articulate its regional peculiarities and particularities. From a farm perched in Jefferson County near Ontario's gray waters, a young woman began sending out her bits of imitative verse and Yorker dialect sketches. Marietta Holley began in the early 1860s to capture the quaint idioms and verbal quirks of the upcountry rustics. Her poetry mimicked the lachrymose verse of the sentimental scribblers, but her vernacular sketches were fresh and authentic. Mark Twain's publisher was so captivated by the force of Holley's renderings and the marketability of her brand of dialect humor that in 1871 he commissioned her to produce a book-length work about the inhabitants of Jonesville, a fictitious rural community in the North Country. Populated by transplanted New Englanders, Jonesville bears the shape of eastern institutions, but underlying and circumscribing a sort of Puritan rectitude is an audacious, exuberant, sometimes cantankerous spirit.

Embodying that spirit is Holley's persona, the narrator of the Jonesville stories, "Josiah Allen's Wife." The garrulous Samantha Smith Allen is a hard-working farm wife of middle age. At two hundred ten pounds, she outweighs in heft, intellect, and spiritual ballast her spouse Josiah, a one-hundred-pound widower with two children. This tidy household, with a string of relations and neighbors, forms the center of the Jonesville circle. Samantha recounts the homely events that set the rhythm of North Country life: planting and harvesting; quilting and putting by; worshipping, mourning, and celebrating. These first sketches are vignettes of rural pleasures. Unlike most of the region's writers who followed her, Holley used the social events of a rural district rather than the struggles of work on the land as her background. The Jonesville stories have a sense of place created by the frequent use of real place and family names as well as specific local manners, customs and bits of speech, but Holley left it to others to recreate the countryside. Hers is a social landscape. Samantha introduces us to the characters of Jonesville, so we hear their idiosyncratic tones, their jibes and diatribes set against the rustic eloquence of Samantha's own "allegorin' and episoden'." Josiah is most often the contrary voice as he exaggerates (or fabricates) a tale or sputters his wrong-headed notions about Samantha's favorite causes: women's rights and temperance. Samantha also recreates the bustling talk of her friends and neighbors, particularly at first the sentimental spinster Betsey Bobbet, thereby assailing us with *My Opinions and Betsey Bobbet's*.

The opinions of this first book predominantly concern women's rights. Samantha is for them; Betsey (and Josiah) are not — or at least are in favor of different rights. Samantha advocates suffrage for women, economic freedom that will allow women to marry for love rather than money, and a redefinition of women's sphere. Betsey, a skinny spinster with no ambition but to marry some man — any man — provides both an example and a foil. Like the rest of Holley's fiction, this is a conversational book with occasional narrative bits that move the characters along. For the most part, reading Samantha's novels is like listening through a thin wall, being privy to the conversations of small town characters.

For example, early in this first book, Betsey drops by unannounced to spend the day with Samantha. Reflecting on the trials of the Christian martyrs, Samantha determines to do her duty and make Betsey welcome, even though she recognizes that Betsey has only come in hopes that she will encounter a widower whose children Samantha is caring for. Betsey settles into her needlework; Samantha tackles her housework. Betsey begins:

> "I have come to spend the day. I saw their deah Pa bringin' the deah little twins in heah, and I thought maybe I could comfort the precious little motherless things some, if I should come over heah. If there is any object upon the earth, Josiah Allen's wife, that appeals to a feelin' heart, it is the sweet little children of widowers. I cannot remember the time when I did not want to comfort them, and their deah Pa's. I have always felt that it was woman's highest speah, her only mission to soothe, to cling, to smile, to coo. I have always felt it, and for yeah's back it has been a growin' on me. I feel that you do not feel as I do in this matter, you do not feel that it is woman's greatest privilege, her crowning blessing, to soothe lacerations, to be a sort of a poultice to the noble, manly breast when it is torn with the cares of life."
>
> This was too much, in the agitated frame of mind I then was.
>
> "Am I a poultice Betsey Bobbet, do I look like one? — am I in the condition to be one?" I cried turnin' my face, red and drippin' with prespiration towards her, and then attacked one of Josiah's shirt sleeves agin. "What has my sect done" says I, as I wildly rubbed his shirt sleeves, "That they have got to be lacerator soothers, when they have got everything else under the sun to do?" Here I stirred down the preserves that was a runnin' over, and turned a pail full of syrup into the sugar kettle. "Everybody says that men are stronger than women, and why should they be treated as if they was glass china, liable to break all to pieces if they haint handled careful. And if they have got to be soothed," says I in an agitated tone, caused by my emotions (and by pumpin' 6 pails of water to fill up the biler), "Why don't they get men to sooth'em? They have as much agin

time as wimmen have; evenin's they don't have anything else to do, they might jest as well be a soothin' each other as to be a hangin' round grocery stores, or settin' by the fire whittlin'."

I see I was frightenin' her by my delerious tone and I continued more mildly, as I stirred down the strugglin' sugar with one hand — removed a cake from the oven with the other — watched my apple preserves with a eagle vision, and listened intently to the voice of the twins, who was playin' in the woodhouse (62–63).

Betsey's voice minces along with the affectation and sentimental mewing of popular culture that was slowly making itself felt in the larger towns, a perversion of the simple dialect and pioneer virtue that the folk trusted and relished as their own; Samantha struggles to moderate her sermonizing.

With the publication of Holley's early novels in the 1870s, the North Country was at least heard by the rest of the state and New England. Though the precise location of Jonesville might be difficult to determine, the characters were types who could be found in any number of the villages that broke up the countryside along the Salina Road and St. Lawrence Valley. While Samantha's sentiments regarding women's rights were not widely shared in the North Country, the wave of feminist thought generated in nearby Seneca Falls at the 1848 Women's Rights Convention had riled up the populace much as abolition and temperance had but with less unanimity. The feminist arguments won some audiences, but it was the homespun wisdom, vernacular humor, and rustic comedy that made *My Opinions and Betsey Bobbet's* a commercial success. The books which followed capitalized on all these elements, often adding the interest of travel to well-known attractions: the Centennial celebration, the World's Fair, the St. Louis Exposition, and capital cities around the world. The counterpoint between Samantha's rusticity and the sophistication of those she met along the way made for good fun. Her travel books are not, however, her best, except perhaps for *Samantha at Saratoga or Flirtin' With Fashion,* one of the better sellers of 1887, and *Samantha on the Race Problem,* her 1892 novel about the effects of manumission in the South. The books which center especially on New York State settings, *Samantha at Saratoga* and *Samantha at Coney Island and A Thousand Other Islands* are vivid portraits of the North Country character defined against intruding tourists and downstaters, illustrating the mild enmity toward outsiders that pervades upstate and its literature.

Holley's prose pieces are truly more like sketches than short stories. A thin narrative strand is merely a device that permits characters their social commentary and criticism, character delineation, and "soarin' into eloquence." Holley's contemporary, Philander Deming, displayed the same gift for sketching by quick, sure strokes and clear voices. However, as Holley was weaving the roughly textured, homespun adventures of the Allens' circle, Deming was creating the concise, chiselled prose that mirrored the harsh realities of North Country living.

Philander Deming was born in Schoharie County, south of the Erie Canal line that is typically considered the lower boundary of the North Country, but like Holley, he was a child of the farm. As a young man, he taught school in the winters and spent summers in the northern Adirondacks operating a saw mill with his brothers. As many Yorker sons would if they were able, Deming went back to New England to college, and was, in fact, the first and only North Country writer before 1900 to have a college education (O'Donnell, "Regional Fiction" 34). After graduation from the University of Vermont and Albany Law School, he traveled as an expert court reporter. Then in 1872, the same year that Holley was converting reluctant feminists with laughter, Deming was recognized as a noteworthy young writer by William Dean Howells, and his first short story was published in *Atlantic Monthly*. Only three slim volumes of fiction followed, but the stories are wonderfully crisp and spare, unsentimental with a sense of interior frostbite and blight that is reminiscent of the stories of Mary Wilkins Freeman. There is in the pieces none of the homely metaphor and exaggerated big talk that Holley used. Deming's prose is bevelled, carefully accurate, precise. The stories are taut and tough minded; the sketches are haunting. Many pieces begin with a sharp, realistic thrust with none of the meandering that characterized the folksy openings of other upcountry writers. One startling story titled "Willie," narrated by a young boy, commences harshly: "It frightened us a good deal when we found the little dead boy" (*Adirondack Stories* 106). Deming's years as a court stenographer had given him opportunities to study characters of the North Country and record their voices in dramatic circumstances. Thus in his stories, the themes closest to the nub of the North Country conscience emerge: fierce self-reliance; the preeminence of local and personal justice over legislated jurisdiction; the plight of women in a region physically and culturally inhospitable; and the perverse consequences of living an interior, insular life. Deming followed the typical impulse to place events in a specific locale, often not merely naming a city like Burlington, Vermont, but placing his characters on a particular hill, overlooking a certain well-known vista. "A Stranger In the City" is set not merely in Albany but on a short block on Jay Street. Despite this penchant for naming, Deming included in his fiction few details of the land. The rootedness is verbal, not physical, yet the characters have a common distaste for travel beyond their own precincts that recurs often in the works of other writers in the region. It is a prejudice that underlies the idea that cities — or even large towns—are alien, dangerous, and degenerate. Nearly all the events take place within the confines of a small village, and those characters who undertake journeys rarely go farther than Albany or Burlington and back. Even then, Albany is described as "Gomorrah on the Hudson," and is the scene of deceit, alienation and moral poison ("A Lover's Conscience," *Pathfinder* 112). With their preference for staying at home, North Country folk distrusted transients. Perhaps most feared were the gypsies who rambled through the region two or three times a year. They fascinated the children but frightened the mothers into posting guard on chicken coops as well as their little ones. Even as the lumbermen from French Canada, Australia, and Europe trickled into the mountains, this essential distrust of outsiders was unabated. The foreigners, suspected of everything and carefully isolated, rarely melded with the New England-bred Yorkers, yet they provide colorful minor characters for the region's writers, perhaps because they are so much the outsiders.

The Emersonian notion that travel was tiresome and useless held firm. Typically, Holley and Deming traveled very little outside the regions of their births, though they both made for themselves two homes. Holley built her estate "Bonnie View" on the land her grandparents had claimed, but she also maintained a residence at the Murray Hill Hotel in New York City. Deming established his bachelor life in Albany while keeping another home in the Adirondacks. Like them, Irving Bacheller felt a deeply rooted need to be on the land even when the imperatives of a literary life required otherwise. He seemed to speak for all the people of his region when he deplored moving about: "There is too much travel. . . . Men can get more in a ten acre lot than in racing around the world. How much travel do you suppose Shakespeare had?" (Samuels 555).

The separateness that North Country Yorkers felt was at once boon and bane. The rights of the individual were guaranteed implicitly, including the right to be as odd as one liked so long as one stayed within the district. Thus Deming described "An Adirondack Neighborhood":

> There was a freedom in the neighborhood that I have never found anywhere else. The mountains and a hundred miles of woods shut us out from the busy life of "the States." The vast dim landscape below to the northward was "only Canada." The isolation was considerable.
>
> The neighborhood was not a small place: we knew literally everybody for a dozen miles around. It made it very much of a home indeed, and very pleasant, to have so wide an acquaintance, and to never meet strange faces. There was an utter lack of formality.
>
> I am telling about the neighborhood as it was many years ago; but so far as a mere description of the place is concerned, I might just as

well tell how it is now. For the place does not change. It is as wild and
free as ever (*Adirondack Stories* 162-63).

The tolerance of others' eccentricities was tempered by a firm sense of local justice, sometimes almost a vigilante warrant. In part this community
concern for monitoring individual conduct was a vestige of the New England Puritan tradition that the Yorkers brought with them. It had, however, deepened and shaded into a morbid fascination with minding everyone else's business.

As a consequence of the isolation, there was often lingering loneliness and the pressure of unrelieved reflection—a habit of mind that led
to unvoiced desperation and morbidity. The fascination with the peculiarities of a character was only reinforced by the fact that, as Deming notes,
the circle of human contact was small, the circumference of community
severely limited. One knew few people but knew them thoroughly. Besides
that, in such a limited circle, normal human vices were more visible, and—
loving colorful talk—North Country folk did a good deal of discussing
and cussing each other. Furthermore there was almost an incestuous quality in their lives: a woman's lover might well turn out to be the village justice or constable to whom she would have to appear when her husband
beat her. The convolutions of human relationships turned in upon themselves until the workings of a small sphere of conscience became a micro-
cosm of moral conflict. Within it private judgment was swift: ostracism,
a sound beating, a quiet hanging in a distant woodlot, or self-inflicted punishment. In one of Deming's *Adirondack Stories*, "Lost," a four-year-old
boy wanders from the clearing around his home. Word passes along the
trail until every man in the area, even distant neighbors who don't know
the family, arrive to search the forest. Without waiting for a lawman or
posse, they inch over the terrain. When days pass and the boy is still missing, the townspeople begin to mutter ugly suspicions about the father, finally accusing him of killing and burying the boy. As they are about to
pass judgment, without due process or evidence, the body is found and
the father exonerated. Yet there is faith in private justice, a seeming lawlessness in the North Country, as if by virtue of their being pioneers the
inhabitants share a code unto themselves. This justice is not peculiar to
Deming's work, of course. Even Holley, in her laudatory vision of rural
life, notes the tendency. In a digression at the outset of *Samantha At the
World's Fair,* Samantha recounts the rape and murder of a little girl by
a drunken hired man and the lynching party that tracks the killer for several days before cornering him in a swamp, a story based on a real crime
in the county.

This righteous lawlessness made the upcountry a natural haven for social and political mavericks like John Brown. Though segregated from the rest of the nation, the people debated and advocated the political issues current beyond the margins of the North Country, demonstrating moral solicitude for the national community while retaining their solitude. There was a deep awareness of the ethical life going on beyond the mountains and a willingness to pronounce opinion on political matters. Upstate had been, in Thomas F. O'Donnell's terms, a "germinating ground for politicians," including four presidents: Martin Van Buren, Millard Fillmore, Grover Cleveland, and Franklin D. Roosevelt ("Regional Fiction" 41).

The presence of real political figures — and the assumption that they were accessible to the thoughtful men and women of the North Country — was an important informing principle in the literature. Beginning with Holley's first novel, whenever Samantha undertakes a journey, she plans to visit with the local politicians and social activists. When Samantha journeys into New York City, it is to see Horace Greeley who was to run for president. Though she admired his principles and agreed with him on nearly every subject, she differed with him on "biled vittles, Wimmen's Rights, and cream biscuits" (*Betsey Bobbet* 247). With naive arrogance typical of North Country folk, Samantha is sure she can persuade him on the central matter at least. Along the way, she meets Schuyler Colfax and Ulysses S. Grant and calls on Victoria Woodhull, Elizabeth Cady Stanton, Dr. Mary Walker, Susan B. Anthony and Theodore Tilton, the movers and shakers of the 1870s. In every encounter she holds forth on her opinions with characteristic eloquence, lengthy but affectionate, assured that she need only tell them where they've gone astray and they'll chirk up and toe the line. In the later works, Samantha insists on calling on all sorts of famous people, believing that they are — or ought to be — interested in her rightminded assessment of the world's problems and practical suggestions for simple remedies.

Of course Holley's argument with politicians, once the slaves were freed, was primarily over suffrage for women. Even the temperance issue was subsumed since Holley, like most feminists, assumed that women would enact prohibition when they got the vote anyway. Holley's feminism, nurtured by the wave of reform movements, was probably rooted in the real hardships of woman's lot in the region as well as Holley's own limited opportunities as a girl. Besides the physical threats to settlers' wives of panthers and wolves, there was the awful certainty that life was likely to be short, painful, cramped, and lonely. The isolation of rural homesteads was relieved for the men by trips to town and communal harvesting, but the women suffered the ache of a brooding, desolate life. The number of suicides among North Country women in the decades after 1855 is testimony to the futility they felt: brides hanged themselves; mothers drowned their baby daughters and then themselves in farm ponds; women prematurely aged with unnamed illnesses drank lethal doses of laudanum. The tales Philander Deming created barely touched on this element of rural life, but he could not ignore, particularly in his story "Joe Baldwin," the disdain for women and marriage that too often prevailed (*Adirondack Stories*). Typically the women in Deming's stories are thinly drawn, starched examples of self-sacrificing wives and long-suffering mothers. The occasional sentimental heroine is apt to be a girl reared in the city who perpetuates some deceit or trickery to achieve her aim, a female who has lost her country honesty by separation from the land and pioneer values.

Like his precursors, Irving Bacheller was conscious of the predicament of women in the northern region, though because of his exuberant optimism and romantic bent, he rarely depicted the haunted lives of up-country women. Himself born on a farm in the St. Lawrence Valley, on the upper curve of the lowlands settled by the migrating Vermonters, Bacheller certainly witnessed the awful waste of women. However, most of the women characters he drew, beginning with the angelic Mrs. Brower in *Eben Holden,* are virtuous, patient mother-women.

> I can see this slender, blue eyed woman as I write. She is walking up and down beside her spinning wheel. I can hear the dreary buz-z-z-z of the spindle as she feeds it with the fleecy ropes. That loud crescendo echoes in the still house of memory. I can hear her singing as she steps forward and slows the wheel and swings the cradle with her foot:
>
> > "On the other side of Jordan,
> > In the sweet fields of Eden,
> > Where the tree of Life is blooming,
> > There is rest for you."
>
> She lays her hand to the spokes again and the roar of the spindle drowns her voice.
> All day, from the breakfast hour to supper time, I have heard the dismal sound of the spinning as she walked the floor, content to sing of rest but never taking it (149).

These were the kinds of women sentimentally elevated to rustic sainthood. Though born on the farm, Bacheller had little enthusiasm or part in the real labor of the homestead. Perhaps because of that and his relocation to Canton and thence to New York City, his pictures of the life are nostalgic and idyllic, highlighting the singular and colorful aspects much like a local colorist, but dimly sketching the drudgery and hardship, thereby creating characters that are "idealized but not falsified" (Samuels 245–57). It isn't until *The Turning of Griggsby* that the realistic side of the North Country pastoral is made evident. In this he recognizes the plight of these women:

> Wifehood was still a form of bondage. . . . In love and fear the wives of the Yankees were always growing. They found a certain joy in trouble. Sorrow was a form of dissipation to many, disappointment a welcome means of grace, and weariness a comforting sign of duty done. Their fears were an ever present trouble in time of need. They were three—idleness, God, and the poor house . . . these willing slaves suffered from injustice more profound than did their dark skinned sisters of the South (Samuels 435).

Despite the relentless toil, the connection with the land was crucial to the men and women who settled it. Separation from that soil brought both release and terror. When David Brower sells his farm to move the family into town, it is the beginning of the end for him, but a peculiar liberation for Elizabeth. Her husband announces the completed sale, then tells her she ought to be glad as she sits rocking silently. "Yes," says she sadly, "it's been hard work. Years ago I thought I never could stan' it. But now I've got kind o' used t' it." More silent rocking and then she begins to laugh (*Eben Holden* 251).

The close-mouthed, flinty character of the farmers is equally evident in the voices of Deming's and Bacheller's characters. That women suffered silence and withdrawal from their men is noted even in Eben's narrative. A local poet recounts to him how a widower had approached him and asked him to write a verse about his just-deceased wife. The poet asks him to tell him about her:

> "'Wall,' said he, after he had scratched his head an' thought a minute, 'she was a dretful good woman t' work.'
> "'Anything else?' I asked.
> "He thought agin fer a minute.
> "'Broke her leg once,' he said, 'an' was laid up fer more'n a year.'
> "'Must o' suffered,' said I.
> "'Not then,' he answered. 'Ruther enjoyed it layin' abed an' readin' an being' rubbed, but 't was hard on the children.'
> "'S'pose ye loved her,' I said.
> "Then the tears come into his eyes an' he couldn't speak fer a minute. Purty soon he whispered 'Yes' kind o' confidential. 'Course he loved her, but these Yankees are ashamed o' their feelin's. They hev tender thoughts, but they hide 'em as careful as the wild goose hides her eggs (101).

The surface chill is Yankee inheritance reinforced by cold habit. The North Country winters last from October to May, and the summers, though splendid, are fleeting. On shallow soil overlaying limestone, land quickly worn out by the new farmers, the impact of so short a growing season was enormous. Still, as Holley and Bacheller would have us know, the North Country spirit meets the challenge with characteristic perseverance and humor. Carl Carmer, encountering a farmer on the edge of the Adirondack–Lake George region, commented that the man must be grateful for such a splendid summer day since the season wasn't long in that clime. The farmer replied seriously, "Only lasts about fifteen minutes," paused a few beats and added, "and *they* seem to come around lunchtime" (315). Even in his laconic answer he just can't resist a bit of play, a chance to relieve the dull silence with banter. Talk as fun pervades Bacheller's works. *Eben Holden* is a book of voices. The narrator's speech with its cultivated cadence is set against the clipped vernacular of Vermonter Eben Holden and then contrasted with the varieties of dialect in the region. As one character in Eben's newly adopted home insists: "What are the two great talents of the Yankee — talents that made our forefathers famous the world over? . . . It's war an' speaking', they are the two great talents of the Yankee. But his greatest talent is the gift o' gab. Give him a chance t' talk it over with his enemy an' he'll lick 'im without a fight. An' when his enemy is another Yankee — why, they both git licked" (139).

The best parts of the novel are Eben's stories to the young boy he carries out of Vermont in a pack basket. The tales are full of dialect, fancy, the supernatural, and sheer fun mingled with moral lessons. The animal stories, folk legends, and mythic tales of a fearsome "night man" are bested only in his creation of "the Swift." This creature lurks just out of sight, waiting for a child to misstep or wander from Eben's supervision. It is the incarnation of the horrible threat that surrounded pioneers in the North Country, a being regarded with a dual sense of delight and dread. Eben Holden had claimed the boy from a family calamity in a Vermont town and spirited him away in the night. Their plunge into the Adirondack Mountains and eventual emergence into the region of Faraway, Paradise Valley, is a recounting of the settlement of the North Country. Like many newcomers, Eben and the boy saw the St. Lawrence Plain as heaven, the promised land. Much later when the boy asked Uncle Eb what kind of place heaven is, Eben responded:

> "Fer one thing," he said, deliberately, "nobody'll die there, 'less he'd ought to; don't believe there's goin' t' be any need o' swearin' er quarrel-in'. To my way o' thinkin' it'll be a good deal like Dave Brower's farm — nice, smooth land and no stun on it, an' hills an' valleys an' white clover

a plenty, an' wheat an' corn higher'n a man's head. No bull thistles, no hard winters, no narrer contracted fools; no long faces, an' plenty o' work. Folks sayin' 'How d'y do' 'stid o' 'good-by,' all the while—coming 'stid o' goin'. There's goin' t' be some kind o' fun there. I ain' no idee what 'tis (212).

Eben's unorthodox view of heaven was probably not atypical in the district. There was ample space for all sorts of latitudinarian opinion. Mostly political free spirits and Universalists, the settlers brought with them considerable tolerance in religious matters. The fire of religious "isms" that swept across New York State in the second quarter of the nineteenth century barely scorched some upper regions and bypassed a few altogether, dug in as they were and surrounded by a kind of natural firebreak. When one of the wandering preachers strode into town, he was as likely to be turned out as not, though as Deming noted in "Lida Ann" (*Adirondack Stories*), one occasionally would be so taken with the women or the life that he would settle in. For the most part, such religious excitements fueled the hearthside debates: "When such an idea got into a lonely village it would buzz there all winter, like a big fly in a glass bottle" (Deming, *Pathfinder* 162). Occasional violence against one of the revivalist groups was usually tempered with the laissez-faire notion that a person might shift his affiliation with a sect as he thought prudent without anyone else becoming particularly distressed about it (Cross 9, 308). Eventually, good-humored sufferance and respect for the individual reasserted itself. Practices among denominations and congregations varied, though all were characterized by the moral intensity inherited from their Yankee forebears. There was little value placed in the fine distinctions of doctrine. In the far reaches of the state, religion was relative and dogma was practiced with pragmatism and moderation as Eben's anecdote, set in Vermont but typical of the North Country, makes clear:

"I recollec' a man by the name o' Ranney over'n Vermont—he was a pious man. Got into an argyment an' a feller slapped him in the face. Ranney turned t'other side an' then t'other an' the feller kep' a slappin' hot 'n heavy. It was jes' like strappin' a razor fer half a minnit. Then Ranney sailed in—gin him the wust lickin' he ever hed.

"'I declare,' says another man, after 'twas all over, 'I thought you was a Christian.'

"'Am up to a cert'in p'int,' says he. 'Can't go tew fur not 'n these parts—men are tew powerful. 'Twon't do 'less ye wan' t' die sudden. When he begun poundin' uv me I see I wan't eggzac'ly prepared.'

"''Fraid 's a good deal thet way with most uv us. We're Christians up to a cert'in p'int (400).

Along with Eben's celestial vision of the region, there is an important awareness of place such as Holley and Deming had created in their works. Like them, Bacheller locates the events in specific townships, but he moves beyond these earlier writers in creating by sensual detail and loving description a sense of the landscape as well as character. He not only maps the territory, he colors it. *Eben Holden* is full of the textures and hues of seasons, the effects of passing weather on the characters of upstate, and the peculiarities of the climate and land. In these Bacheller was true to the facts of North Country living. The summers reveal

> a valley reaching to distant hills and a river winding through it, glimmering in the sunlight; a long wooded ledge breaking into naked, grassy slopes on one side of the valley and on the other a deep forest rolling to the far horizon; between them big patches of yellow grain and white buckwheat and green pasture land and greener meadows and the straight road, with white houses on either side of it, glorious in a double fringe of golden rod and purple aster and yellow John's-wort and the deep blue of the Jacob's ladder (58).

With equal reverence, Bacheller sketches the long winters, conjuring the danger of being lost in a sudden blizzard, trapped while horse-drawn plows spend days trying to clear a way, and then the sudden thaw that hit like July and sent the sledge careening across ice-crusted fields. For all the terror and threat, there was joy in the challenge. While Bacheller does not quite make the landscape a character, he renders even the frozen countryside with great vitality.

His novel *Darrel of the Blessed Isles* is a winter book written with a keen eye fixed on the details of snow, ice, and leaden days. The landscape reflects the interior frostbite of the people; their survival becomes a metaphor for the struggle against the silence and desolation of the region. A single image is emblematic of their struggle to endure: a lone man walking across a snow meadow seems like one rising and falling on turbulent waves, occasionally disappearing and presumed lost (136). In this work Bacheller looks with a naturalist's eye at woodland lore, always ending in a lesson on human survival. Perhaps because of the frigid quality in this novel, there is an elegiac tone to it. As in much of Deming's work, the plot is borne along by well-intentioned lies, misunderstandings, and ill-placed allegiances that lead to strangely unsatisfying revelations. In this work there is less of the grim patience for "the reveille of spring" (*Eben Holden* 95). This harshness had appeared before in Bacheller's writing. For all the frolic and adventure in *Eben Holden,* there is an occasional glimpse of the coarseness and vulgarity of many of the later settlers and their heirs. Abe, the itinerant butcher, is a frightening example with "his bloody work and noisy oaths. Such men were the curse of the cleanly homes in that country. There was much to shock the ears and eyes of children in the life of the farm. It was a fashion among the help to decorate their speech with profanity for the mere sound of it, and the foul mouthings of low minded men spread like a pestilence in the fields" (109).

This consciousness of the darker side of rustic manliness reinforced the author's concern with leadership. Lacking faith in an inherent nobility in common folk, he believed the rough masses required an elite corps of leaders, a kind of aristocracy. In *Silas Strong, Emperor of the Woods,* the title character embodies this distinction between rustic man and rural aristocrat. Silas is torn between his need to make a living as an Adirondack guide taking people into the woods and to protect those forests from rape by loggers and railroad builders. The old voices of the North Country were being silenced or drowned out by encroaching twentieth-century civilization. In contrast to Eben or Holley's Samantha, Silas Strong is nearly mute. He says as much as possible with as little talk as possible. He is a one-word man with a stammer. In a scene with his beloved, when he is courting, the tendency to Yankee terseness has been refined to a fault:

> "All w-well?" he inquired, soberly.
> "Eat our allowance," said she, sitting near him. "How's Miss Strong?"
> "S-supple!" he answered. Then he ran his fingers through his blond hair and soberly exclaimed, "Weasels!"
> This remark indicated that weasels had been killing the poultry and applying stimulation to the tongue of Miss Strong. Silas had sent her fowls away to market the day before.
> "Too bad!" was the remark of Lady Ann.
> "Fisht?" By this word Silas meant to inquire if she had been fishing.
> "Yesterday. Over at the falls—caught ten," said she, getting busy with her knitting.
> "B-big?"
> "Three that long," she answered, measuring with her thread.
> He gave a loud whistle of surprise, thought a moment, and exclaimed, "M-mountaneyous!" He used this word when contemplating in imagination news of a large and important character.
> "How have you been?"
> "Stout," he answered, drawing in his breath (39–40).

The author's sense that the dialect was losing its peculiar strength is clear in his later works, particularly in *Winds of God* (1941) where Bill Seavey, also a guide, speaks both the rural vernacular and a more cultivated, educated speech, claiming, "The city folks wouldn't want me for a guide if I talked as they talked. . . . They want something different — a half-wild man with the bear and panther in his manners" (41). Seavey accepts the pain of being two-tongued, but with characteristic stoicism declares "there's a man way down under my vest. . . . I call him the Honorable William L. Seavey" (41). It is that character who finally emerges. The later transformation of the rough-hewn trapper into articulate statesman reflects the author's belief in a breed of leaders who might be identified not just by their virtues but their voices.

Bacheller was as politically conservative as most North Country folk and as much of a hero-worshipper. Just as Holley revered Henry Ward Beecher and Horace Greeley, Bacheller — and his characters — elevated certain men of power and wealth to political pedestals. However, while Holley was firm in believing in a democratic, widely based governmental system in which all people, including women, were participants, Bacheller did not trust the common folk to make intelligent, well-reasoned choices. In Bacheller's works one finds the opinion that the folk need heroes not just to emulate but to follow (Samuels 449ff.). With *Light In the Clearing,* in which New York Governor and U.S. Senator Silas Wright is hero, he published the first of his novels based on the lives of famous Americans. The North Country seemed spoiled by the rapacious railroaders and loggers. Bacheller began to look beyond the mountains for his heroes.

Nostalgia for the antique purity of the North Country connected the artistic visions of the nineteenth-century authors and linked them to the newer generation of upcountry writers. In 1926, the year Marietta Holley died, Scribner's began publishing the short fiction of another young writer, Walter Edmonds. Born in Boonville, the son of a prominent attorney, Edmonds left the North Country early to attend prep school in New England. His talent was nurtured there and at Harvard where he wrote the first Scribner's piece. His first novel, *Rome Haul,* placed him as an Erie Canal writer and set his reputation as both a novelist and chronicler. It is for his canal stories and *Drums Along the Mohawk* that he is best known, but within his canon there are a few works set in the North Country that resound with the characteristic echoes of the region's history. Like the other writers discussed in this brief study, Edmonds created people who live by a code: "the Yorker-based philosophy of individual worth and dignity, of common-sense approaches to the problems of living, and of simple pleasures which sometimes show how very close sadness is to laughter, tragedy to comedy" (Wyld 47). These characters embody the same endurance and integrity that had previously defined the fictional inhabitants of the region, but to these qualities Edmonds added another.

There is about his characters a vague sense of seignorial nobility, a belief that the old landed families, however land-poor now, constitute a kind of gentry with rights and obligations that include maintaining — if not expanding — their holdings and providing heirs to continue the squire-archy. These men and women are larger than life, totems of the enormous power, endurance, and virtue in the region's people. At the opening of *The Big Barn,* the patriarch of the Wilder clan dozes in the spring sunshine on his "verandah" (what Eben and Samantha would call a porch):

> An ant on its spring marching came upon the mountain of his cowhide boot. For a while it considered the phenomenon, its horns erect. Then it laid hold with its hands and began to climb. It went slowly, using the crossed laces as a ladder until it reached the smooth curve of the doeskin breeches over the great knee. There it paused once more to gain its breath. Then, gathering itself, it made a rush to gain the summit, and saw the whole man before it, the heavy chest rising and falling evenly in sleep. The ant stayed there marveling to itself with its hands (1).

The ant's journey seems to suggest the Wilder family's migration into the Black River hills. More importantly, from this ant's perspective, the man and the land are one: powerful, mountainous, marvelous. Though it may have taken a century, the Yankees finally have merged with the land. They do not merely inhabit it: they are the land. In the last pages of *The Big Barn,* old man Wilder tells his daughter-in-law Rose not to bury him in the graveyard but by a rock that looks over the meadow land: "'Bury me deep down and don't mark me any way at all. When it comes time to turn the meadow into corn or barley, plough me over.' He stirred, as if he felt the web of heavy pasture rooting in his heart" (332).

The land endures. Even though the men and women accept their mortality and surrender gratefully to the final merging, they strive to create on the land enduring structures. For Wilder, that means a family and the barn. The one he intends to build is bigger than anything ever conceived of by local folks, a building so huge that it is compared to the Ark, and everyone is stunned at the idea. Yet such a grand scheme is not just one writer's fancy. Set in 1860, the novel is a fictionalized account of an actual barn-raising north of Boonville (Wyld 68). Even now the northern region is strewn with remnants of stone houses and elaborate compounds built by families aiming to leave a birthright for the cycle of generations. Edmonds recognized that impulse, adding it to Bacheller's belief in the emergence of a natural aristocracy. Thus he recreates not the simple, plain-spoken rustics of Holley and Deming, but a towering squire who oversees the hill folk, acting as baronial guardian for them. Both Bacheller and Edmonds use as motif the education of a youth, but whereas Bacheller's boys

are usually travelling about to find their fortunes, Edmonds' characters
are forever coming home to find themselves. Place is everything.

Set in real places, using the names of actual towns, streets, creeks,
and families, Edmonds' narratives are rooted more deeply in the soil of
the upstate region than any of the other writers. The land, with its history
of seizure and settlement, binds the members of a clan. Families are nearly
regal in their rural manors. There is about them the mark of aristocracy,
however rustic. The Boyds of Black River, for example, being old gentry,
have about them an air of gentility that has nothing to do with fashion
or parlor refinements. At the horse races in Syracuse, Teddy, the narrator
and only a shirt-tail relation, notes

> even from the paddock gate I could recognize the Boyds among [the crowd]
> as clearly as if they wore a family uniform. For there was something old-
> fashioned about even their best clothes, a shabby gentility in the black
> silks of the women and a country cut to the men's coats. And they all
> kept together, and they didn't talk like the backers of the other two horses,
> but sat silently, their eyes moving in unison as the grey horse circled the
> track (*The Boyds of Black River* 114).

It is this notion of aristocracy and class-consciousness that in part
attracted Edmund Wilson back to the solid stone house in Talcottville that
he had inherited from his mother. Although Wilson, like Edmonds, kept
a place near Boonville, he was never a North Country person. For him
the hills at the edge of the Tug Hill plateau were enchanted with childhood
memories, but they were fleeting, evanescent summer recollections, not the
character-founding daily experiences of living upstate. Associated in his
memory with a manorial quality, the Stone House centered among wood
frame dwellings signified endurance and continuity. Even in his early essay "The Old Stone House" he recognized that it and the antique spirit
it represented were not realistic alternatives to his oppressive present. The
walls stood intact, but the interior was dilapidated and rank with musti-
ness, filled with objects no longer useful except as curios. Finally he acknowledged that the North Country life was lonely, poor, and provincial,
not so different from the life outside the region in the twentieth century.
Nevertheless, like the Boyds and Wilders in Edmonds' novels, Wilson clung
to place, determined that it would never, despite severe financial troubles,
pass out of his hands in his lifetime or out of his family afterward (Costa
65). Wilson always felt noblesse oblige: "And it seems to me that every
upstate New Yorker whose family belongs, or once belonged, to this land-
lord class retains something of this feudal mentality. They have never been
able to get over the conviction that they ought to have the say as to what
is for the good of the lower orders" (*Upstate* 12).

To be among these folk he would make the trip from Wellfleet, usually in late spring, noting how different even now New York looks to one coming over from New England, seeing the open spaces, uncramped valleys and blue, bare-topped mountains much as his forebears must have seen them (76–77). In some mystical way Wilson felt connected to the hillside walkers: "Even when I don't remember them, it is as if I had always known them" (270).

The insular, almost incestuous, character of North Country communities was one Wilson approved: "Everybody was related to everybody else or, at no matter what distance from one another, were neighbors or very old friends. They had grown out of the country like elms" (Costa 45). As old as the trees were the peculiar habits of mind that Wilson, not entirely sharing them, could identify, notably the penchant for brooding and a fascination with the sordid bits of rural living that local folk indulged. They were characteristics that Edmonds, with all his concern for grace, could not ignore. The proud families retain their code of private justice as well as their preference for solitude. Peddlers, city folk, even people from beyond the next valley are kept at bay or invited off the land. When one of their own transgresses, justice is quickly dispatched. In *The Big Barn,* one man finds another consorting with his wife; he tracks, kills, and buries the malefactor, sowing spring rye over the grave (296–302). Whatever else may happen, the land will go on.

The moods of the landscape shape the characters and the narrative. On the day when the bride arrives at the Wilder Farm, the countryside seems to dominate the scene as if to imply that this human drama, crucial as it is to the family, is only a passing moment:

> The sun was now so low over Tug Hill that in the valley the shadows cast by the trees merged with the dusk; but on the western upland, along which the road from Utica and Rome ran straight toward the High Falls, the eye of the sun was still visible. A red sheen marked the puddles in the ruts, and the crowns of the eastern hills and the clouds above them still carried a pink flush.
>
> The small pastures on either side of the road were marked off by snake rail fences; but the cattle had not yet come forth from the barns. There was no sign of life on the earth; and in the sky only four crows flying one behind the other over the lip of the valley, but they flew soundlessly. The whole land seemed overhung with silence (24).

The rough language of the hillside walkers and lowland settlers is silenced. In Edmonds' books there are the quiet, sober voices of settlers' children who have left the land and returned to it bringing with them more cultivated talk. The servants and tenants still utter the cropped sentences and homely vernacular of the late nineteenth century, but even theirs is more refined than the broad dialect of Holley's sketches or Bacheller's "B' Gosh" stories (O'Donnell, "History" 57). Yet with whatever grandeur the new generation acquires, the old values hold fast. There is less of the elegy in these works by Edmonds and more of a hymn to endurance. Like the spiders who continually spin intricate webs in the Boyd barn, the characters weave relationships of kin and obligation that are generations old.

It is the women in these two novels who bind the families together, who are responsible for the continuance of the clan. As Wyld has pointed out, the books are dominated by men (128–29). In spite of that, the women are clearly drawn as vigorous, single-minded characters with as much responsibility as the men. They are exceptional, particularly compared with the women that Deming or Bacheller drew. In *The Big Barn,* the bride who comes from Boston to the Wilder Farm north of Utica is really not a city-bred maiden at all. Born in Rome, New York, she returns to the upcountry. The subsequent struggle to meet the Wilder men on equal terms as well as carry on the tradition of inheritance is virtually a declaration that there is something inbred in North Country women that even urban gentility can't hinder. Edmonds was conscious of the predicament of women in the northern regions. When Rose, who has taken hold of the running of the place as old man Wilder has asked her to, finally gives birth to a baby girl, the first and only legitimate grandchild, Wilder is disappointed: he cannot consider her the heir. So dismal is the realization that the baby is a mere girl that even Rose apologetically tells her father-in-law that she is disappointed, but that at least the child can carry on the grandmother's name (267). It is small comfort.

Among the Boyds of Black River there is an old antagonism between the men and women. The Boyd men are preoccupied with their horses, hunting, and fishing, always redolent with the smell of "horses and tobacco and clean hay" (5). The women are equal to the match, particularly Kathy, the daughter of the old Ledyard Boyd's best friend. After dinner at the Boyd house, she withdraws to the rose-colored parlor, a "rather pathetic" room, "a mausoleum" full of Boyd women, the only place where there was space for them (33). The room is darkened and defined by the male presence: "Outside the door of this room is their big living room with its big furniture and its smell of men and tobacco. And on the other side is their verandah where the men drink. The roof throws a shadow on the light in this room" (32).

It is a position of powerlessness that Marietta Holley's Samantha would have railed against and one that Kathy won't tolerate. A woman may as well be a drudge as a doll; Kathy chooses neither. She insists on hunting and fishing with the men. Taking the reins, she fights hard against the old habits of constraint. However, there is no peace or surrender, only truce. When Kathy and Doone Boyd's child is born during a critical horse race, there is an elaborate strategy to keep the news of Kathy's labor from Doone. When the race is over, a single voice is raised above the screeching and cheering of the crowd, announcing "It's a girl" (151). This time, there is no disappointment. Edmonds has given the North Country's women their due just as he has its men. In his chronicle of upstate life, he has recreated the wild, free, exuberant spirit that enabled the Yankess, with their big talk and bigger ambitions, to settle the York State wilderness.

Settle but not tame. Within natural boundaries, bolstered by the habit of isolation, the North Country character remains much as the pioneering Vermonters forged it. The highways that Edmund Wilson bemoaned now cut through farmland and forest bringing the rumble of business and tourism, but the traffic moves on. The North Country resists change and cherishes its past. Summer people come and go, leaving the stern features of the landscape and the people untouched. Traces of the old values gleam in the quiet talk across a rail fence, around the stove at the corner store or post office, and in the seemingly aimless chatter at farm auctions. The people still relish a good story, embroidered with fabulous detail, carefully timed to hook the listener and catch him. Good talk is sport. Ambitions are smaller now, scaled down to the hard reality of worn out soil and a diminished economy, but the old independence and self-sufficiency persists. A stranger is met with silence, held respectfully at arm's length until his measure has been taken, his lineage established. Then the stories begin again.

Works Cited

Bacheller, Irving. *Darrel of the Blessed Isles.* New York: Grosset and Dunlap, 1903.
———. *Eben Holden: A Tale of the North Country.* Boston: Lothrop Pub. Co., 1900.
———. *The Light in the Clearing.* Indianapolis: Bobbs-Merrill, 1917.
———. *Silas Strong, Emperor of the Woods.* New York: Grosset and Dunlap, 1906.
———. *Winds of God.* New York: Grosset and Dunlap, 1941.
Carmer, Carl. *Listen for A Lonesome Drum: A York State Chronicle.* New York: Farrar and Rinehart, 1936.
Costa, Richard Hauer. *Edmund Wilson: Our Neighbor From Talcottville.* Syracuse: Syracuse University Press, 1980.
Cross, Whitney R. *The Burned-Over District: A Social and Intellectual History*

of Enthusiastic Religion in Western New York, 1800–1850. New York: Harper and Row, 1965.

Deming, Philander. *Adirondack Stories* (1880). Freeport, N.Y.: Books for Libraries, 1970.

———. *Story of A Pathfinder* (1907). New York: Garrett Press, 1969.

———. *Tompkins and Other Folks: Stories of the Hudson and the Adirondacks* (1885). New York: Garrett Press, 1969.

Edmonds, Walter Dumaux. *The Big Barn.* Boston: Little, Brown, 1930.

———. *The Boyds of Black River.* New York: Dodd, Mead, 1953.

———. *Rome Haul.* Boston: Little, Brown, 1929.

Holley, Marietta (Josiah Allen's Wife). *My Opinions and Betsey Bobbet's.* Hartford, Conn.: American Pub. Co., 1873.

———. *Samantha At Coney Island and A Thousand Other Islands.* New York: The Christian Herald, 1911.

———. *Samantha At Saratoga or Flirtin' with Fashion.* Philadelphia: Hubbard Brothers, 1887.

———. *Samantha At the World's Fair.* New York: Funk and Wagnalls, 1893.

———. *Samantha On the Race Problem.* New York: Dodd, Mead, 1892.

O'Donnell, Thomas F. "The Regional Fiction of Upstate New York." Diss., Syracuse University, 1957.

———. "Literary History of New York, 1650–1958," *Richards Atlas of New York State.* Phoenix, N.Y.: Frank E. Richards, 1957–59, pp. 55–60.

Samuels, Charles Edward. "Irving Bacheller: A Critical Biography." Diss., Syracuse University, 1952.

Wilson, Edmund. *Upstate: Records and Recollections of Northern New York.* New York: Farrar, Straus and Giroux, 1971.

———. "The Old Stone House." *The American Earthquake.* New York: Doubleday, 1958.

Wyld, Lionel D. *Walter D. Edmonds, Storyteller.* Syracuse: Syracuse University Press, 1982.

9   The Erie Canal and the Novel

LIONEL D. WYLD

Y OU MUST HAVE HEARD OF IT," Herman Melville wrote in referring to
the Erie Canal in his novel *Moby-Dick,* and it seems clear that by
the middle of the nineteenth century most Americans were aware of upstate New York's inland waterway. Like other great accomplishments, the
"Clinton Ditch" exerted a widespread influence on people and culture. It
particularly influenced the economy of New York State and the westward
development of the United States. Upstate New Yorkers saw villages grow
into cities and new towns spring up in the wilderness, farm incomes in-
crease and food prices in the cities go down. It opened the Midwest to
a vast immigration by New Englanders and as a technical endeavor created, perhaps more than any other factor, an American civil engineering
profession.

Completed in 1825, the Erie was a great human achievement. Stretch-
ing 363 miles from Albany to Buffalo, the canal connected the Hudson
River, and thus New York City, with the Great Lakes. The longest con-
tinuous canal in the world, it had to be dug through all sorts of terrain,
mosquito-infested marshes, river valleys, and rocky escarpments. In several places solid rock was assaulted by "powder monkeys" directed by self-
made engineers with no prior knowledge of canal building. The locks
around the Cohoes Falls and up the Niagara Escarpment at Lockport were
magnificent engineering constructions for so young a country. At the eastern end of the canal, twenty-seven locks were provided in the short distance
from West Troy (Watervliet) to Schenectady in the Cohoes-Waterford area;
at the western end the famous "Lockport Five" — five pairs of locks that

allowed boats to go through lockage in both directions, up and down, at the same time—evoked awe in foreign and native tourists alike. In all, the canal engineers built eighty-three locks, as well as numerous aqueducts to carry water traffic over rivers and streams. Their efforts saw the dawn of the Canal Era, a mania of canal building throughout the eastern United States and the Ohio territory.

In the Erie's eastern section the canal builders used the valley of the Mohawk River, "the river flowing through mountains," as the Indians called it. British Shakespearian actor Tyrone Power reflected the thoughts of countless other foreign travelers in the early 1830s when he noted in his *Impressions of America* that "no valley in the world can present charms more varied or more beautiful." As General George Washington toured the Mohawk Valley after the Revolution he felt it could be the pathway to empire, and the Erie Canal had much to do with fulfilling his prophecy. The central upstate New York region, already made secure in history by settlement and critical colonial battles, became a bustling commercial catalyst with the opening of the Erie—the Grand Western Canal, as New Yorkers proudly hailed it.

Tourists to America called the canal "the eighth wonder of the world," and upstate New Yorkers proudly hailed their canal as the longest and best in the world. It was indeed the "Grand Western Canal," though local folk were more often apt to call it "the Big Ditch." That sobriquet reflected the average person's pride, too, when one considers that the prism of the "big" ditch was only 40 feet by 28 feet by 4 feet. Yet, songs were sung about it, and stories and tales sprang up among the boatmen and other workers on the towpath. The Erie Canal became a legend, part of folklore as well as history.

From its inception the Erie Canal got into literature, in both the general and more specific meanings of the word. There were songs, travelers' accounts, diaries, newspaper stories, and eulogistic verse; and there were also short stories, plays, and novels that used the Erie Canal as setting or its boaters as characters. Early American writers, from William Dunlap and Nathaniel Hawthorne to Mark Twain and William Dean Howells, found in the Erie something interesting and usable. Theatre manager and playwright William Dunlap can be credited with the first "Erie drama" in his *A Trip to Niagara* (1818). James Kirke Paulding wrote the first short story to include the Erie (see Paulding's *The Book of Saint Nicholas,* 1836), and a juvenile book, Jacob Abbott's *Marco Paul's Travels and Adventures in the Pursuit of Knowledge on the Erie Canal* (1844), is the first longer fiction about the canal. The canal novel, however, is a more modern phenomenon.

While the Erie Canal seemed to be a fruitful field for literary exploitation, the early appearance of canallers or the canal in fiction rarely formed an essential or extensive part of a work's narrative structure. It was not until *David Harum* (1899) that a full scale regional treatment appeared in a major literary work. Edward Noyes Westcott's extremely popular novel, which featured a typical upstate New Yorker as the title character, showed the possibilities for exploiting the characters and the canal background of "Erie country." But it remained for Walter D. Edmonds' *Rome Haul* (1929) to begin a major trend. Edmonds' influence was very large. In the 1930s he wrote dozens of short stories and several novels, beginning with *Rome Haul,* that depict the canal country and its people with a cultural and historical authenticity. Samuel Hopkins Adams turned his talents to Erie fiction, too, with *Canal Town* (1944), *Banner by the Wayside* (1947), and *Sunrise to Sunset* (1950). From Westcott's time on, an impressive number of novels have been written about the historic Erie, with Edmonds and Adams in the forefront.

Edmonds Starts a Trend

In numerous short stories, two novels and a novelette, the Grand Canal of New York State provided Walter D. Edmonds with major theme, setting, and a wide variety of characters. If the canal and its boaters are considered in their larger influence, there is hardly a work by Edmonds, right up to his National Book Award novel in 1975, that does not reflect the effects of his Black River Valley boyhood and his deep-rooted interest in the canal days. Samuel Hopkins Adams, who followed Edmonds in creating a successful literary genre out of the canal novel, saw the towpath as "a moving marvel of humanity" (as an Adams grandfather put it). It was a feeling equally shared by Edmonds.

Edmonds found it very easy to write his first Erie novel. During his college years, he published a number of canal-set stories in the *Harvard Advocate,* and when he left Cambridge with his bachelor's degree in 1926 he already had sold a story to *Scribner's.* At the urging of Professor Charles Townsend Copeland, his composition instructor at Harvard, and of *Atlantic Monthly* editor Ellery Sedgwick, Edmonds enthusiastically began writing a book about the canal period in upstate New York. He titled it *Rome Haul.*

Sedgwick promised to print a manuscript if delivered in four months. Edmonds, then twenty-five, completed *Rome Haul* in three. "By the first of November," he recalled later, in writing an introduction to a Modern

Library edition of the novel that resulted, "I was installed in a room with a typewriter, and the second morning I wrote 'Rome Haul' at the top of the page, 'I' under it, and under that 'The Road and the Peddler.' 'In 1850 the road to Boonville wound out of the Tug Hill country . . .' No fresh start, no hesitation: I finished the first chapter by lunch time. That morning at breakfast I had thought of a peddler describing the Erie, saying of it, 'it's the bowels of the nation, it's the whole shebang of life.' I thought it was good for an opening chapter, and it turned out to be good for the whole book." Actually, he produced a book even longer than Sedgwick had anticipated, but with pruning (by *Atlantic* editors, Edmonds happily recalls) *Rome Haul* was published amid warm reviews. Edmonds had set out to write a novel of the upstate New York canal country, and he succeeded admirably well: canal life pervades the pages, which reflect the commercial as well as the human sides of canalling in the mid-nineteenth century. As it turns out, the book was a literary pioneer in another important respect. *Rome Haul* is the first adult novel to deal in its entirety with the Erie Canal, and it became a model for Erie-inspired fiction.

Because Edmonds' novel is critical in literary history to the concept of what I have called "the canal novel," it will be helpful to discuss Edmonds' Erie novels at some length. Only by treating *Rome Haul* and other early Erie-related works in some depth can the distinguishing characteristics of this class of fiction be adequately perceived.

Edmonds told me that he drew upon a number of sources in writing his novel: tales he had heard from old boaters in Boonville and along the Black River Canal, family scrapbooks of newspaper clips from the 1850s and 1860s, and the book *Old Towpaths* (1926) by Alvin Harlow. Edmonds' novel deals with people who earn their livelihood from the Erie Canal or who are otherwise significantly affected by it. The novel is set in 1850, with the heyday of passenger packets past and freight hauling the canal's chief activity. It was also a time when railroads like the New York Central seriously began to contest canals for both passenger and freight. His basic theme, apart from the time and canal setting, is that of finding one's self, of maturing. As one notes in subsequent Erie fiction, Edmonds' included, the hero rises quickly through opportune circumstances to a successful and rewarding position (essentially in the manner of the Horatio Alger formula). For *Rome Haul,* it is an orphan named Dan Harrow, who comes from the Black River country to take a job as hoggee [canallers' term for towpath driver boy] and who soon becomes the captain of his own boat, the *Sarsey Sal.* The tone for the novel is set by a peddler at the outset, as young Harrow learns of the significance of DeWitt Clinton's canal. "The Erie is a swarming hive," the peddler says. "Boats, coming and going, passing you all the while. You can hear their horns blowing all day long. As like as not there's a fight at every lock. There's all kind of people there, and all going all the while. . . . There's freight going west and raw food east, all on the canal; there's people going west, New Englanders, Germans, all them furrin folk, and there's people coming east that've quit. But the canawlers keep a-moving."

This freneticism is well depicted in *Rome Haul*: the Erie is the "swarming hive"and "whole shebang of life" the old peddler describes. Edmonds creates a plethora of characters, major and minor, to populate his novel, providing a realistic and essentially humanistic portrayal of the melting pot that was early America. His concern with people, particularly the ordinary citizens, as my *Walter D. Edmonds, Storyteller* (1982) shows, has become an important trademark of Edmonds as a writer.

The wide-eyed youth Dan Harrow feels that all of America and much of Europe seems to be on the Erie Canal. When he acquires the *Sarsey Sal* from a captain whom his father had known, he enters fully and purposely into what for a farm lad is essentially an alien world of boating. Molly Larkins provides the romantic conflict. Taken on board the *Sarsey Sal* as cook, she has left another boater, Jotham Klore. "He's a sort of bully," she says. Eventually, Harrow fights Klore in a climactic event that becomes a characteristic of the canal novel. *Rome Haul* is unified around three conflicts, the first of which is the man-woman conflict of Dan versus Molly. A second, Dan versus Jotham Klore, develops from the first. The third is really a background conflict, centering on the rivalry between canallers and railroaders, since the novel depicts that period of upstate history when the canal faced competition from the economic and technological efficiency offered by the railroads.

His experience on the canal is a maturing one for Dan Harrow. Molly Larkins seems the catalyst in the process, but they part at the novel's end when Dan decides to leave the canal. In the novel, unlike the stage and motion picture versions of Edmonds' book, Dan loses Molly when he quits the canal to return to farming. The outcome of his fight with Klore is a victory for the shy and nonbelligerent Dan only in a minimal sense, for in winning the fight he makes up his mind to leave the canal and thus also his girl. A secondary character, Fortune Friendly, sums up the situation between the two men with a characteristic Yorker terseness: "It don't seem right," he said. "Each one thought he was fighting for her. And neither one won." Edmonds' novel not only captures the brawling and buoyant spirit of an era in American history but also, importantly, presents basic human issues in a way that transcends a narrow regionalism. The universal themes of maturing, of love, and of struggle against personal and environmental adversaries are there.

This first canal novel is important literarily, I think, because it is a regional novel in the best sense. Furthermore, it seems to have opened the way for a surprisingly large number of novels "in which the great upstate area provides an identifiable, significant background," as Thomas F. O'Donnell suggested in his doctoral dissertation on "The Regional Fiction of Upstate New York" (Syracuse University, 1957). In particular, Edmonds proved to be an influence on other authors to find themes, characters, and settings for stories and novels that have resulted in a considerable canal literature. *Rome Haul* established — with its canal bully, its canal argot, its climactic hero-versus-bully fistfight — conventions that have been more or less followed by other writers dealing with the Erie and its boaters.

As "The Farmer Takes a Wife," the novel was successfully adapted for Broadway in the 1930s and as motion pictures in 1934 and 1952. *Rome Haul* was reprinted in *Three Stalwarts* (1962), which included two other Edmonds novels.

His next novel was *The Big Barn* (1930), which according to Howard Thomas in his *Black River in the North Country* is a fictionalized account of the building of a barn near High Falls, north of Boonville, The old peddler from *Rome Haul* appears briefly, and Dan Harrow also appears again, although he has no major role. The Black River Canal, which was built to connect the North Country with the Erie at Rome, New York, serves as background, and some of the characters had worked the canal or served as canal commissioners. The story is essentially about Ralph Wilder, whom Edmonds describes as "a handsome old desperado" tied to the tradition of farming. His grand project, of course, is his building the big barn of the title. While not a canal novel, this book bridges Edmonds' two major novels about the canal, *Rome Haul* and *Erie Water* (1933).

In *Erie Water,* Edmonds' third book and second canal novel, the Erie Canal is a symbol of technological progress and democratic achievement. It was built largely by ordinary people unskilled in engineering but distinguished by considerable initiative and common sense. *Erie Water* is the story of building the canal from start to finish (1817-25). Edmonds said that two volumes of the laws of the State of New York "formed the bones of my description of digging and building locks," and there is a fair amount of documentary history about the book. In fact, it is "so historically accurate," Edmonds later reflected (in his Introduction to the Modern Library edition of *Rome Haul*), "that it is a wonder anyone ever read it as a novel." As might be expected with the Erie Canal project so epical to the development of the state and nation, Edmonds' novel contains historical figures like DeWitt Clinton, Benjamin Wright, Jemima Wilkinson, Myron Holley, and Joseph Smith. The principal fictional characters are two young persons, Jerry Fowler, who comes from the Lebanon Valley, and Mary Goodhill, an English redemptioner, whose papers Jerry buys at the outset. As in *Rome Haul,* the plot and setting are both canal connected. Fowler is hired by a Utica contractor, Caleb Hammil, to help build the first locks. Hammil, like most of the canal workers, didn't even know what a canal lock looked like when he won a $17,000 contract for building the first Erie locks and aqueducts. "I'm a contractor and no mechanic," he admitted, with Yorker common sense and good humour. "I've never seen one. But they've got them down in Massachusetts, so I guess we can build them."

Through such characters Edmonds traces the building of the canal from the initial spadeful of earth dug at Rome in 1817 to the completion of the job with the famous combines, or paired locks, at Lockport six years later. "You and I started the first lock," an engineer tells Fowler. "It would be fun to build the last on the line." And that is what they do.

Erie Water is more than documentary history. Like so much of Edmonds' writing, the novel is good history *and* good fiction. The narrative, said one reviewer," is much like the canal itself [and] does not grow monotonous but proves to develop something interesting all along the way." Its folklore is honest. The reader learns of an "ether plant" that can soothe an aching tooth; of ladies' conversation over buying calico cloth in Philetus Bumpus' general store; of "christening" a new horse; of the hard life in a digger's shanty; and of the reaction to the whole business of canal contracting. "Afore this damned canal a man just said he'd work," said a worker. "Now he signs a paper." The novel is important for Edmonds' treatment of a plethora of problems, many of them monumental in the days when the profession of engineering was yet unborn: building locks without plans; running a canal bed on an aqueduct over the Genesee River or the Mohawk, or carving it out of bedrock around a mountain; enduring malarial fever while building the canal through the Montezuma swamp; and overcoming other difficulties hostile environments presented. Edmonds not only provides the reader with an insight into the technical side of canal building but also conveys a sense of the jubilance and pride citizens felt in being part of a pioneer endeavor.

In 1940 Edmonds published *Chad Hanna,* a novel about circus life in upstate New York in the 1830s that first appeared serially in the *Saturday Evening Post.* While it may not fit the normal pattern of a canal novel, the presence of the Erie and of canal boaters is much in evidence. One of Edmonds' best novels, *Chad Hanna* is pure entertainment. Like *Rome Haul,* it went quickly to Hollywood as another vehicle for Henry Fonda to play a leading Edmonds character. Chad is a child of the Erie, an orphan who throws his lot in with Huguenine's circus as it travels from village to village in central upstate New York. We first meet Chad in the canal town of Canastota; and the vernacular, humor, folklore, and enterprise of Jacksonian America, when New York was the western frontier in the young United States, are all present in the novel.

Of Edmonds' shorter novels, *The Wedding Journey* (1947) is all Erie, as he writes of a newlywed couple en route to Ohio aboard a packet from Schenectady. The title suggests comparison with William Dean Howells' *Their Wedding Journey* (1872) for obvious reasons, but Howells' bride and groom, while traversing the same route in upstate New York, rode the train rather than a canal boat. In the Edmonds story the times are accurately depicted, and nostalgia dwells in the pages: one feels inevitably the passing of the times when everything was slower paced. Roger Willcox urges the packet's captain to make the trip to Buffalo in four days, and Captain Harrow agrees. "Four days?" he tells Willcox. "Well, I'll give you a run for your money, mister. Maybe I'll shade it under four days. It's a light trip and we're out to bust time wide open." He acknowledges that the company has given him a hundred dollars to pay any fines for exceeding the four-mile-an-hour legal speed limit.

When Edmonds began writing, fiction in the United States was in a period of change, as Sherwood Anderson and other writers with an interest in locality began to be felt in American literature. Their "first-hand examination" and "wholly American" representation, as critic H. L. Mencken pointed out in *Prejudices: Fourth Series,* were the hallmarks of a new literature. From the time of his earliest work at Harvard College, Edmonds' stories and novels drew upon upstate New York and, especially, upon the people and the culture of the so-called Canal Era. Because he is primarily an artist, wrote Dayton Kohler in an *English Journal* article, "the work of Walter D. Edmonds goes beyond a local realism. Beneath his faithful use of local color he attempts to express the essential truths of human experience." For this reason Edmonds is important as a humanist, and this is also perhaps one reason why his stories so often appeal to young readers even when he is writing for adults. While he once said that he never wrote a children's book, he won a Newbery Award for *The Matchlock Gun* (1941), a previously published "adult" short story, and a National Book Award for *Bert Breen's Barn* (1975). Along the way he "sired" the modern canal novel, for which Union College justly recognized him with an honorary doctoral degree as "the second builder of our Grand Canal."

Sam Adams' Canal Romances

Like Edmonds, Samuel Hopkins Adams had a good deal of "canal" in his blood. His great-grandfather, Abner Adams, was a canal contractor;

a grandfather, Myron Adams, whose stories about canal days form the basis for *Grandfather Stories* (1955), continually reminisced about the Grand Canal for his grandson's benefit; and the family name was given to one of the western canal hamlets, Adams Basin. Adams himself wrote many of his stories at "Wide Waters," the Hopkins residence at Auburn, New York, not far from the Erie towpath.

After graduation from Hamilton College, he took his first job with Chester Lord of the *New York Sun*, worked a while for *McClure's Magazine*, and then free-lanced stories, detective fiction, and muckraking medical articles. The latter, documented in *The Great American Fraud* (1906), helped get the Pure Food and Drug Act passed and earned Sam an honorary membership in the American Medical Association. Indefatigable to the core, he wrote several biographies, including one of his fellow Hamilton alumnus Alexander Woollcott. Hollywood took sixteen of his novels and stories, including the one that won an Academy Award as "It Happened One Night." The most interesting thing about Adams, however, is his turn to upstate regionalism that began at an age when many persons are retired. At 73 he published his first Erie novel, *Canal Town* (1944). That launched the irascible Adams on an entirely new career, or at least one which took a new direction.

"The plot," Walter Edmonds wrote in reviewing *Canal Town* for the *Atlantic*, "is the least important element of the novel. What counts is the elaborate, colorful, and affectionate portrait of a canal town in its growing pains. Obviously, Mr. Adams has not only gone back to the sources but has lived with them for a long time." The town is Palmyra in the 1820s, when the digging of "that vast Clintonian enterprise, the Erie Canal," Adams writes, "brought with it to Western New York not only progress and prosperity but unforseen upheavals." With authentic detail Adams depicts the "upheavals" on several frontiers — the engineering one of building the Erie, the medical frontier of coping with swamp fever and cholera epidemics which faced the Erie project, and the socioeconomic frontier of expansionism and growth. Scepticism went side by side with enthusiasm, however. "The canawl! The canawl!" jeers one character. "I'll spit you all the canawl you'll get!" Ejecting his tobacco juice, he continued in what Adams calls his "hoarse basso" to chant a rhyme of the period: "Clinton, the federal son-of-a bitch / Taxes our dollars to build him a ditch."

In *Canal Town* Adams drew upon his experience with detective fiction and medical journalism, as well as his long kinship with the Erie. Focusing upon Dr. Horace Amlie, a class of 1818 graduate of Hamilton College, and Aramintha "Dinty" Jerrold, who becomes his wife, the novel is rich in characters caught up in the effects of what Adams calls "the alien irruption" the coming of the canal represented. Genter Latham and his daughter Wealthia represent the prevailing social order, and Silverhorn Ramsey, "canaller by trade," the spirit of adventure on the new canal. Silverhorn's love affair with Wealthia, and her pregnancy and death, may be viewed as an allegory of the effect of the canal on the old social structure. Genter Latham and his socially elite position are completely shaken by the book's end, while Dr. Amlie and the canallers have created a more democratic social order in the canal town.

Other characters are authentic to the times. T. Lay, an archetype of frontier mercantilism, "trafficked in anything and everything vendible." Ephraim Upcraft is an honest lawyer who buys "uncurrent notes." The Rev. Theron Strang is Palmyra's respectable clergyman, and the Rev. Philo Stickel is an itinerant revivalist who discourses on "The Seven Plagues of the Erie." They are, he avers, harlotry, blasphemy, bastardy, drunkenness, rioting, and chills-and-fever. (The last one "counts as two," he said.) Various other persons fill the novel as well, and the use of canal argot and regional speech provides examples of the vocabulary of the times.

Adams' regionalism, along with his deep feelings for the Old Erie, are well illustrated in a scene where Dr. Amlie, as a young doctor newly arrived in a bustling canal town, rides out to see for himself the building of the Big Ditch. The novel speaks of the great cut as it pushed slowly east and west (by starting the Erie project at the proposed canal's approximate midpoint near Rome, New York, building time was minimized as the canal construction could proceed both east and west at the same time.) Amlie saw a hundred men and a score of horses sweating and straining, "dragging dredges, plucking out recalcitrant stumps as a dentist plucks out a broken root." With pick and shovel the canal workers dug out obstructing boulders, fashioned towpaths and berms, "toilfully embodying the dream of DeWitt Clinton, the pride of the Empire State, the longest, deepest, mightiest canal in all history." Amlie felt his pulse stir when a gang of workers, pushing their new Brainerd wheelbarrows, lifted their rough voices in a song of the Ditch: "We are digging the Ditch through the gravel /Through the gravel and mud and slime, by God! / So the people and freight can travel / And the packets can move on time, by God!" It was a vision of expanding America, he thought, and he hummed along with them.

Banner by the Wayside (1947), which came next, is the story of the Thalia Dramatic Company. In the 1830s this traveling troupe, with its great "T" flag, brought "illusion and delight," said Adams, "to the dark fringes of civilization." The novel is pure costume romance. The New York *Herald Tribune* reviewer said the novel "has the same relation to reading that ice cream has to eating — rich, healthful, tasty and appropriate at any time for anybody." The spicy, coarse chatter of upstate New York in canal days is there, and many characters and incidents are drawn from Erie legend. The relatively simple plot revolves about the protagonists, Endurance "Durie" Andrews, a foundling, and Jans Quintard, whom she meets at Harvard College. Her upbringing, by a chauvinist bookseller who felt that marriage was a diatribe, resulted in a feminist desire to matriculate at her foster father's *alma mater* in Cambridge, where, as a matter of course, she finds Jans Quintard aligned with the Corinthians, whose motto, *Caveat puella,* is chauvinistically masculine, too. As an actress Durie later becomes Thalia's "Le Jeune Amour."

The Erie Canal is a constant backdrop to the "T." From the time Durie sets out on the towpath with a worldly wise female companion, the novel takes the reader along the canal and into hamlets in upstate New York. At one of the inns, Durie's friend raises her glass in a ribald toast. "Here's to path and berm and free passage west," she said, "and may our roads never spread wider than a spinster's knees." As she travels the towpath, Durie meets a twenty-year-old hoggee employed by Captain Bully Suggs of the *Water Witch,* who turns the lad out while withholding his $10 season's wages, but then she meets Deacon Gildersleeve of the *Peace-on-Earth,* whose hoggee, in contrast, was so well clad that he was "a phenomenon in that ill-used calling." The deacon, one notes amusedly, freighted rum and whiskey. Dinty also meets the *Merry Mount,* "the dandiest Durham on the Erie," with a crew of Harvard roisterers who later follow the theatre troupe from town to town to watch her performances. Adams' novel includes other curious characters, too—like Mr. Gospel, keeper of Auburn's famed state prison; Lucky Seven Smith, a bounty hunter; Pig Baker, the municipal swineherd of Albany; and Four-skate Pilkington, who escaped from a Pennsylvania sheriff by a demonstration of quadrupedal skating on the Susquehanna that took him across the state line into the more friendly New York.

New York's cholera epidemic of the 1830s occupies the concluding chapters. Many persons felt that the plague followed the Erie, and, with the uncertain state of medical science of the period, the price of camphor (a popular "defense" against cholera) went up to five dollars a pound along the canal. Since boats were suspected spreaders of the disease, a burned-in letter "C" served to brand those thought to be carriers. In an article written for the *New York Folklore Quarterly,* Adams provided the historical details upon which the events in his novel are based, and he later included a story about the plague in his *Grandfather Stories.* In *Banner by the Wayside,* medical supplies are run up the canal by Jans and Four-skate, who at one point find their way into Syracuse blocked by fearful and adamant town officials. Although the governor himself had given them a warrant for priority passage through all the Erie's locks, Syracuse officialdom was unmoved. Knowing how badly the people needed the drugs, Quintard marshals the crews of several canal boats to help get the medicine to the city docks. Eriemen, loyal to the tradition of the canal and always eager for mayhem, responded willingly. Before long, Quintard's boat was snugged up at Salinas Basin, and the anticholera drugs were distributed. In the doing, *Banner by the Wayside* also gets its "canal novel" fight scene.

Sunrise to Sunset (1950) is a novel about the Troy mills. More than a hundred pages go by before *canawlers* or the word "Erie" appears, yet it is very much a canal novel. Across the Hudson River from Watervliet (which served as the Erie's eastern terminus) Troy was a very active canal town in the hurly-burly 1830s. It was there that many of the boatyards were located and where canallers often showed up, fresh off the boats with pay from Utica or Buffalo in their hands. The plot concerns the love of Obedience "Becky" Webb, a young factory worker, for Guy Roy, a manufacturer of the first detachable collars. As a child, Becky becomes a bobbin-doffer in the Eureka Mills, owned by Gurdon Stockwell, "the most influential mill owner in Troy." Although Stockwell thinks of himself as a man of principle and the townspeople consider him a pillar of the community, Guy Roy seems to demonstrate much more concern for his fellow citizens. In some ways Becky and Guy have affinities with Dinty Jerrold and Horace Amlie (in *Canal Town*): both Becky and Dinty are children when they first meet their beloveds, and both all but worship the men; both men are high-principled persons, though not necessarily appreciated by the townsfolk in the respective novels; and both are innovators, too, who bring about enduring social reform.

Sunrise to Sunset (the title refers to the working hours of the mills) has ingredients similar to Dreiser's *An American Tragedy*: a factory girl's pregnancy, a surreptitious disclosure to the lover, an attempted abortion, and the girl's death — accidentally, ironically, at the hand of the lover. Furthermore, Gurdon Stockwell's story is an American tragedy of the 1830s, for Adams provides authentic details about the tragic situation in early American mills. The principal role of the Erie boaters in the novel comes in a scene of mob violence. The townsfolk, bent on lynching an innocent man whom they assume to be a murderer, are reinforced by the canallers, fresh in off the boats and eager for mayhem. Stockwell ameliorates the townspeople with his oratory, but the boaters are eager for a fight. Just as the canallers are rallying to help out "Judge Lynch," a seasoned canaller — a packet captain in a resplendent uniform — tells them, "Hold your broadside."

"Trigg! Bull Trigg!" The words passed through the crowd accented with respect.

The man was built like a bull: vast chest, bulky shoulders, neck like a tree-bole supporting a craggy head. He stood above Stockwell's six feet by a good three inches and looked to outweigh him two stone or more. Solid and uncompromising, the man with the gun said, "What do you do on my premises, Captain Trigg?"

"Will you put down that gun and run me off?"

"No. I am no brawler."

"I'll lay you a test."

"State it."

Captain Trigg asked if Gurdon Stockwell would fight him, with the alleged murderer going to the winner. Stockwell wanted to be sure he understood the Erie captain. "If I fight and best you," he asked, "will this mob disperse peacefully to their homes?" The crowd roared its disapproval, crying "Hemp for both of 'em." Trigg was not to be put off. "Tell you what," he said to Stockwell, "I'll make a bargain with you just the same." While he admitted he couldn't speak for the frenzied mob, he told Stockwell that he had "thirty-forty rough-and-tumble Erie men here." If Stockwell bested him, the canallers would fight for Stockwell against the mob. The canallers agreed, with a "Right-o, Cap!" and the "The Ee-rye-ee forever!" As Adams put it, "Little did the canallers care on which side they fought, just so the battle was a good one."

The ensuing fight between the wealthy mill owner and Bull Trigg provides *Sunrise to Sunset* with its version of an Erie novel's big fight. It is short and violent. When Stockwell does indeed best Trigg, the canallers join forces with the Stockwell men: "We're your men," they said, "you're the boss." A man's word was his bond on the Old Erie.

Adams wrote other Erie books, fiction and nonfiction. His *The Erie Canal* (1953) for the Landmark series of junior books has become a classic of its kind; and his collection of reminiscences in *Grandfather Stories* is a potpourri of canal lore. In his *Chingo Smith of the Erie Canal* (1958), an Horatio Alger tale for younger readers, an upstate lad rises to the position of packet skipper ("the youngest shipmaster on Erie water"). The story opens in "Eighteen Hundred and Frozen-to-Death" (1816), known as the year without a summer, as a waif named Chingo Smith travels with other delinquent youths (called "runagates" in the vernacular of the day) who roamed the towpath. In a construction job digging Clinton's Ditch, his first meeting with the canal's mud and mire disillusions him so much that he is turned against the canal and all it stands for. But he takes an old cinderwench's advice about education being "the biggest thing in the world."

Chingo seeks out the Learned Tinker, a mender of pots who teaches him to read and write. He next learns self-defense from prizefighter Terrible Tigg, a skill that proves useful more than once along the canal. He even overcomes his early dislike of the canal, as he gradually comes to feel he is part of a glorious enterprise. By novel's end a reader will have discovered that Adams' *Chingo Smith of the Erie Canal* is as rich in social history and canal lore as are his and Edmonds' adult books.

In several of the novels in Samuel Hopkins Adams' wide repertoire, we find a deep sense of the grandeur and greatness which the Erie Canal represented to nineteenth-century America. As much as any other writer he was able to capture the meaning of the Old Erie in its heyday. With his novels and stories based upon New York State's colorful past, it is not difficult to realize how Sam Adams could recall that as a boy he "had nothing but pity . . . for those unfortunate children who lived in canal-less regions."

Fiction for All Ages

Other novels about the Erie canal period were published both before and since the work of Edmonds and Adams. In addition to adult novels, books for younger readers abound. Canal-based stories seem to have a natural appeal for children and teenagers, just as the canal itself once had. A flourishing part of American literature, they can be both entertaining and educational, offering many different, interesting facets of boating life. Enid LaMonte Meadowcroft's *Along the Erie Towpath* (1940), for example, is typical of the modern juvenile novels which deal in their entirety with the canal. In this novel David Burns, one of six orphaned youngsters, runs away from his Aunt Polly to take a canal job on the *Flying Cloud* at thirty-five cents a trip; later works for the book boat aptly named *Encyclopaedia;* and finally is reunited with his brothers and sisters in Buffalo, where the family watches DeWitt Clinton and the *Seneca Chief* begin the celebration marking the opening of the Erie Canal in 1825. There's even a young reader's mystery novel set on the canal: *Canalboat Mystery* (1963) by Lois Benedict, who grew up near the Erie's western terminus. Both Random House's Landmark and the American Heritage Junior Library series include books on the Erie, as does Grosset and Dunlap's "We Were There" series.

James Kirke Paulding's short story, "The Ride of Saint Nicholas on Newyear's Eve," and Jacob Abbot's novelette, *Marco Paul's Travels and*

Adventures in the Pursuit of Knowledge on the Erie Canal represent the earliest fiction about the Erie. Abbott's story involves a young boy whose tutor, named Forester, seeks to interest the boy "in the acquisition of knowledge" by travelling on the canal. This field trip approach to education works well, for Marco Paul finds much of interest along the Erie. Aboard a westbound boat from Albany, he learns about packets and line boats, feeders supplying water to the canal and waste weirs carrying water away from it, and weighlocks where a boat's cargo weight was determined. He and Forester also became acutely aware of the sleeping problems aboard a crowded packet, as well as the sometimes humorous ways passengers resolved their dilemmas. Juvenile and didactic though it is, *Marco Paul's Travels and Adventures* is an early part of the literary history of the canal novel.

It was more than half a century later that a major novel appeared that drew significantly upon the canal. Edward Noyes Westcott's novel, *David Harum*, as already indicated, is important for its delineation of the stereotype of a congenial, eccentric upstate New Yorker. Based on an actual person (David Hannum, of Homer, New York), the novel's David grew up in central New York and worked on the Erie Canal in his adolescent years. When he quit the canal at twenty-one "to go into other things," he worked as a lock-keep and later concluded that his canal experience "was putty thorough, take it all 'round." The novel is more important to the literary history of upstate regionalism than to a discussion of the Erie novel *per se*, although these are often not mutually exclusive. In the 1930s *David Harum* went to Hollywood about the time Janet Gaynor and Henry Fonda were doing Edmonds' *Rome Haul* as a Fox Film. Will Rogers played the title role, but the Erie Canal was not even mentioned in the screen version.

Among the books which Walter D. Edmonds cites as having had an influence on him is Herbert Quick's *Vandemark's Folly* (1922), a semi-autobiographical novel about a Dutch-American youth who migrated westward to Iowa. The novel opens with a young Jacob Teunis Vandemark marvelling at canallers. "I used to go down by the canal and watch the boats go back and forth," he says, adding that he often sat on a stump by the towpath "so close to it that the boys driving the mules or horses drawing the boats could almost strike me with their whips, which they often tried to do as they went by." There was a lock nearby, but he seldom went near it, he said, because "all the drivers were egged on to fight each other during the delay at the locks, and the canallers would have been sure to set them on me for the fun of seeing a fight."

When he was thirteen, Jacob ran away from home to become a hoggee for Captain Eben Sproule, and for several years he witnessed canal life both good and bad from Buffalo to Albany. But Jacob was caught

in another current, that of the westward movement. He moved to the call
of the prairie winds, far from Erie country.

Nebraska Coast (1939) by Clyde Davis is also concerned with emigra-
tion west, in this case to "Nebrasky" in 1861. When Clint Mcdongall's father bought a canal boat to make money hauling, his mother saw little
good in the plan or in the Erie. Their pastor, she said, held that "canal-
boating can't last much longer. All the rotten characters in the country
are being gathered right on the Erie Canal," but the elder Mcdongall went
right ahead repainting his boat "a flaming scarlet and the cabin yellower
than a lemon." Clint became towpath driver and his older brother, Allen,
was steersman. "It was all very exciting," the lads found, and the reader
can gain an insight into the appeal the canal seems to have had for youth
in its heyday.

The Ring Buster (1940) by James Monroe Fitch is a novel about the
days of young Grover Cleveland, when Samuel J. Tilden was governor of
New York. It is also a canal novel. Its protagonist, Tim Brady, "born on
the wrong side of the Canal," fits the Horatio Alger mold, as he rises from
towpath hoggee to greater things. The locale is western New York in the
1870s, and the boy-girl plot (she's from the right side of the canal) is equally
Alger formula: when the eighteen-year-old Tim Brady saves Mary Wade
from the clutches of a canal bully in the Gasport area, the ensuing romance is never in doubt.

The Ring Buster is a good example of Erie fiction: the times are depicted appropriately, the characterizations are decently drawn, and typical
canal types fill the pages. Bill Wade, Mary's brother, is a canal engineer
who collects evidence against a "Canal Ring"; Ezra Baldwin and Silas
Latham are nefarious contractors engaged in maintaining and repairing
sections of the canal. Jerry Sykes is a Twainian town drunkard, Red Moll
a down-to-earth tavernkeep who used to be Jerry's wife, and Bud Haynes
a one time canal bully who throws in with the do-gooders and marries
a Wild West circus woman named Lotta Tubbs. Grover Cleveland plays
a prominent part as a Buffalo lawyer, and the later president's morality
and sense of rightmindedness in government pervade the novel. Governor
Tilden (the "ring buster" of the title) was a warm advocate of the canal.
"I am proud of the Erie Canal," he says. "It has made New York an empire
within an Empire. . . . There is something about the canal that appeals
to the hearts of the people."

While few novels reach either the critical acclaim or the popularity
of those by Edmonds and Adams, it should be clear that the Erie Canal
has made its mark in literature as well as in history. Its influence on literature other than the novel has been considerable, too — in poetry and drama,
and in numerous children's books. In the early nineteenth century, Wil-

liam Dunlap put actresses and actors into roles on *A Trip to Niagara,* and minstrel shows and reviews such as *The Grip* (which featured the tune "Oh! Dat Low Bridge!") kept canalling days in the public mind. Regional dramatists in the twentieth century continued to ride Erie water. Canal lore plays a part in "A Dam for Delta" (1957) by Thomas F. O'Donnell, a one-act play produced by the Utica College Gaslighters. A "gang from the Erie canawl" join other Yorker characters in viewing the marvelous hoax of 1869 in *The Cardiff Giant* (1949) by A. M. Drummond and Robert E. Gard, in which the boaters sing the ballad "the E-ri-e."

Yet the Erie Canal, as previously noted, has been of greater influence on fiction writers than on those of any other genre. In the area of junior books and young adult literature alone, the canal has provided setting, characters, and themes for a large number of books. Novels about the canal—both for adults and younger readers—seem to share a number of conventions and motifs, many of them traceable to the canal novels of Edmonds and indicative of that writer's influence on the genre. While there is no definitive model for a "canal novel," the following motifs and conventions are well-established:

1. The setting is the Erie Canal or a village along the canal, as in *Sunrise to Sunset, The Ring Buster, Rome Haul,* and *Erie Water.*

2. The dialogue is filled with what I have termed "canalese" or canal talk, including authentic colloquialisms and regional speech common to the period, and terms or expressions that are the recognized vernacular of boaters.

3. The plot involves a ragamuffin (like Chad Hanna or Chingo Smith) or a naive country lad (Dan Harrow, Jerry Fowler, etc.) who becomes successful as a result of combining native Yankee/Yorker ingenuity with the opportunities offered by the Erie enterprise. The kind of plot, in its general theme, is really a version of the Alger rags-to-riches formula set on Erie water.

4. The plot involves a befriended runaway. Examples of this narrative element include Jacob Vandemark befriended by Captain Sproule (in *Vandemark's Folly*); Tim Brady befriended by the Wades (*The Ring Buster*); Obedience Webb protected by Guy Roy (*Sunrise to Sunset*); and Chad Hanna taken in by the Huguenines who owned the circus in *Chad Hanna.* Similarly, juvenile heroes like David Burns (*Along the Erie Towpath*) and Chingo Smith (*Chingo Smith of the Erie Canal*) benefit from meeting Samaritans along the towpath.

5. There is a major fight scene, often forming an important part of the narrative. Begun by Edmonds in *Rome Haul* and evident in the works of Fitch and Adams, depictions of the fighting canawler reflect the brawling times as well as the sometimes exaggerated folklore surrounding the

now nostalgic days of Erie boaters. Fights among boaters, between boaters and rafters, or between both of them and the seemingly universally disliked locktenders were apparently common occurrences along the canal, where tempers ran high and patience was short. Sometimes, it has been alleged, fighting (as in the old West) simply was a way of exerting one's masculinity, or just breaking the monotony of the dull routine of an ordinary boater's unglamourous life. At any rate, a confrontation between hero and canal bully is often an integral part of a canal novel. When Dan Harrow and Jotham Klore meet in *Rome Haul,* for example, it is as much a showdown as that occurring in any Western novel or screen play about the old West.

The canal novel can adventurously recreate another age, when the nation was young in spirit and many a youngster aspired to be into canalling. It was a time when the towpaths of the East teemed with all manner of folk, from boaters and other working men and women to fashionable tourists and immigrant passengers. Fiction about canal times in upstate New York now has a substantial literary history. By any standard, the canal novel has been a popular genre with writers and with the reading public. In the hands of a talented romanticist like Samuel Hopkins Adams or a master storyteller like Walter D. Edmonds, it makes a worthy contribution to regionalism and our literary tradition.

Literary Versions
of Ethnic History
from Upstate New York

10

JOHN M. REILLY

To ACQUIRE DESIGNATION as an ethnic American is also to be given a
historical role. One will of course be part of a minority, except possibly within an established neighborhood enclave, and the object of study
and concern for the majority society. It will be equally the case that the
others for whom one is a social issue will have seen to it that the difference
from the norms of language, appearance, faith, or custom that makes up
ethnicity is accompanied by some degree of social prejudice and economic
hardship. Settlement and development of the United States proceeded by
forced transportation and immigration, events of a magnitude and consequence that transformed history from the actions of a select heroic band
into a mass experience. Every migrant, every settler and worker became
a participant in the making of the nation; all issues of social change became linked to the mass experience. To the ethnic American, therefore,
the most personal feelings and conduct have their historical dimension,
for in its prospects and limitations individuality derives from the historical peculiarity of immigration to America.

Unquestionably a sense of the historical significance of ethnicity motivates readers of fiction written in relation to the ethnic experience. Aware
of the absence of ethnic writing from the canon of American literature
established by anthologists and designers of school curricula, readers may
well seek out works that promise to portray underrepresented people. If
those people are like oneself, the desire to read an Irish-American, a Polish-
American, or an Italian-American writer amounts to a wish to legitimate
common experience as eligible for literary status. If the writer is ethnic
but not of one's own background, the wish might be as simple as wanting
to know how others have endured the conflicts of culture in America. Some-

times the desire for authentication or for documentary information is accompanied by a political motive as well. Expression of ethnicity in the readily apprehensible form of narrative fiction gives popular currency to the values and outlook of the community. This motive is the source of the concern of partisans for positive images and the cause of such dismay as that described by Philip Roth in *The Ghost Writer* when Nathan Zuckerman's family recoils in painful anticipation of the contribution Nathan's short story will make to anti-Semitism. There also may be a moral motive for reading ethnic fiction, namely, the assumption that an ethnic vantage point on American experience has exceptional credibility by virtue of the fact that those who have paid their dues in suffering or demeaned status see reality with spectacles that penetrate delusion and sentimentality.

Legitimation, documentation, reinforcement, perception of truth—each of these presumed functions of ethnic fiction is laudable, but none is based upon entirely accurate suppositions about how literature works. It is no wonder there is confusion of motives, for it is after all by its capacity to intensify the representation of experience that fiction is such an appealing way to examine the living of ethnic history. Yet that very intensity results from what might be called the unreality of literary means. The writer disturbs and deforms the conventional or natural way of using language. This may be apparent in manipulation of the sequence of time, the devising of scenes carrying a heavy burden of symbolism, or the lavishing of detail in portrayal of character; but even in innocent, seemingly reportorial writing there is at the very least an unreality of selectivity. Readers are correct to seek ethnic history in fiction, but it is necessary to say that the history is enacted in the writing and in the reading. The mass experience that becomes the source of ethnic identity is background reference for the fiction, while in the foreground of the narrative itself a writer, using the chosen means of literature, organizes an interpretation or version of ethnic reality that is at one and the same time the author's attempt to cope with the historically generated issue of ethnicity in America and an invitation for readers to experience the peculiar reality of the interpretation.

By this reasoning, then, the significance of upstate New York ethnic writing does not lie in provision of pictures of specialized ethnic experience in Rochester, Utica, Gloversville, or Albany. In devising a plot, choosing details, and projecting a voice, the writers enact their own historical situation, and by adopting a literary form and then modifying or reforming it in accordance with their conception of experience, the writers carry upstate ethnicity onto a historical stage where the purpose of action is creation of an affecting narrative capable of representing the writer's own sense of ethnicity. Four authors publishing over a period of forty-five years in the twentieth century serve to illustrate the process of creating the ethnic narrative in upstate New York.

Joseph Vogel began publishing short fiction in 1926, the year he graduated from Hamilton College. Working as a reporter on a trade paper and later as editor of a business magazine, he made time after hours to write stories, several of which appeared in the famous *American Caravan* anthologies. Like most prose writers, however, Vogel's chosen form was the novel. He reports writing and discarding four attempts at long fiction before 1935 when Alfred A. Knopf published *At Madame Bonnard's.* The reviews were everything a young writer might wish, and together with other successes showed the possibility of Vogel being very much part of the contemporary literary scene in New York. Besides regular publication in the influential little magazines, he also secured fellowships at Yaddo in 1932 and 1938 and one from the Munson-Williams-Proctor Institute in his hometown of Utica. These awards enabled him to complete his second novel, *Man's Courage,* which appeared in 1938, again as a publication by the prestigious firm of Alfred A. Knopf. There was a third novel, too, *The Straw Hat,* but by the time he completed it, Vogel had found it impossible to maintain his family any longer without full-time employment and therefore entered federal service as an employee of the Bureau of Prisons. The job was so demanding that it effectively ended his writing career until many years later, when he became a writing instructor at Ohio State University (MacDonald).

The outline of Vogel's career shows him in the familiar environment of the writer of the 1930s serving an apprenticeship among his peers, seeking with them the outlets for his creative work that are necessary to become a functioning writer if not an established one. He found sufficient success to certify his talent as genuine, but not the luck, support, or sales to enable him to survive in the mainstream of American writing, and it is important to note that his writing career does show him to be part of that mainstream. *At Madame Bonnard's*, his first novel, is constructed on the pattern of the venerable group tale, recounting experiences of lodgers in a New York City rooming house. The structure is an excellent means of opening up the novel to allow rendition of a cast of particularized characters while suggesting a commonality of experience that offers suggestions of a collective identity. At one and the same time such a construction embodies the supposition of literary realism that character is both individual and representative and also provides the new writer readily managed access to a traditional way of telling a tale. The characters and experience could very well be ethnic, but, as the use of the group tale in war stories or disaster tales indicates, the significance of the form does not demand any commonality beyond proximity. It would require the application of a writer's specialized purpose to convert the form into support of an ethnic theme.

That specialized purpose appears in Vogel's second novel, *Man's Courage,* which displays Polish-American ethnicity in the development of the character of the protagonist Adam Wolak, a massive man whose dependence on physical strength and elemental love of nature links him to the peasantry. Resident for eighteen years in Genesee — that is, Utica — Adam is presented with the opportunity to become a citizen of the United States by Mrs. Janis, a political appointee of Alderman D'Amico, whose interest in helping immigrants rests on the addition they can make to the numbers of voters indebted to him. The lessons Mrs. Janis gives Adam are patronizingly simplistic. She explains, for example, that America is not a democracy but a republic: "A Democracy is direct rule by the masses, and when you have such a government you can be sure you have no respect for life and property, what you have is mobocracy. A Republic, on the other hand, is a representative form of government, where representatives are duly elected for their capability, and when you have that, as opposed to government by the masses, then you have respect for law, justice, and progress" (65). The reason for making the point about a republic, Mrs. Janis assures Adam, is to show him how fortunate he is. Unlike a native-born American, he does not have to live twenty-one years under the government before he can vote. "Just think, an uneducated immigrant comes here from the old country, where all he knew was poverty and misery, and after only five years he can enjoy the full privileges of citizenship" (65–66). And, in case he does not fully comprehend representational government, there is the example of Genesee, the first ward of which is represented by Joseph D'Amico. "He's a wonderful man! He has accomplished marvels for the first ward!" (66)

The parody of American civics lessons is matched by the satiric representation of Adam's experiences in the relief station where, since he is unemployed, he must endure the delays and misunderstandings of a bureaucracy contemptuous of those who seem unable to help themselves. Functioning to degrade and suppress people like Adam, the system is his nemesis. At each point of turn in the plot the system demeans Adam, until the legalistic demand for the eviction of his family from a low rent house results in his being shot dead by uniformed marshalls. Actually, there has been a legal error. Families with a sick child cannot be evicted, but correction of the ironic error, even if accomplished before Adam's death, would hardly soften the point that the organized agencies of society, including the church, are the foes of this ethnic hero. They have no intention of permitting him entry into complete citizenship and use their ethical and political teachings as means of controlling the perceived threat of the people presumed to be unassimilable. On the level of plot, then, *Man's Courage* works to portray an irresolvable conflict arising from ethnic difference, a conflict that eventuates in victimization; yet for several reasons it would be inappropriate to describe Vogel's narrative as exclusively a tale of the victim.

Though he perishes in conflict, the protagonist lives a life enriched by contact with other immigrants and nurtured by his family. He is no mere brute, as those who mean to control him assume; nor is he powerless, as his fate suggests. Adam Wolak rages justifiably, sustains an ethical outlook on life that keeps him from temptation, and demonstrates a capacity for commitment to his fellows; thus he is a humanized character directed by values and feelings that give his fated end a quality of tragedy. Moreover, the narrative voice — a traditional third person — identifies with Adam's perspective so that the powerful presentation of the crushing system of organized welfare and politics is associated with the evaluation made by Adam himself. The evident parody of the citizenship lessons and the actions of the directors of relief programs, recounted with such extremity that they become satiric, appear infuriatingly ridiculous because the novel has established Adams as a dignified, worthy man. Adam may be marginal to the agencies of society, but he is the ethical norm providing the measures of conduct properly attributed to a hero.

Observation that the novel places an immigrant peasant in the role of tragic hero within a plot of victimization does not exhaust the ethnic significance of the narrative, for *Man's Courage* works also as social criticism and, beyond that, as an exploration of the historical experience of ethnicity. The conflict between Adam and the destructive system constitutes a struggle between visions of life. The vision contained in the simplistic behavior of Mrs. Janis and the relief workers amounts to a bare ideological treatment of people. It is driven by a fear of the immigrant working class to distort American political philosophy in order to justify denial of sympathy and humane treatment. It asserts the accepted notion that one's initiative can overcome adversity in order to universalize exploitation. In that respect the values of a majority society are abstracted for use as means of forestalling acceptance of the minority. In his opposing view, Adam values a fuller way of life, an ideology that has place in it for all.

The conflict between a reductionist ideology and a full way of life finds its fullest play through the provision of a special historical context for the events of Adam Wolak's life. As the novel opens, Adam has received a letter written in German and dispatched from Czechoslovakia that contains news of his brother's role in the revolt of Viennese workers against the Dollfuss government in 1934. As the letter relates events, it becomes clear that Andrew Wolak had died in a struggle betrayed by reformism. The workers' unity and heroism would have prevailed had not the leadership compromised the socialist values that instigated revolt. Since Adam does not read German he must have someone else read the letter, and, when he does, news of the glorious battle of a workers' army inspires the immigrant neighborhood and wins for Adam fame as the brother of a workers' hero. It is against the background of these events that the plot of *Man's Courage* evolves, making clear that Adam's resistance and rage against the dehumanizing system in Genesee is an equivalent to Viennese revolt. The radical orientation provided by the letter gains reinforcement in the narrative from explanatory statements such as one on solidarity of workers presented by an organizer for unemployment councils (227–28) and from principled action such as Adam's refusal to take a job at Alderman D'Amico's business when he discovers that the unionized workers are on strike.

The effect of providing a historical context of workers' struggle is to establish the troubles faced by Adam Wolak in Genesee as part of a pattern of broader social issues: his individual experiences are cast always in collective terms. What happens to Adam is everyone's fate. Appropriately, then, after Adam's death the novel moves to its close with scenes showing how his funeral generates a collective wrath, producing in his victimization a spirit to achieve a genuinely democratic society.

In his study *The Radical Novel in America* Walter Rideout classifies *Man's Courage* as a bottom dog novel (185), a category of works about the lowest group in society. While the unemployed immigrant would seem the lowest social order, Vogel's novel can hardly be said to portray the lumpen proletariat. Wolak is out of work, but he lives his social role within an environment that replaces what it lacks in material sustenance with active values. His world is complete in culture, despite the denial of political citizenship. Still, in reading *Man's Courage* one is aware of absences in the narrative of an immigrant's life, and it is perhaps these that led Rideout to consider the novel a representation of deracinated life. There are few details of language or custom, little reference to traditional ways of life, or to the problem of adjusting inherited patterns of conduct to the new American experience. In place of an expected ethnic texture we find references to economic class that direct us to view Wolak's career under the aspect of political economy, which simply means that Vogel's narrative is determined both by desire to relate immigrant experiences and by the imperatives of class analysis. The result is a formulation that takes ethnicity as a given bedrock for the story but conceives historical identity more broadly. Regardless of how one may view ethnicity in the hierarchy of variables that signify identity — and we are reminded that in *Beyond the Melting Pot* Glazer and Moynihan assert that their investigations show ethnicity and religion to be the primary designations for residents of New York City in the 1960s (314–15)—the point at issue here is neither accuracy in reflecting the findings of empirical studies nor personal agreement. Rather, critical study demands that we see Vogel's selection of a genre of fiction as *his* way of encountering history, the form he gives to the experience of being an ethnic American.

A strongly contrasting formulation of the ethnic story appears in Jerre Mangione's *Mount Allegro,* which employs an autobiographical voice in an account of successful assimilation into American mainstream society. That assimilation can be accomplished without painful separation from one's roots is signified by the dominance in *Mount Allegro* of a secure narrative voice that memorializes the author's Italian-American neighborhood in Rochester. Mangione organizes his story into categorical chapters on religion, superstition, love and sex, family relations, law and crime, etc. Centering each chapter on richly detailed anecdotes involving family and neighborhood friends, he reports behavior and conversation characterizing the texture of first and second generation Sicilian immigrant culture.

A chapter on language illustrates the function of the categorical chapters. "Talking American" is its title. Family content is provided by accounts of his mother's attempt to keep the native language pure by forbidding the children to speak English in the household and by recollection of his father's pride in achieving mastery of the new language. Of course, his father's way inevitably becomes the way of the community, as is made clear by references to the change dialect undergoes in America. There is, for example, the word *baccauso* which Mangione testifies he used for a lifetime under the impression that it was an authentic Sicilian word until he visited Sicily and mystified Sicilians there by using the word. As it turns out, the word, referring to "toilet," was obviously derived from "backhouse," used by early immigrants to earlier, rural America, passed on to other American Sicilians when they arrived in Rochester, and incorporated into daily speech (52). Linguistically, therefore, adaptation of culture proceeds naturally as part of a process of change that leaves its effect but requires no reflection or self-consciousness.

Until the chapter entitled "American Pattern," the eleventh of fourteen in the book, personal chronology plays little part in Mangione's narrative. With that chapter, however, he relates the move from his neighborhood that accompanied adulthood. Here he explains that like other children of Sicilian parents he was disturbed by the contrasts between the Latin and Anglo-Saxon worlds, felt embarrassed at things his relatives did in public that seemed vulgar, and developed a distorted attitude toward other Americans because of the resentment Sicilians felt about the overcompensating behavior of the sons of poor Italians who became professional men in the community. The presentation of these complex feelings, however, is neither confessional nor painful. The cultural conflict and its emotional burden are generalized as though they were recorded by the mind but failed to affect the inner self in any way that requires reconsideration.

Chronology becomes fully assertive in the final chapters of *Mount Allegro*. "New Bread, Old Wine" tells of Mangione's attendance at Syracuse University, experience accompanied by observation of the aging of his home community, while the last two chapters, based upon a trip to Sicily before World War II, allow him to offer a comparison of the native land and America. Where earlier parts of the book range over time to select incidents so that they seem to compress years in their categorical discussions, the later chapters stretch the time of university study and the visit to Sicily in order to amplify the overt theme of the evolution of an Americanized Sicilian culture and the latent autobiographical theme of Mangione as a representative of that successful amalgamation. In Sicily his interest is captured by character types he recognizes from his Rochester home, but there is no romantic nostalgia. The apparent poverty of the "blighted land" forestalls any desire to heroize Sicily. In place of such feelings there is longing to return to America, his true home.

The anecdotal materials of *Mount Allegro* become personal testament, because each tale and vignette is related in the consistent voice of a reflective narrator who has incorporated the experience of the ethnic community into his own being. As the topical construction of chapters indicates, Mangione reports rather than enacts a process of self-development. In place of an inductive narrative building toward the conclusion of maturity, *Mount Allegro* proceeds deductively with the present self of the narrator as the reference point. In its tone that narrator's voice conveys mastery and the achievement of a distance that permits reasoned control of events that once might have been difficult. Cultural conflict has been overcome and replaced with conviction that amalgamation of cultures can be the satisfying outcome of life in America.

Mount Allegro achieves its effects because the narrative's voice is that of a Sicilian whose mastery of the American language has enabled him to become an accomplished writer. The existence of his book certifies the theme of successful amalgamation of culture, so that with his personal narrative the ethnic Jerre Mangione takes his role upon the historical stage to play the part of a representative man.

To be entirely accurate, the formulation of *Mount Allegro* must be described as a memoir rather than an autobiography, for that older term describes a work of historical witness to notable and illustrative happenings. The self serves as an armature for the memoir, but the subject is less

the unfolding of personality than it is passage through events and relationships that may be known also from other, perhaps more objective, writings. The memoir is the form Mangione chooses for his later volumes, *The
Dream and the Deal* (1972) and *An Ethnic at Large* (1978). These recollections of the Federal Writers Project and the literary milieu of the 1930s
and 1940s show the same secure narrative voice and synthesis of chronology and topicality in structure as does *Mount Allegro,* suggesting by the
similarity that in the selection of a genre allied to historical writing, Mangione assumes the role of a spokesman whose observations of inevitable
cultural change and amalgamation are a template for all ethnic American
experience.

Obviously fiction must establish its connection to history in more
indirect ways than the memoir. The most essential means available to the
fictional genres to introduce a historical discussion into narrative is creation
of characters whose traits and career typify the movement of historical
forces. Such typical characters are the subject of Helen Barolini's panoramic novel of Italian-American experience related through four generations of women whose lives stretch over the century from the foundation
of Garibaldi's New Italy to the time of the American 1960s generation.
The titular character of *Umbertina* (1979) presides in the novel as founder
of the family in America and, by that accomplishment, a source of the
experiences with which her granddaughter and great-granddaughter must
cope.

Umbertina's unusual place in the establishment of a commercially
successful family in upstate "Cato" (not the village west of Syracuse but —
like Vogel's Genesee — Utica, this time with a proper classical twist) figures
as an illustration of differential history that perceives how experiences
among immigrants vary according to gender. In Umbertina's story it is
necessity and a will to survive that motivates her when she takes over direction of the family from her husband Serafino Longobardi, whose health
and ability are sapped in two efforts to make a place in America. As a
woman, Umbertina has no recourse to physical labor to establish herself
in the new land. Rather she must depend upon resourcefulness in applying
herself to available women's tasks among which is, of course, cooking.
From cooking lunches for her husband and other workers she develops
a grocery store and, in time, an importing business that also handles
steamship tickets and even offers banking services to the immigrant community. Single-mindedly she pursues business success without distraction
by sentiment or concession to the social hardships enunciated in a running
commentary by Domenico Saccà, a socialist sensitive to the poverty of
immigrants and their class status. To Umbertina a view of the world that
depends upon class analysis is no more sympathetic than is the tendency

of the poor immigrant to cling to the comfort of the familiar and known. For her the ultimate social unit is the family, and in the circumstances of late nineteenth-century America that is sufficient. Devotion to material success, however, is not without cost. Umbertina is seen in the early pages of the novel as a sensitive, loving woman. Becoming one-dimensional as a consequence of her strength and will, she has found no time for conduct that is not directed to the goal of providing material success for the family. Her children have been educated, while she has remained illiterate; in her strength she has created submissive daughters; in her zealous work she has isolated herself, so that while by the standards she understands as American she has won success, there is no one to whom she can tell the story. Indeed, "at times the doubt came to her whether she had really won, after all. . . . She had seven living children and twenty-seven grandchildren, but to none of them could she really speak" (145–46).

Umbertina's deathbed regret, expressed by her last word "Castagna," a reference to her home in Italy, is the substance of her legacy to a progeny whose stories contain and carry forward Umbertina's. The prologue of the novel, in which her granddaughter Marguerite has a session with her psychiatrist, establishes Umbertina's living presence throughout the narrative, for in analyzing a dream that appears to deal with the need to find her essential self, the analyst instructs Marguerite to seek her truths in the family past. The fact that the interview occurs in Florence and that Marguerite has for eighteen years been married to the Italian writer Alberto Morosini and resident in Italy reinforces the linkage between past and present. The American transplant, disabused of the romance with which she had come to Italy shortly after World War II, discontented with her life because she feels it has been false, and convinced that she must divorce Alberto if she is to be herself must, after all, find out what that self is. She longs for the strength her grandmother had but knows she must above all resolve her relationships with the past if she is to go forward with her life.

The project of the fictional character Marguerite is autobiographical. She must find the materials in her past that can constitute a life in the present. The purpose of her creator, the novelist Helen Barolini, is psycho-historical. By representation of the self-absorbed Marguerite she aims to dramatize the emotional and psychic content of an Italian-American woman's conflicts and identity.

By enclosing the account of Umbertina's immigration to America and her material success between the prologue that introduces her granddaughter and the portion of the narrative that follows Marguerite through her troubles, Barolini folds the present over the past to establish the realm of the novel concerning Marguerite as devoted to consciousness rather than the objective reality in which Umbertina accomplishes her material success. In this way Barolini absorbs the conventional plot of American success stories into narration that uses the conventional plot as background against which to play the more complex problems of psychological survival in the modern world. In its own way this is as much a critique of ideology as is Vogel's parodic presentation of civics lessons. Against the backdrop of rags-to-riches Barolini constructs a narrative proposing that the way of living which popular ideology presumes to describe is for Americans at the very least problematic and eccentric rather than simple and linear.

Casting her characters as women and ethnic, Barolini might be said to be writing realistically, mining experiences that she knows well. Yet there must be an element of choice here, too, and the choice is an innovation upon if not a critique of realism. As noted earlier, concentration upon the lives of women endorses the principle of differential history. It also repudiates the supposition of realism that implies by its emphasis upon empirical rendition of scene and character that the details present in a story constitute the world; what is absent is not objectively real. Giving voice to the women who have usually been given minor roles in realistic fiction and setting them in the center of interwoven narratives so that their experiences and thoughts form the substance of the novel is to define the women as historical actors and to modify our understanding of other texts in which the women were not subjects. Similarly, Barolini's representation of ethnicity as a continuing issue in a genre — realistic fiction — depending so heavily for episode and scene upon the interaction of individuals also modifies the assumptions of fiction. Again the accomplishment resembles Vogel's, but where he uses class identification to link individuals, Barolini displays the power and effect of collective experience through presentation of the way the social experience of an ethnic group shapes individual mentality. Vogel's outlook is socioeconomic, Barolini's social-psychological, each in its own way setting the stamp of ethnicity upon the novel.

The story of Marguerite, the dates of whose life are given as 1927–73, is the most personally psychological of the three narratives in the book. Where Umbertina appears to be representative of the immigrant generation, despite her remarkable individual drive, Marguerite's career in the novel characterizes her by dissociation from her family and preoccupation with introspection. In defiance of her parents' respectability she had eloped as a young woman, and when that marriage was annulled she had immersed herself in sexual adventure. She experiences deracination in remarriage to Alberto, scion of an old Venetian family, and in the relationship with a lover she behaves as a woman desperate to feel the intensity of living on the one hand but pursuing feeling destructively on the other hand. There is, of course, suggestion that Marguerite's anomic condition is the consequence of the bourgeois life into which she was born, but the historical sources of that life escape her ken. She is an heir for whom grandmother Umbertina worked so hard; her fate is to have only the social status Umbertina earned. Practical necessity lacks the power to force Marguerite's energy into a struggle for material survival, and lacking a project greater than herself she cannot organize her resources toward a goal. Absorbed by psychic problems consequent to her inherited class position, and unable to resolve them, she has no reference point for identity and certainly for felt connection to her ethnicity.

It is Marguerite's daughter Tina, born in 1950 and named for her great-grandmother, who achieves a promise of resolution and with it provides to the readers Barolini's thoughtful consideration of the value of ethnicity in American life. Tina is a child of her 1960s generation. Prolonging her studies into a Ph.D. program as much for protection from life as for love of the Italian literature she studies, she benefits from her family's affluence at the same time that she feels critical of them. Still, she has a role model from the past, and finds requisite discipline in the present. Above all, Tina understands the message of Umbertina's life: make a choice.

Three passages in Tina's portion of the novel illustrate her growth to maturity. In the first, she speaks of her ethnic identity to Jason Jowers, a young man she is beginning to realize she loves. "You see," she says, "I have these two things in me that are beginning to be worked out, my work and my Italian-American identity." Jason reminds her that she has always gone to great lengths to make it understood that her mother was American, her father Italian. None of the melting-pot Italian for her. Tina admits the charge, then adds:

> I'm excited by being near Umbertina's birthplace—and excited by her, by her story. Up till now I ignored all that part; my mother's family just wasn't up to my father's side and so I ignored them. But the fact is, you see, that my father's Venetian side is like being Wasp in the States; all well and good, but dying out, enervated, obsolete. The interesting part is the rise of all these new people who get where they are not by privilege or family or connections but just by sheer guts and working hard. I'm beginning to like the southern part of me. (359)

Significantly, Tina makes this statement following a trip to Calabria; the physical journey to her roots has awakened a psychological awareness that she may be shaped by the character of Umbertina whose own character was formed in Calabria.

The second passage relating to the attitudes toward ethnicity appears in a comment by an Italian sociologist about American expectations of

Italy. Tina expresses conventional regret that it is too bad the Italians are losing some of their natural ways of doing things. "Sometimes," she says, "when I see the Italo-Americans, I think it's too bad they left at all." The sociologist replies ironically, "Yes, *that's* the really hard nut to crack, isn't it? You could never have come back to show off your superior taste if they hadn't gotten out in the first place. And they got out to better themselves and use plastic if they want to. But when you come back, you're sorry they're still not what they used to be. *That's* the conundrum of your trip. They advanced you to the middle-class — but you want them to stay peasants" (382). The comment is severe but just, for Tina has another step to take in comprehending Italian-American history.

The opportunity for that comes when she is back in America, planning to marry Jason and staying in his family's home on Cape Cod. She recognizes an equivalence between the old stock Anglo-Saxon Jowers', descended from sea-farers, and the Venetian family of her father, which also gained its wealth and pride from the sea. The Morosinis had been in decline since the early years of the century, while the Jowers' appear to retain their vigor. Yet both Venice and Cape Cod will inevitably return to the sea; by extension of the image, the families will pass too. One need not decide if there is more merit in the ways of one family or the other. What one must do, though, is choose to live a present that accepts the gifts of the past. Symbolizing resolution, Tina plants some rosemary — the family women's plant ever since Umbertina set it in the ground of New York — in the yard of the Jowers home on Cape Cod.

Barolini's novel agrees with Mangione's autobiographical narrative. In the amalgamation of heritage available in the social conditions of America lies strength and security. What Barolini adds, and what distinguishes her novel as an exploration rather than an application of conclusive ideas, is the drama of personality formation. All of the technical choices regarding rendition of time, selection of character, and innovations on the conventions of realism have been made with an eye to discovering the means to account for the evolution of contemporary ethnicity from its origins in immigration and its passage through the homogenizing mainstream of American bourgeois culture. It is entirely fitting that the dramatic account of the choices necessary to sustain life and identity should itself be visibly marked by the evidence of choices of craft, for it is thus that the narrative *Umbertina* becomes the counterpart of the story it tells.

Typified characters such as those in Barolini's *Umbertina* are especially effective for rendering the processes of ethnic history as a central theme of fiction. If, however, a writer wishes to explore subjects other than cultural conflicts or the issues surrounding assimilation, ethnicity must be treated obliquely. Such is the case with William Kennedy, whose trilogy of novels uses the Irish-American city of Albany as setting but occupies the foreground of the narratives with particularized stories of singular character.

A native of Albany, William Kennedy prepared for his career as a novelist by working as a professional newspaper writer. The evident disposition in the novels for collecting and relating tales of neighborhood and political life in the capital city was consistent with the investigative work required for the sort of writing journalists reasonably consider to be history as it happens. Relish for the tale and the speaking voice in which it is normally delivered marks each of Kennedy's Albany novels as well as his most recent book, *O Albany!* (1983), which is a compilation of appreciative accounts of the city's character. Reviewers have been as impressed as other readers by Kennedy's facility for chat and gab, the flow of verbal energy. This man renews the novel by restoring to it the elemental power of storytelling which we associate with the grand sound of a Dickens or a Twain or a Faulkner. Narrative impulse dominates the novels of Kennedy in the way in which in face-to-face encounters the personality of the storyteller dominates the tale, making experiences compelling and characters intriguing by force of the style in which they are presented.

Yet to say Kennedy's writing has elemental power is not to say it is simple, and it is certainly not to imply that it is achieved without art. The measure of the art is its success in making us overlook the fact that the smallest, most localized passage appears authentic because Kennedy has selected diction and construed syntax so that it deviates from the empirical commonplace with a precision that creates unique sound within the echo of expected ordinary language. The effect is to heighten our awareness of language without allowing us to feel that it has been elevated beyond our norms of usage. He helps us to know what we know.

Since *Legs* (1975), the larger structures of Kennedy's fiction have shown a fascination with the interpenetration of history and the telling of the tale. The historical character of Legs Diamond and his shooting on Dove Street in Albany provide the spine of the plot which is fleshed out by the novelist applying imagination to vivifying the life of Legs in his last days. This is not, however, in the conventional sense of the term a historical novel which stresses recreation of costume and setting with a salting of revelation about "the way he really was." Rather, the extent of invention in the narrative makes it into a historical text in its own right instead of a derivation from preceding texts.

Similarly, the next novels in the Albany trilogy, *Billy Phelan's Greatest Game* (1978) and *Ironweed* (1983), also build upon the possibilities of fiction as history. When you think about it, you realize that we know history by the increment of texts: papers, newspaper accounts, research reports, and interpretation upon interpretation. As we pore through these varied writings, the original event elusively slithers through references, cross references, disputed documentation, and corrected accounts, each of them a product of someone or other writing. Perhaps Kennedy sensed the evasiveness of the object when he worked as a newspaper reporter sifting evidence for his daily columns, but in any case his novels show he is fully aware now that fiction offers the chance for substantial historical "truth" precisely because its techniques require the devices of simulation.

In the story of Billy Phelan, a newspaperman — Martin Daugherty — has the privileged position of narrative center. Son of a famous Irish-American playwright, Martin in his personal story conforms to an Oedipal pattern made startling, even rollicking, by the fact that his lust for the maternal figure directs itself toward the woman who had been his father's mistress and the cause of popular scandal, and by the fact that son Martin's desire is satisfied not by just one sexual episode but also in a second opportunity that Martin finds as irresistible as the first. The experiences are replete with bad conscience, reference to castration imaged by reference to the accident that crippled Albany's Henry James the elder, a guilty sense of his parents' observing him while he copulates, and philosophical reflections on the synthesis of generations; but there is also a recognition of sex as fate: "He loathed himself for his own psychic mendacity, for trying to persuade himself he had other than venereal reasons for jingling everybody's favorite triangle. Hypocrite! Lecher! My boy!" (214) The parodic allusion to Baudelaire, and perhaps T. S. Eliot, in the last three words serves as well as any passage to characterize Martin Daugherty, for it shows the self-reflexive mind that seeks the meaning of experiences and the detachment that suits him to be the observer whose interest in the hustler Billy Phelan allows Martin to serve as the historian of Billy's career in the sporting life of depression Albany.

Two additional father-son relationships appear in the texture of the novel. One is that of the McCall family, in which the father is head of the Democratic political organization and the son is kidnapped. The second is the surrogate relationship that develops between Billy, who becomes marked as a man who knows more than he will tell about that kidnapping, and Martin, whose access to the influential columns of a newspaper allows him to redeem Billy from ostracism. These relationships interweave the story of the characters with the broader history of Albany. Calling upon a kidnapping that can be known and documented from sources outside his novel, Kennedy fuses his fictional characters with the record. The line between history as history, which is to say empirically documented happenings in the past, and literature as literature blurs, and the story we read in the present with all of its attendant interpretive detail of subjective thought and feeling becomes the source of our knowledge about everything that it tells.

The historical investigations of Kennedy's novels are related to ethnicity in a fashion very different from Barolini's. The characters are Irish-American, the political organization of Albany is founded on Irish votes, and the neighborhood in which the novel is set is Irish. This pervasive Celticism also dominates Martin's life as son of a playwright described by George Jean Nathan as "more significantly Irish-American than Boucicault or Sheldon" (174). The Irish-American milieu envelops characters and events so completely that conflicts and crises are intraethnic rather than between groups.

The point is emphasized by *Ironweed* (1983), which relates the background of Billy Phelan's father Francis. Francis plays a role in the previous novel where the outline of his life as a baseball player, a negligent father who accidentally caused his infant son's death, and a man who accidentally killed a strike breaker by throwing a fatal stone is recounted when he returns briefly to Albany with a woman companion as down-and-out as he is. In *Ironweed* Francis, once more back in Albany, becomes the protagonist and the instrument of Kennedy's further experimenting with the subjective side of history. The circumstances of Francis' life are associated with the possibilities of Irish working-class life, but from the start Francis' story is his own, representative of the experience of guilt.

Francis has a place in Irish-American history and senses it when he reflects upon his connection with the Daughertys. There was Emmett Daugherty the immigrant, denied a chance to disembark at Albany because of the threat of cholera. Emmett became a labor organizer and leader who lived to see the Irish in control of Albany. Then there was Edward Daugherty, father of Martin and author of the play *The Car Barns* which tells of Emmett radicalizing Francis Phelan and inspiring him to attack scabs. In the play Francis is said to be "liberator of the strikers from the capitalist beggars who owned the trolleys" and is identified with Emmett Daugherty as a Divine Warrior (206). By throwing the first stone in the battle of labor during Albany's trolley strike, Francis became the principal hero. Yet that instrumental role has persuaded him of his guilt for the deaths that ensued, so "he lived all his life . . . unable to see any other force at work in the world that day beyond his own right hand" (206). When he reflects on the past in *Ironweed,* Francis can no longer see broad significance in the remembered events. The story he pieces together is individualized, representative of the experience of personal guilt, not the life of the Irish. A remarkable story it is, too, weaving Francis' memories together as he projects them onto characters created out of the force of imagination in service to psychological need. Opening in a graveyard where he con-

verses with the dead, Francis reanimates the past so successfully that he
re-presents the past in the persons of ghosts who, appearing to be inde-
pendently real, challenge and decry Francis. By generating these figures
out of his past, Francis is generating himself insofar as the ghosts are the
source of the guilt upon which his identity depends.

The rich texture of the Albany novels inspires interpretation. One
yearns for opportunity to discuss them with other readers. Ultimately, however, they stand on their own, just as do *Man's Courage, Mount Allegro,*
and *Umbertina.* All of these texts fulfill themselves without any need for
expert decoding to reveal their intent, and they certainly deserve better than
to be supplanted by a variety of paraphrase that would make them "easier
to read." As objects of critical study they require only acknowledgement
that they are in themselves interpretive products of their authors. As though
in testimony to diversity, each production is different. In some the biography of the author might explain the literary choices, in another perhaps
the author's gender, or the special circumstances of the ethnic group's experience. Common to all, though, is a precedent decision to confront the
issue of ethnicity. In daily experience one may not have a choice about
accepting ethnicity, but in the mind it is different. One chooses ethnicity.
All the more so when it comes to projecting the mind into a literary project. Once the choice has been made for ethnicity, we have the object of
our critical study: the range of technical decisions necessary to convert
perceptions of ethnicity and assumptions about its significance into the
system of a literary text. In this brief examination of four writers who have
chosen an ethnic literary project I have tried to suggest that here we have
such a breadth of formal development, such a subtle connection of literature to life, that no study of upstate New York can afford to overlook its
ethnic writers as a source of vital history.

Works Cited

The American Caravan: A Yearbook of American Literature. Edited by Van Wyck
    Brooks, Alfred Kreymborg, Lewis Mumford, and Paul Rosenfeld. New York:
    Macaulay, 1927. Subsequent volumes edited by Kreymborg, Mumford, Rosen-
    feld as *The Second American Caravan* (1928), *The New American Caravan*
    (1929), *American Caravan* (1931), and *The New Caravan* (1936).
Barolini, Helen, *Umbertina.* New York: Seaview Books, 1979.
Glazer, Nathan and Daniel Patrick Moynihan. *Beyond the Melting Pot: The Ne-
    groes, Puerto Ricans, Jews, Italians, and Irish of New York City.* Cambridge:
    MIT Press and Harvard University Press, 1963.

Kennedy, William. *Billy Phelan's Greatest Game.* New York: Viking Press, 1978.

———. *Ironweed.* New York: Viking Press, 1983.

———. *Legs.* New York: Coward, McCann & Geoghegan, 1975.

———. *O Albany! Improbable City of Political Wizards, Fearless Ethnics, Fabulous Aristocrats & Spectacular Scoundrels.* Albany: Washington Park Press; New York: Viking Press, 1983.

MacDonald, P. R. "The Writer Who Disappeared." *Escutcheon* 3 (Winter–Spring 1968): 5–8.

Mangione, Jerre. *The Dream and the Deal: The Federal Writers' Project 1935–1943.* Boston: Little, Brown, 1972.

———. *An Ethnic at Large: A Memoir of America in the Thirties and Forties.* New York: G. P. Putnam's 1978.

———. *Mount Allegro.* New York: Crown, 1972.

Rideout, Walter B. *The Radical Novel in the United States 1900–1954: Some Interrelations of Literature and Society.* Cambridge: Harvard University Press, 1956.

Roth, Phillip. *The Ghost Writer.* New York: Farrar, Straus and Giroux, 1979.

Vogel, Joseph. *At Madame Bonnard's.* New York: Alfred A. Knopf, 1935.

———. *Man's Courage.* New York: Alfred A. Knopf, 1938.

11   Early Days of the Folklore Renaissance

LOUIS C. JONES

T HE FIRST RECOGNITION that there existed in New York a long tradition of folklore came from the country's first two masters of narrative: Washington Irving and James Fenimore Cooper. As between literature and scholarship, in New York, folklore has been closer to the former than the latter. Many of those who have collected and published and taught folklore have been teachers of English or American literature. It is only recently that trained folklorists have replaced them, but it should be remembered that the trained folklorist in America is a late comer.

Washington Irving came to American literature with a professional admiration for Richard Steele and Joseph Addison and especially Oliver Goldsmith. He too would write a clean, uncluttered prose, project a gentle, humane humor, a patient sympathy with the vagaries of the human mind. His awareness of folklore, as Harold Thompson has pointed out in *Body, Boots & Britches* (118), came with his genes and his upbringing. Having a native Scot for his father and a Scotch maid to sing ballads and tell him tales of the old country when he was a child gave him a taste for the folklore he discovered rambling along the Hudson, dawdling in coves and Dutch villages. Later he came to know Sir Walter Scott and to wish to do for the Hudson what Scott had done for the Tweed.

Irving made adoptive use of the folk motifs he found current in the Hudson Valley. Interestingly enough these same types and motifs were still current as recently as the 1930s and '40s when Harold Thompson's students and mine were collecting in New York State. Pirate lore and tales of buried treasure such as he used in *Tales of a Traveller* and the devil as seen in "The Devil and Tom Walker" were to be heard of in scores of current folk tales. The ghosts and evil spirits encountered in "The Legend

of Sleepy Hollow" and especially the major motif, the hoax, loom large
in our archives. With more than an interest in the purely verbal, Irving
describes the ways of life, the way a room was furnished, the foods the
people ate, the style of architecture, the frolics and dances, the music and
everyday labors. In short, his stories are seasoned with valuable accounts
of folk life.

The second literary pioneer, James Fenimore Cooper, six years
younger than Irving, came from a similar background. They were both
sons of federalist fathers, men of wealth whose fortunes disappeared shortly
after their deaths, forcing the sons to write for a living. And both writers
were financially successful in their craft, both famous not only in this country but in Europe where both stayed in the 1820s and early '30s. There
were also strong differences of temperament: Irving, gently humorous and
often melancholy, while Cooper was more rigid, peppery, and contentious.

Warren S. Walker, a onetime student of Harold Thompson's and
mine, has made a long-term study of the folk elements in the novels of
James Fenimore Cooper, and I shall lean on his excellent scholarship. He
sees Cooper's use of folkloristic elements as a device to "add texture, a
dimension of realism . . . sometimes it provides comic relief; at still other
times it is used thematically" (24). It is material interwoven with the other
elements of his narrative, seldom the dominant, as for example the supernatural often is in Irving's stories. Certainly the descriptions of folk life
and customs are the outstanding traditional components. Church raising,
clearing the forest, shooting of passenger pigeons, seining for Otsego bass,
and the description of Pinkster, the holiday of the slaves in Dutch times,
these are scenes which are invaluable records of common occurrences ne-
glected by most other writers. Walker emphasizes Cooper's attempts at
dialects and his use of proverbs, mostly from the British tradition. Cooper
was also alert to naming patterns, especially those of blacks, Indians, and
Yankees. He writes, too, of various types of men who are popular in folk
legends in this country: the frontiersman, the Indian killers (he must have
heard stories of Tim Murphy, Tom Quick, and Nat Foster as a boy) and
pirates. He uses supernatural motifs far less than Irving, and usually these
are beliefs of simple characters such as sailors before the mast who carefully avoid the seafaring taboos and believe wholeheartedly in such matters as ghost ships.

So we see Cooper utilizing five major folkloristic areas: folk life and
custom, folk speech, legendry and, finally, the supernatural. These two
great literary pioneers were not only aware of the folkloristic level of their
culture but embraced it as they strove for a completeness in their narratives. They were not collectors or scholars but artists and men of their time
using the raw literary materials available to all and recognizable by many.[1]

Sixty years or more ago I found in my father's library an attractive two-volume work by Charles M. Skinner called *Myths and Legends of Our Own Land.* Later I found a companion volume, *Legends and Myths Beyond Our Borders,* published two years later. Bibliographical references uncovered two other related titles, one as late as 1925, but I have been unable to discover anything about the author. I am concerned here with the first of these books, *Myths and Legends of Our Own Land,* a collection of 267 narratives, averaging about 700 words each. Of these, sixty have New York State settings, "gathered from sources the most diverse, records, histories, newspapers, magazines, oral narrative in every case reconstructed" (1, 5). Nowhere does he provide us with the specific source, although it is sometimes as obvious as Irving's *Tales of a Traveller* or *The Sketch Book* or Cooper's *The Spy.* However, these sixty stories are, to my knowledge, the first general collection of New York folklore that we have. For the most part they are local legends, but they include pseudo-Indian lore (tales the white man superimposed on the Indian), tales from the Revolution, stories about place names, some from as far west as Painted Post and Horseheads, and a number of supernatural tales of ghosts, buried treasure, and witchcraft.

Note that Skinner says that in every case the story is "reconstructed," in short, rewritten in his own easygoing and comfortable style. He is deliberately producing a piece of literature, although where we have the source at hand he stays close to it, seldom altering the facts or even the details. The New York material is followed by the other 78 percent from New England, Pennsylvania, the South, the Midwest, the Rockies, the Pacific Coast. It becomes then a very early nationwide collection of traditional local legendry, with the same kinds of emphases we have already described. This is not what the modern scholar wants to accept as folklore, since it is too far from the spoken word of the tradition bearer, but in the 1890s very few were recording the words of the tradition bearers.

The first volume about New York State folklore by an author with academic training in folklore was Emelyn Gardner's *Folklore of the Schoharie Hills* of 1937, but Miss Gardner had done her field work in summers from 1912 to 1918. The work became her Ph.D. dissertation. Describing her field methods, she writes: "Since I am unable to write shorthand, I regret to say that often the language is my own. But I always took copious notes from which I wrote the stories within a short time after they were related to me. If I heard a tale a number of times, I was able to catch much of the vernacular. In case informants were requested to proceed slowly or to repeat passages, they became conscious and stilted or forgot altogether, so that I had to let them proceed in their customary manner, which included a rapid tempo. . . . I have made no attempt to reconstruct or to improve the tales which were told for my entertainment" (100). It would take many inventions and many a long year before the inconspicuous tape recorder could be put on the table and forgotten, but even when that time came there would still be informants who shied away from it and froze into confused silence.

Schoharie County has an interesting history: settled by Palatine Germans, by Dutch, English, Irish, and Scots, dominated by the patroons until the Down-Rent war of the 1840s, mountainous, much of it isolated, much of it little changed from the previous century at the time Miss Gardner was collecting. Quite understandably she often made comparisons to other sections of the Appalachian piedmont. She also brought a new dimension to her study in that she searched for parallels for her narratives in the folk literature of Europe, using Stith Thompson's "The Types of the Folk Tale", published in *Folklore Fellows Communications*. There was no such guide for the songs, games, and folk beliefs, but she tenaciously traced the history and appearances of each item. New York State material had never before been put into this international context and the result was — indeed, still is — impressive.

Miss Gardner found at least two folk heroes still alive in the oral tradition. The first was Tim Murphy from revolutionary times who shot General Fraser, the leader of the Highlanders at the battle of Saratoga, causing the British retreat and the American victory. Murphy was an Indian killer, and there were myriad tales of his outwitting Indians he found in the woods; the most widely circulated tells of how "Once when he was splitting rails, a band of Indians appeared and asked if he could tell them where they would find Tim Murphy. He said he would go help them find him if they would help him split the log on which he was then working. He arranged some on one side, some on the other with their fingers in the crack and told them to pull with all their might. As they were obeying he jerked out the wedge inserted in the log, and snapped the Indians fast. Then he proceeded to scalp them." (26). Every Schoharian Miss Gardner interviewed knew this story, but she also found it in "The Types of the Folk Tale." Another only slightly less colorful character was the great revival preacher, Lorenzo Dow. The story of how Dow "raised the Devil" was told over and over again in frontier New York and especially in Schoharie County where Dow had often preached. The other great source of local legendry and broadside ballads was the Down-Rent war of the 1840s when the tenants refused to let the sheriff and his men sell the farms of delinquent householders.

While she located thirty ghost tales, none of them are very unusual and all can be matched across the state. While there is more witchcraft told of and believed in than one would find in many parts of the state, yet the themes are the most usual ones, concerning the drying up of cows, the failure of butter to come, of cats and millers, black (bad) witchcraft and white (benevolent). There was considerable lore about Dr. Jake Brink who could lift spells and outwit the most potent of the black witches. Miss Gardner gave the tales exhaustive analysis of their origins and parallels. All are of European origin, usually retold in a Catskill setting. The tellers thought of them as local stories and were amazed to discover that they had appeared in books and were told in far-off lands. Some of them were so localized that they had become the "property" of a particular teller and were told only by that person. The section on beliefs covering folk medicine, planting and plant lore, conjuring, marriage charms and taboos and death omens are exactly what one would expect once we had begun to hear from other counties. The important point is that Emelyn Gardner was pioneering and proving what a large part of our folklore is international and universal and how little of it unique.

I did not know Emelyn Gardner, but all the others of whom I shall be writing in this piece were friends or at least acquaintances. Among the closest were Carl and Betty Black Carmer; he dedicated *The Tavern Lamps Are Burning* to my wife and me; we were married at Octagon House and the Carmers were our matron of honor and best man. I wrote the Introduction to *My Kind of Country;* Carl taught in our Seminars on American Culture for many years and was a Trustee of the New York State Historical Association.

Carmer did a year's graduate work in English at Harvard, then taught at Hamilton and the University of Rochester before he went to the University of Alabama where he stayed for six years — asking, listening, watching, noting down. And out of all that came *Stars Fell on Alabama* (1934), a book of experiences, of hearsay, of the lore of blacks and whites, of the magic of place. But Carmer's roots were deep in upstate New York, going back to Dutch immigrants in New Amsterdam crossed later with Scotch aliens from Connecticut. Born in Cortland, raised in Albion, he was — like his father and dozens of other kin — educated at Hamilton College; upstate New York was his kind of country.

Stars Fell on Alabama was a national success. It turned his mind back to York State, and he and Betty Black, whom he had married in New Orleans, began to examine his homeland with a writer's eye and ear. As I wrote long ago, "It was Carmer who first noted the broad band of wondrous happenings that have crossed New York State from east to west, from the Shakers at Lebanon to the Spiritualists in Lily Dale; and it was he who called this path 'The psychic highway.' The wayfarers on that highway were as disparate as they were amazing: Mother Ann Lee, Prophet Joseph Smith, the spiritualist Fox Sisters, the Public Universal Friend" (*My Kind of Coun-*

try xii). It was not only of religionists he wrote, but of Indians, revolutionary soldiers, cavaliers, rascals, and saints in *Listen for a Lonesome Drum* (1936) and *Dark Trees to the Wind* (1949).

He was editor of The Rivers of America series and contributed two volumes, *The Hudson* (1939) and *The Susquehanna* (1955). In all of these books he followed much the same pattern: "He combined his own personal experience and documented research with the oral history of the people of a geographic area to emphasize events as the people remember them as having happened. . . . Carmer knew that what people believe to have happened can have an equal influence on the course of events as what did happen" (*My Kind of Country* xiv). In short, he was concerned with folk history.

He was a great raconteur, and audiences loved to listen as he wove spells with his poetic prose, for while he published only two volumes of poetry there were imagery and rhythms in both his prose and his speech. The wide popularity of his books with their variety of subject matter suggested subjects to a whole generation of younger writers, Henry Christman, Whitney Cross, Lionel Wyld, to mention the first names that come to mind. Each of these men expanded Carmer's chapters into full-length volumes.

Carmer was a romantic in many ways, casting an aura over the state, yet never far from the gritty speech of its people. This was literature which utilized folklore, staying close to the material in both vocabulary, rhythms, and viewpoint but not concerned with the folklore scholar's concern with minutiae. He was the inheritor of the Washington Irving tradition, and yet it was sheer accident that led him and Betty to buy their fabulous octagon house only a few blocks from Irving's Sunnyside.

Harold W. Thompson and Carmer became friends at Hamilton College where Thompson was in the class of 1912 and Carmer in '14. Their paths and interests were tangential and mutually encouraging, but neither influenced the other very much beyond that. Their friendship rested on their common experiences at Hamilton and Harvard, their love for New York State, and their interest in folklore and folk life and in people, especially oddballs and eccentrics.

First and foremost Thompson was a teacher and dedicated to any student who showed any life and intellectual curiosity. At Harvard he studied under the true giants of the English Department: Bliss Perry, William Allan Neilson, George Pierce Baker and, most important, George Lyman Kittredge, whose course in the English and Scottish ballad nurtured the first generation of American folklorists. At first under Neilson and then Perry he wrote his dissertation on the Scotch romantic Henry Mackenzie, a work later expanded to *A Scottish Man of Feeling* (1931), written under one of the first Guggenheim fellowships. He received his doctorate in 1915 and joined the faculty of the New York State College for Teachers (now SUNY Albany) and was there for a quarter of a century before he went to Cornell. As an undergraduate he had been organist at Hamilton, and he was soon organist and choir leader at the prestigious First Presbyterian Church in Albany. He was teaching English and American literature at the college and teaching music, leading the chorus, teaching and coaching debate and on the side serving as review editor of *Diapason,* the magazine of organists. All this he accomplished with gusto, humor, and unrelenting energy despite a life-long major handicap of severe nearsightedness.

I never knew by what stages he moved into the folklore field. His work in Scottish literature, his studies with Kittredge, his own Scotch grandfather, his admiration for Irving, Cooper, Whitman, Sandburg, Frost, his own abilities as a storyteller, all these may have been factors; but also his political sympathies were to the left, rather than to the right and its more aristocratic traditions. I first came to know him slightly in the 1920s; he was an acquaintance of my father's and I took a course in summer school with him in 1928, but it was not until I went to teach at the college in 1934 that we became close friends. He began teaching American Folklore about that same time and I sat in on his one-semester course.

There was no textbook; I have always assumed that it was the first undergraduate course in American folklore, so textbooks were far down the road. But there was shortly a shelf in the library which began to grow. All students did a term paper based on the oral tradition they could discover in their own family, neighborhood, or community. There was a wonderful mix of students at State from century-farm families to refugees from Hitler. Thompson stressed "folklore in America," making it clear that the folklore but recently come from Europe was just as welcome as that which had long been here. The psychological impact of this assignment was remarkable for hundreds of students, especially for children of first-generation Americans who had been urged to forget their origins, to drop the hyphen, never to learn the old world language. Suddenly all that tabooed part of their lives had value, and old grandma who had been kept in the shadows became the most important part of one's life. For a quarter of a century, at Albany and at Cornell, three semesters a year, to classes never under a hundred students, Thompson brought his enthusiasm, his scholarship, and his infectious delight.

It was from this mass of student-collected material that he wrote *Body, Boots & Britches* which came out in 1939, shortly before he was badly hurt in a train wreck on the New York Central. The book was his telling of the legends, tall tales, folk history, songs and ballads, canal and pirate lore, place names and proverbs as remembered by the older stocks. He had planned later volumes of folklore brought from Europe and Africa to New York State, where it began a whole new life of its own, but the accident brought on years of ill health, and his move to Cornell involved huge classes and the supervision of scores of doctoral dissertations. So he never finished the larger plan he had well in mind.

I shall shortly return to later contributions Thompson made to this field, but it seems to me that it was in the classroom, especially teaching teachers and teachers-to-be, that he created a great network in New York State of key people sympathetic to and appreciative of folklore. He created an audience that is still with us and whose children and students know and enjoy it. *Body, Boots & Britches* — the best book of York State folklore that we have — expanded that audience beyond the classroom to the state at large.[2]

Our correspondence shows that Thompson and I had begun to talk of a New York Folklore Society as early as 1938 when I was finishing my graduate work at Columbia, but his move to Ithaca, his ill health, my concentration on my dissertation, and the war all pushed the plans aside, but we were both accumulating good materials for a journal, for I was teaching folklore in his old spot at Albany, three times a year and in extension classes. By the summer of 1944 I had, at Thompson's suggestion, approached Dixon Ryan Fox, President of the New York State Historical Association (as well as of Union College) and found him most receptive to the idea that the new society should be born at a meeting of the Association. It took place at the luncheon meeting held at the Trinity Methodist Church in Albany on October 6, 1944; a few hours later Thompson presided at a session devoted entirely to papers on New York folklore: he spoke on Dutch traditional lore; Moritz Jagendorf spoke on John Darling, about whom he was to write his best book; Wheaton Webb described his field research in the Schenevus valley; and I talked about ghosts. We elected officers for the new society: Thompson was president; Elaine Lambert Lewis, who had done folklore broadcasts for the Brooklyn Public Library, was vice-president; Victor Reynolds, the University Publisher at Cornell, became secretary and treasurer. I was elected editor of the *Quarterly,* which was guaranteed five years of support by President Ezra Day of Cornell.

The *Quarterly,* whose first issue came out February 1945, will shortly celebrate its fortieth birthday under its later name, *New York Folklore.* I served as editor for five years, then Thompson took over. Many others have followed us, and with the years its character has changed, tuned to the changing tides in folklore studies generally; we were concerned with the gathering of oral lore before it was forgotten, later generations were most concerned with theory and significance. The *Quarterly* saw the publication of many a piece of research by Thompson's students and mine, but much more remains unpublished in our huge archives now housed together in the Library of the New York State Historical Association in Cooperstown.

Writing of the '40s brings to mind a number of men and women who were active in those early years. In the late '30s a New York City teacher, Norman Studer, and his wife opened a summer camp for city children back of Phoenicia called Camp Woodland. They wanted their young charges to experience as much of early Catskill folk life as possible, and they saw that they met and listened to the old folks who were their neighbors. They learned about the old crafts like cutting bark and tanning, the domestic arts, lumbering, square dancing, and the old songs which men like George Edwards, rich in folk repertory, taught youngsters from the streets of New York. At the end of the summer they held a folk festival that became a wonderful experience for the mountain dwellers, the children, and the rest of us who joined them. Sadly, in the McCarthy years the Studers were hounded out of the Catskills and the camp burned. A happier result of Camp Woodland is the books on Catskill music written over the years by Norman Cazden, who was one of the music counsellors at the camp and who recorded the local singers.

Up along Lake Champlain lived Marjorie Lansing Porter, editor of the *Essex County Republican* in Keeseville and historian of Plattsburgh and of Clinton County. She made a remarkable collection of folksongs now housed at SUNY Plattsburgh. Another northern woman, Edith Cutting, an early student of Thompson's at Albany and at Cornell, published *Lore of an Adirondack County* (1944) and a collection of rural lore called *Whistling Girls and Jumping Sheep* (1951). She also assisted Thompson in editing *A Pioneer Songster* (1958), the texts from the Stevens-Douglass Manuscripts of eighty-nine songs that a family had gathered from 1841–56.

In the early '40s there were two men who never met or knew each other but who were writing very similar weekly contributions to their local newspapers, Warren G. Sherwood in the *New Paltz Independent and Times* and Wheaton P. Webb in the *Worcester Times*. Sherwood was older, born in 1902, raised on an Ulster County farm, had gone to Cornell then came home to teach. When I first knew him he was living alone in a small cabin, digging graves, picking apples, and grabbing whatever odd jobs came along, sometimes drinking far more than was good for him. But he was also writing a history of the town of Lloyd, searching out old maps, forgotten diaries, and correspondence. He was entranced by the history of Pang Yang, which was settled by followers of Jemima Wilkinson, the Public Universal Friend. They had once headed for Penn Yan, but never got there and built their stone houses just back a few miles from the Hudson, west of Highland.

If they didn't get to Jemima, Sherwood was convinced, she came to them as "the woman in white" whenever one of them died — and long afterward when Pang Yang was only stone walls overgrown with trees and brush. Sherwood saw her himself once — for he was what Robert Frost called "an old believer."

His contributions to the *Independent* were in both prose and verse. Some were local folk history but many were anecdotes, folk ways and old customs, weather lore, and the food of the countryside — apple pie, for example. My favorite piece, for a very personal reason, is in prose and is called "When Pa Died." He sent it to me in manuscript when my own father died, then years later asked for it back to publish. All the details of a country funeral are there along with that sense of the end of something big in one's life that every son feels at the death of his father. Sherwood died in 1947 at the age of 45, his work only begun, but he left us his *Poems from the Platte Binnewater 1940-1947*. brought together and published by Mabel E. L. Lent, his successor as historian of the town of Lloyd.

When I was a senior in college my freshman roommate was a red-headed youngster who was determined to be a clergyman and was still so determined after a year of living with me. Wheaton Webb was interested in literature and the supernatural and poetry and bad puns. Neither of us knew anything about folklore as such, but both of us gravitated toward it after college. One of his early charges was in the Methodist Church, Worcester, New York, Otsego County. He also preached in some of the more isolated communities back in the hills and took his pastoral duties very seriously, especially spending time with oldsters who told him neighborhood yarns, the ways of life that had gone by the board. As "The Old Whittler" he published a column nearly every week for a year and a half, beginning in May 1941. I have mentioned that Webb was a speaker at the birth of the Folklore Society; his "Witches in the Cooper Country" was the first article in the first issue of the *Quarterly*. Later he published a children's book full of village ways called *Uncle Swithin's Invention* (1947), but I cherish most my folder of his slightly fay, endearing letters, these from a Doctor of Divinity with a reputation for inculcating a new vigor to each church he came to serve. Sherwood and Webb, so very different, shared the same warm love for their countryside, its legendry, and its folk ways, but most of all for the people who were their neighbors, living and dead.

In 1946 I was awarded a Guggenheim Fellowship to do a book on the folklore of the supernatural in New York, largely based on the field work of my students. I took my family to the dulcet climate of St. Croix in the Virgin Islands. In the first month I wrote a juvenile called *Spooks of the Valley* (1948) which retold the ghostlore of the Hudson Valley. The next month I flew back to the States to meet with Stephen C. Clark, Sr., who was about to become the Chairman of the Board of the New York State Historical Association and who offered me the position of its Executive Director. This involved responsibility for two museums — Fenimore House and The Farmer's Museum — oversight of a new and rapidly growing junior program, a quarterly journal, a library (then housed in one room). In none of these areas had I had any experience, I was not a historian, knew nothing about museums, but happily there was in place a small but able staff: Janet MacFarlane, Acting Director and Curator; Mary Cunningham, Editor and creator of the junior program and librarian; and George Campbell, a one time farmer who had been largely responsible for the collection at The Farmer's Museum. Stephen Clark had other plans: he wanted the Association to develop a major adult education program, he wanted it to strike out in new directions, and he was prepared to provide the wherewithal. Would I like the job? I would. I went back to St. Croix, finished my writing, which included an adult book on New York ghostlore called *Things That Go Bump in The Night* (1959), and returned to Cooperstown by May of 1947.

A year later we opened the first of the annual Seminars on American Culture, the adult education program Mr. Clark had proposed. Nineteen eighty-four will see the thirty-seventh year of Seminars, and practically every year there has been offered a course in some aspect of folk culture: lore, song, art, architecture, crafts, textiles. It was in 1969 that Tom O'Donnell gave a wonderfully successful course in "The Yorker Imagination: Upstate in Literature." There was soon a small faculty cadre which attracted not only students but other faculty. Thompson and Carmer, both Trustees by 1952, were very popular and directly responsible for bringing onto the faculty Samuel Hopkins Adams and Frank Warner. Adams, who had been one of the muckrakers of the early part of the century, began writing novels and short stories of Upstate in the '40s that were filled with folk speech and a plethora of lore from the oral tradition. This was true of his *Grandfather Tales* (1955), stories of the Erie Canal, but equally true of *Canal Town* (1944; folk medicine). As a novelist he was a user and incorporator of folklore, especially of all aspects of folk life. Frank Warner, a North Carolina native, had begun his folk song collecting while a travelling secretary for the Railroad YMCA's. I first met him and his wife Anne when they were living on the ground floor of Carl and Betty Carmer's house in Greenwich Village in the late '30s or early '40s. The Warners spent their vacations up and down the east coast collecting and learning folk songs.

His collecting included work in the Adirondacks where he recorded Yankee John Galusha and Lena Bourne Fish, both treasuries of remembered song. Frank had a phenomenal capacity for reproducing the very voice from which he had first heard a song, so that an evening of his singing had great variety, vitality, and validity. For some years he was a firm fixture of Seminars, and he and Anne were greatly beloved.

In 1963 NYSHA and SUNY Oneonta opened a master's program at Cooperstown with two separate but interlocking programs: one in history museum studies, the other in folk culture or, as the faculty preferred to call it, folk life. Using The Farmer's Museum and the folk art collection and especially the countryside around us, Per Guldbeck, Bruce Buckley, Rod Roberts, and I developed a folk program that was pioneering in many ways for recording every aspect of rural folk life. The emphasis was away from the verbal to the hand-skills, the material objects, and their uses. This coincided with the growth of folk museums, folk research centers, positions for state folklorists, and many of those posts were filled by our graduates. The closing of that program, which came in 1979, was in my view a major mistake, but at the time it seemed necessary to those responsible. Fortunately the History Museums Studies Program has continued.

By now it is obvious that this account is largely one man's memory of the early years of the folk renaissance. Much has been left out because I didn't know about it at first hand, but I was lucky enough to have known most of these men and women as friends and co-workers, and the memories are good. I think we succeeded in making a segment, at least, of our fellow Yorkers aware of the layers and varieties of the folk culture which they have inherited and which requires only to be understood and to be enjoyed.

Notes

1. An earlier article by Warren S. Walker should be noted: "Elements of Folk Culture in Cooper's Novels," in *James Fenimore Cooper: A Re-Appraisal,* edited by Mary E. Cunningham (Cooperstown: New York State Historical Association, 1954).

2. A *festschrift* for Harold W. Thompson has articles about various sides of his character and his career: *Whatever Makes Papa Laugh: A Folklore Sheaf Honoring Harold W. Thompson,* edited by Warren S. Walker (Cooperstown: New York Folklore Society, 1958).

Works Cited

Carmer, Carl. *My Kind of Country.* Introduction by Louis C. Jones. New York: David McKay, 1966.

Gardner, Emelyn. *Folklore of the Schoharie Hills.* Ann Arbor: University of Michigan Press, 1937.

Skinner, Charles M. *Myths and Legends of Our Own Land.* 2 vols. Philadelphia: J. B. Lippincott, 1896.

Thompson, Harold W. *Body, Boots & Britches.* Philadelphia: J. B. Lippincott, 1939. Republished with an Introduction by Thomas F. O'Donnell. Syracuse: Syracuse University Press, 1979.

Walker, Warren S. "Cooper's Fictional Use of the Oral Tradition." In George A. Test, ed. *James Fenimore Cooper: His Country and His Art.* Papers from the 1980 Conference at State University of New York College at Oneonta and Cooperstown. Oneonta, New York, 1981.

Index

UPSTATE LITERATURE

was composed in 10-point Digital Compugraphic Times Roman and leaded 2 points,
with display type in Times Roman, by Metricomp;
printed by sheet-fed offset on 55-pound, acid-free Glatfelter B-31,
Smythe-sewn and bound over binder's boards in Holliston Roxite B,
also adhesive bound with paper covers by Wickersham Printing Co., Inc.;
and published by

SYRACUSE UNIVERSITY PRESS

SYRACUSE, NEW YORK 13210